A History of Jammû

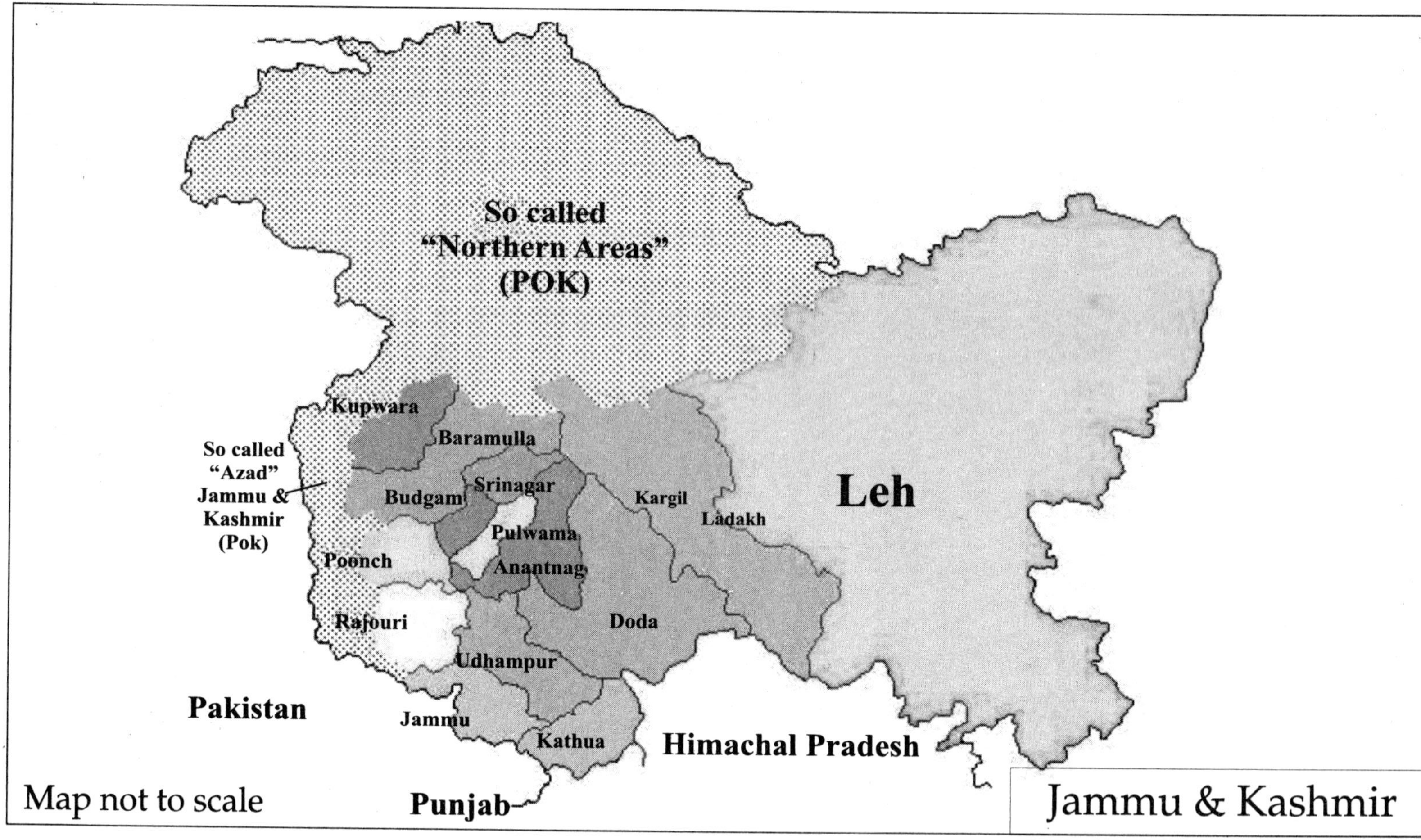
So called
"Northern Areas"
(POK)
Leh
Kupwara
Baramulla
So called
"Azad"
Jammu &
Kashmir
(Pok)
Budgam
Srinagar
Kargil
Ladakh
Pulwama
Poonch
Anantnag
Rajouri
Doda
Udhampur
Pakistan
Jammu
Kathua
Himachal Pradesh
Map not to scale
Punjab
Jammu & Kashmir

A HISTORY OF
Jammû

Parvéz Dewân, IAS

Manas Publications
New Delhi-110 002 (INDIA)

MANAS PUBLICATIONS
(Publishers, Distributors, Importers & Exporters)
4402/5-A, Ansari Road (Opp. HDFC Bank)
Darya Ganj, New Delhi - 110 002 (India)
Phones: Off.: 011-23260783, 23265523,
Res.: 011-41606977
E-mail: manaspublications@gmail.com
manaspub6@gmail.com

2nd Impression 2023 (FP - 2008)

ISBN: 978-81-7049-312-9

495/-

Designed at
Manas Publications
Printed in India at
RK Print Services, Delhi
and published by Mrs Suman Lata for
Manas Publications, 4402/5-A,
Ansari Road (Opp HDFC Bank),
Darya Ganj, New Delhi - 110002 (INDIA)

For the Shamîms

Gp. Capt. (Dr.) Syed Mohamad Shamim and Mrs. Bano Shamim, Rukhsana and Shahid, Qaiser and Tasneem, Anwar and Sunita and, above all, Faez.

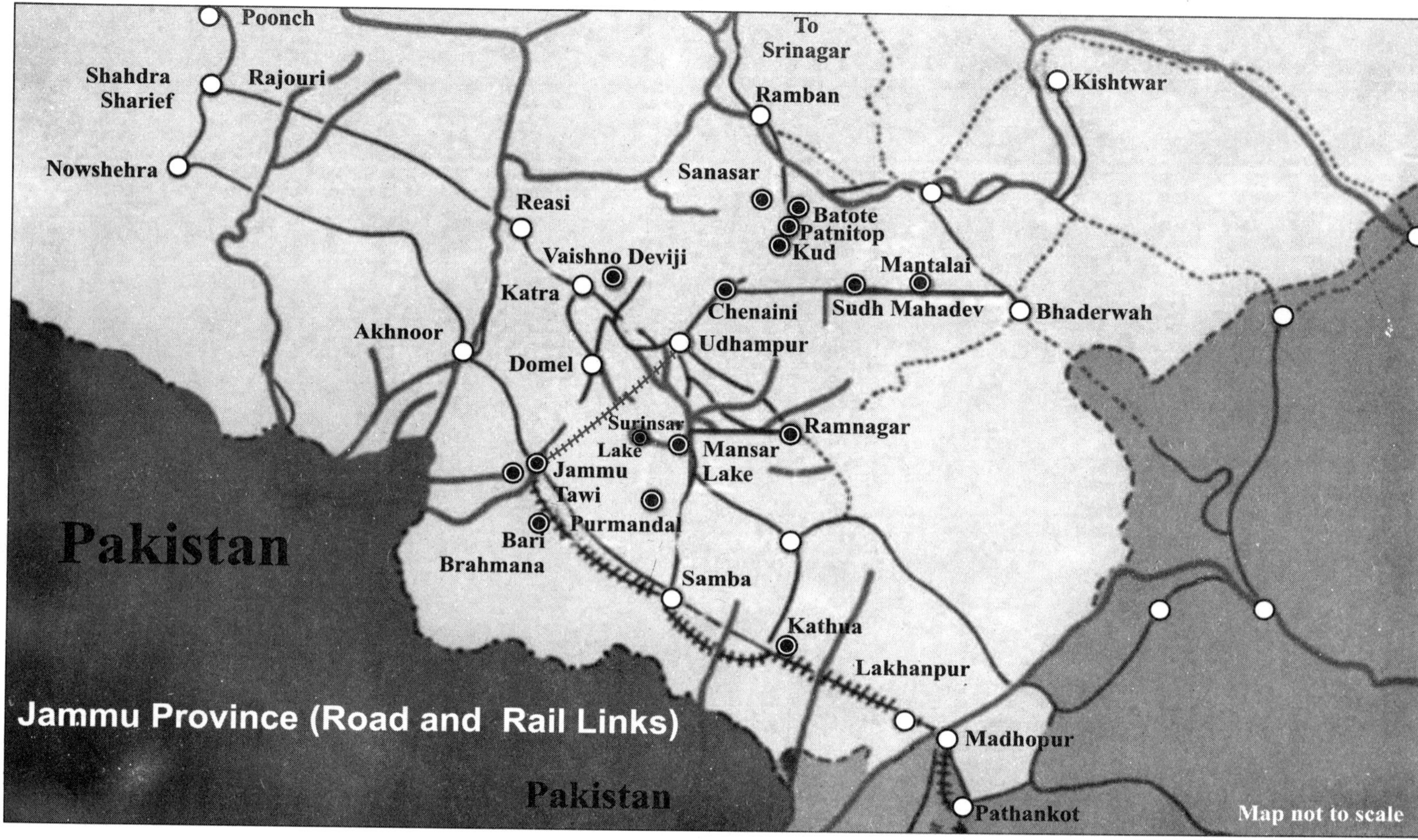

Jammu Province (Road and Rail Links)

Preface

When Adishree Singh suggested that I publish a book exclusively on the history of Jammu, she was echoing the sentiments of many Jammuites. There has perhaps never been a book about the history of the entire province.

This is surprising because the 'Kashmîr dispute' is mostly about the occupied parts of Jammû province, which Pâkistân calls 'Azad' Jammû and Kashmîr. (Pâkistân does not control an inch of the Valley of Kashmîr.) Even the wars of 1948, 1965 and 1971 have mainly taken place in Jammû province.

With this book I have attempted to fill the gap.

Like all historians I have, naturally, relied on what has already been written. But at least a third of this book consists of new materials, based on primary sources.

I have used the results of 20th century archæological discoveries to construct a pre-history of Jammu.

As will become evident, the violent happenings of 1947-49 have been the main object of my investigations. Most Indian historians have ignored that unfortunate period, while Pâkistânis have published exaggerated accounts. Pâkistân claims that almost two lakh (two hundred thousand) Jammû Muslims were killed in those riots—and an even larger number migrated.

In order to arrive at the truth, I examined census records (1931-2001) and also collected anecdotes from the families of the victims of that violent era—Hiñdu, Muslim and Sikh.

I have also tried to cover every important battle fought in Jammû province after 1947, as well as all significant political developments.

With the help of the memoirs of the legendary Malka Pukhraj, a volume compiled by Rehmatullah Rad, and stray newspaper articles, I have put together two nostalgic chapters about Jammû's fabled composite culture, where Hiñdus and Muslims went to the same shrines and 'godmen,' ate the same food and thought the same thoughts.

Parvez Dewan

Acknowledgements

Adishree, the Sheikhs of Julâhâ kâ Mohâllâ, Ranvijay and I had gone on a boat ride through the history of our fascinating state.

During the ride Adishree suggested that I put all my notes and chapters on the history of Jammû together into a book. It was a Saturday and I worked through the night doing just that: cutting and pasting notes on my computer. By the next morning I had printed out a 'limited edition' (all of one copy) history of Jammû for Adishree.

I am grateful to Adishree Singh Jamwal for having inspired this book. Dr. R.L. Jetley, Saleem Beig, M. Ashraf (IAS) and R.L. Bharti (IFS) provided me with invaluable oral histories. Mr. Satinder S. Sahni (IAS) very kindly went through some of the proofs.

Above all, I would like to acknowledge the help given at every stage by Mr. Devender Seth.

List of Maps

Contents

Cover Illustrations

Front cover

'Raja ki Mandi, Jammu'

Lithograph drawn by Sarna, c.1929.

This was the winter palace of the Mahârâjâ of Jammu and Kashmîr.

Back cover

'Poormandal Male or Festival'

A lithograph, c. 1929, 'Drawn by the Hon'ble Charles Hardince.' 'I.D. Hardino Litho.'

'Poormandal' should correctly be spelt 'Purmandal.' The 'pur' here sounds exactly like the 'pur' in, say, 'Jaipur.' By 'Male' the good man obviously meant 'mélâ' (fair).

Both drawings are from the collection of the Nizam, Hyderabad House, New Delhi. Photographs courtesy Sh. Rajiv Makin. Thanks are also due to Anita Bimal and Achint.

1

Jammu State

(Pre-history—A.D. 1100)

In a Nutshell

There once was a king called Agnibaran. He was a descendant of Kush, the elder son of Sri Ram, King of Ayodhya. Agnibaran, his brother and their followers migrated from Oopa, their estate in Ayodhya. They first went to Kangra and then crossed River Ravi to settle at Parole, a village close to the J&K, Punjab border. (There are several references to Parole in the chapter on 'Kathua' district.) This event took place in the later Vedic period according to some historians and 'about the time of Cyrus,' according to others.

Agnibaran's son, Vayu Srava, conquered all lands as far west as the Jammu Tawi. Four other Surajbansi kings followed in succession. The fifth was Agni Garbh. His eldest son, Bâhu Lochan, succeeded him and founded the town and fort of Bâhu, on the left bank of the Tawi, and made it his capital.

Bahu Lochan then tried to conquer territories in the plains. So he went to war with Chandrahâs, the king of Punjab, but was killed. His younger brother, Jambu Lochan, avenged his death and killed Chandrahas.

On becoming the king, Jambu Lochan went on a hunt. When he crossed the Tawi, he found a deer (or a goat) and a tiger drinking water from the same pond. His ministers explained that this meant that the soil of the place was so virtuous that no living being was the enemy of another.

Raja Jambu Lochan decided to found his capital, Jambupura, on that noble soil, on the right bank of the Tawi, overlooking his brother's fort.

It is generally accepted that the brothers—Raja Jambu Lochan and Raja Bahu Lochan-founded the twin cities of Jammu and Bahu respectively in the 14th century BC. (Today, Bahu, which is across the river from

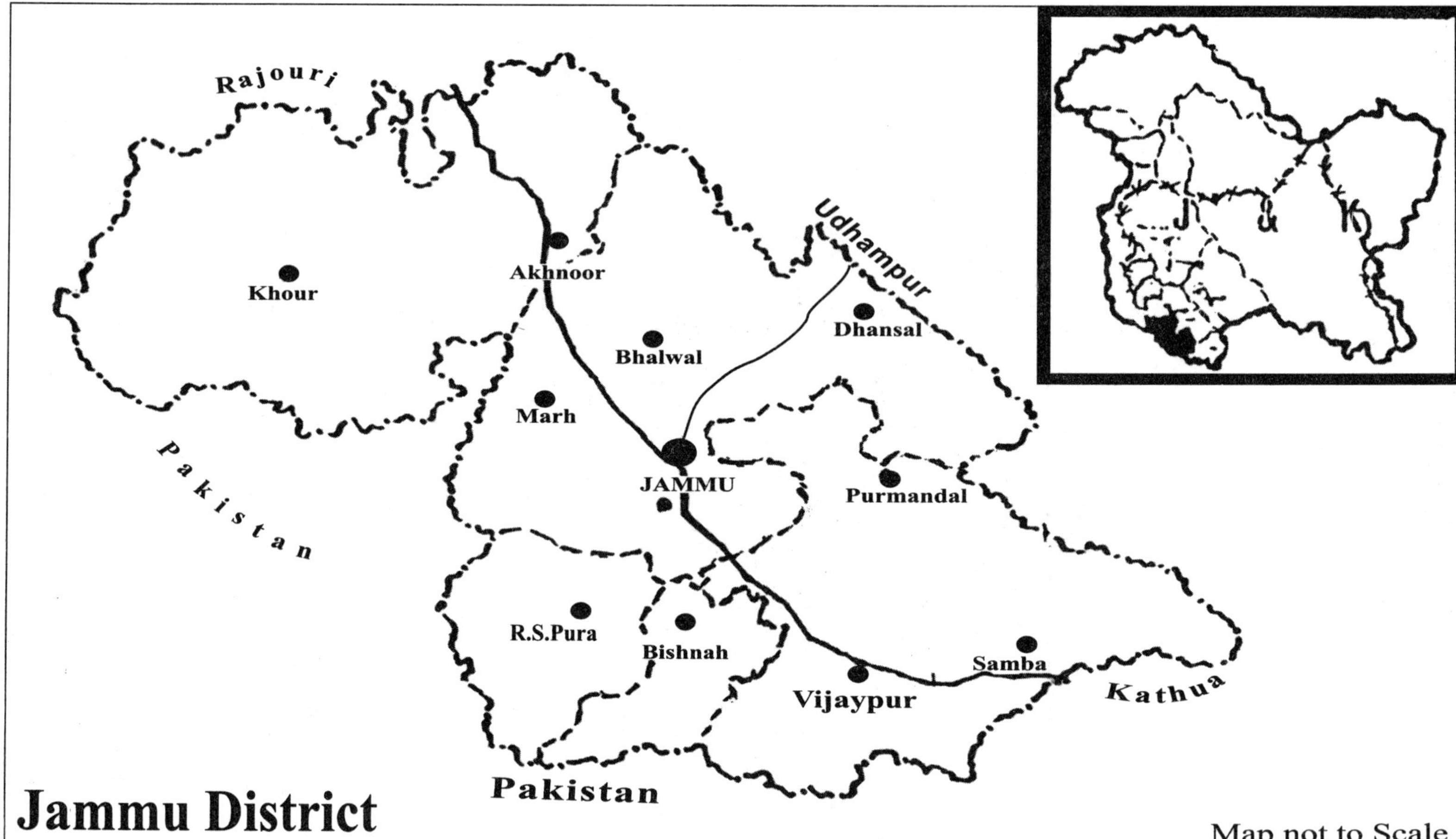
Rajouri
Khour
Akhnoor
Bhalwal
Udhampur
Dhansal
Marh
JAMMU
Purmandal
Pakistan
R.S.Pura
Bishnah
Vijaypur
Samba
Kathua
Pakistan
Jammu District
Map not to Scale

downtown Jammu, is part of Jammu city. It is a major tourist attraction because of its ancient temple, its early 19th-century A.D. fort and the Bâgh-e-Bâhu gardens.)

Jammu province is several times as big as the city of the same name. It has traditionally been divided into a large number of tiny kingdoms. The kingdom based in Jammu city has from time to time asserted control over many (but, till the 19th century, never all) of these kingdoms. Ranjit Dev, king of Jammu proper (A.D. 1723-1783), was one of the few who controlled as many as 22 of these principalities from Jammu city. His successors squabbled amongst themselves. This paved the way for a takeover by the Sikh rulers of neighbouring Punjab.

The great Sikh ruler, Mahârâjâ Ranjit Singh, too, had problems controlling the province. So he sent Râjâ Gulâb Singh, a descendant of Râjâ Ranjit Dev, to put down the rebellion. Gulab managed to conquer much of the present day Jammu province—perhaps that anyone had the first time ever done so—on behalf of the Sikh kingdom. However, after Ranjit Singh's death the Sikh kingdom disintegrated. The British demanded an indemnity of Rs. 1.5 crore (15 million) for the war in which the British had defeated the Lahore kingdom.

Most successors of Ranjit Singh were unable to pay. However, Gulab Singh paid Rs. 75 lakh (7.5 million). In turn, under the Treaty of Amritsar, the British gave him all of the Valley of Kashmir (and some other territories). Gulab Singh became a Maharaja, one of only five in all of undivided India to be accorded a 21-gun salute by the British colonial government.

His son, Maharaja Ranbir Singh (1857-85), inherited his throne, to be followed by Pratap Singh. Pratap, in turn, was succeeded in 1925 by his nephew Maharaja Hari Singh who ruled till the 26th October, 1947, when he signed the instrument of (the) accession of the state to the Union of India.

Pre-history

Archæologists have, since 1935, made major discoveries about Jammu's pre-history. Fossils of almost two dozen species of the human-like Sivapithecus ape have been found in the Shivalik range of Himachal Pradesh (HP), Ramnagar (Jammu) and Pakistan. The stone age of Jammu, seems to have had a culture similar to that of the Soan culture of the Shivaliks of neighbouring Potwar (Pakistan) and the Beas Valley (HP).

Excavations at Lakhanpur (on River Ravi), Nagrota (on River Tawi), Koote (on the Bei) and Ambaran (on River Chenâb) have revealed four terraces. The earliest of these date to the pleistocene period.

The Soan Period: This period has been sub-divided into three sub-periods.

i) *Early Soan*: (Around 1.6 million years BC.) Some simple tools made of pebbles and flakes have been excavated from the first terrace. Implements in the second terrace are similar but show greater diversity and sophistication. The sites: Gurha Pattan and Nagrota (both Jammu district) and Kurro, Pinyani, Sutash and Terra (all Kathua).

ii) *Late Soan*: Flakes found from the third terrace were fully developed.

Sites: Ambaran, Jagatpur, Katrâ, Kishanpur, Mah and Nagrota.

iii) *Final Soan*: (Around 13,000 B.C.) In the fourth terrace were found small pebble tools. In this period chert was used as one of the raw materials.

The Neolithic Period: Polished stone tools from this period have been found in the foothills of the Shivaliks. These include adzes, axes, chisels, grinders, hammerstones, picks and ringstones. They are much like the tools from this period found in Kashmir and Himachal Pradesh. These tools show that the people had started producing food. They had thus grown out of the food-gathering stage.

Sites: Amb Gharota, Dayala Chak, Gurha Pattan, Kurro, Kut, Mah and Malpur.

Archæology: Malpur is a major neolithic site. Mâñdâ is Harappan. Other important pre-historic sites are Ambaran, Guru Baba ka Tilla and Jâfar Chak. Between them we have evidence of civilisation from the sixth century BC onwards.

Paucity of Sources

Among early references to the region are mentions in the *Mahabharat* and the memoirs of Timur. Excavations conducted in Akhnoor, which is in Jammu district, revealed signs of the Harappan civilisation as well as Indo-Greek artefacts. (See 'Ambaran' and 'Mândâ' in the chapter on 'Jammu district.') Fine terracotta Buddhas excavated in the district indicate that Jammu had an advanced civilisation several centuries before King Harsh Vardhan. Other archaeological evidence indicates signs of the Mauryan, Kushan and Gupta periods.

Ferishta, the mediæval historian, wrote about incidents that took place in the first century of the Christian era. Around then Raja Ram Dev Rathor, king of Kannauj, invaded and defeated the king of Jammu, who had to give his daughter in marriage to Rathor's son. So, we have at least that for sure.

Between the first and tenth centuries A.D. we know very little about the state. Two copper plates found in Chamba were the first to mention an independent state called Durgara, which obviously was what we now know as Jammu. These plates date to the eleventh century but talk of things that happened in the early tenth century.

The famous Chambâ copper-plates are the title deeds of Râjâ Asht-varman (A.D. 1030-40). They mention a confrontation with the Durgar people.

(In the chapter on 'Udhampur', in the section about the Mansar Lake, we have discussed a theory about how the words 'Dogra' and 'Duggar' might have originated. Here is a slight variant: Hutchison and Vogel argue that just as the Gujjar tribe derives its name from the Sanskrit 'Gurjar', clearly 'Duggar' comes from the 'Durgara' mentioned on the Chamba copper-plates. But there's no contradiction between the two theories. The Durgara tribe could well have taken its name from the Mansar-Surinsar lakes and the word Dogra was then derived from it.)

Alberuni (Abu Rihan) who travelled in India between A.D. 1017 and 1031 mentions Jammu province. He says that the road from Hardwar to Kashmir passed through Pinjor (near Chandigarh), Dahmala (Nurpur), Ballawur (Billawar), Ladha and the Rajagiri fort, before going up north through the Pir Panjal pass.

The *Rajatarangini* mentions neither Jammu nor Durgara, though it talks about much smaller states. That could be because the capital of Durgara was at Babbapura (now Babor), 27km. east of Jammu, near the left bank of the Tawi. (The ruins of seven stone temples survive at Babor. The Sharda script has been used in these temples. That would date the temples to at least the 13th century A.D. A coin from the reign of King Kalash of Kashmir (A.D. 1063-1089) has been found at Babor.)

Other states in Jammu province mentioned by the *Rajatarangini* include Vallapura (Billawar), Bhadravaksh (Bhaderwah), Kashtavat (Kishtwar), Vartul (Batal: the area between Banihal and Ramban) and Vishalata (the area around Dharamkot) and Jasata.[1]

Bahu, almost certainly, was Jammu's ancient capital. Babor took over much later, perhaps in the eleventh century when Bahu began to be attacked by invaders from the west. Kirti Raja, one of the kings of Babbapura (elsewhere mentioned as the king of Nilapura), visited Kashmir

---

1. Could this be Jasrota? Unlikely. Kalhan started writing the *Rajatarangini* in A.D. 1148. On the other hand, the prince who founded Jasrota is believed to have been born around A.D. 1195. Dates given by Kalhan are mostly accurate to the month and day. However, Prince Jas Dev could have been born a century or two earlier.

in the winter of A.D. 1087-88. This was during the reign of Kalash, to whom his daughter Bhuvanamati was married. That might explain the aforementioned coin.

References to the princes of what is now Jammu district and its neighbourhood become a little more frequent, from this point but mostly with reference to Kashmir. Around A.D. 1114 Prince Vajradhar of Babbapura went on a pilgrimage to Kurukshetra. There he met Kalash's great-grandson Prince Bhiksha Char, whose family had been replaced as the rulers of Kashmir by the Lohara dynasty. Vajradhar supported Bhiksha Char's claim. However, four years later he supported the Lohara King Sussala against Bhiksha Char. The *Rajatarangini* clearly implies that Sussala was the boss and Vajradhar the weaker party.

Now again for more than four hundred years there is little authentic information about Jammu. However, we are told of twenty Rajas having ruled in succession till Raja Paras Ram Dev (1589). After that dates start getting more accurate. The *Vanshawali* (family tree) of the Jammu royal family is one of the few local sources and is fairly reliable. It mentions 120 kings and princes, but has major blanks. It reveals that local as well as foreign kings ruled Jammu. Between 1589 and 1812 there were twelve indigenous kings in Jammu. Hutchison and Vogel, who published in 1932, have used the *Vanshawali* to painstakingly reconstruct the history of Jammu.

The only other local sources are the 19th century *Gulabnama* and the *Tawâreekh e Rajputân Mulk e Punjab* (A History of the Rajputs of the Punjab) by Thakur Kahan Singh Balauria. (In the nineteenth and in much of the twentieth century, all kingdoms in what is now the Jammu province, even Bhaderwah and Kishtwar, were included by writers in the Punjab Hill States.)

Timur invaded Jammu in 1398-9. The *Malfuzat i Timuri*, which records the invasion, and the *Târeekh e Kashmir e Azami* (1417) are the oldest extant works to mention Jammu by its present name. The town was around five hundred years old then. Thus, going by the only reliable source we have, Jammu was founded around A.D. 900. (What was founded before that was probably the Bahu section of the town.)

Alternative versions

Others tell the Bahu-Jambu story slightly differently. They say that the two Rajput brothers who had migrated from Ayodhya in ancient times, first settled near River Sutlej. The clan lived at various places in the Punjab for the next twenty-eight generations. Various kings and dynasties patronised this clan of warriors.

According to this version, Bija Singh (c. A.D. 426), was the first of the clan to have settled in the present Jammu province. He represented the 28th generation and shifted, with his clan, close to Mirpur (now in POK). The clan lived there for thirty-one generations.

In the fifty-ninth generation, around A.D. 1207, the clan broke up into three broad groups. Some members of the family went over to Chamba, while the second branch settled at Teera Kangra. The main branch, consisting of Kripal Dev and his brother Sangram Dev, went over to the Dhahman hills and established their capital, Bahu, there. Later Sangram set up a township of his own across the river from Bahu. This grew into the present Jammu City.

Kashmir's own historians, Hindu as well as Muslim, have chronicled the valley in the minutest detail. We have surviving histories that were written as early as in A.D. 1148; and if the *Nilamat Puran* counts as history then we have a text that dates to the 6th or 7th century A.D. On the other hand for Jammu, Leh and Kargil we have almost nothing to go by. Because of the paucity of sources already mentioned, we have widely differing, rival versions of the history of Jammu. I have mostly gone along with Hutchison and Vogel, because they have adduced more evidence than the anonymous 19th century authors, also British, of the Bija Singh/ Kripal Dev/ Sangram Dev version.

Both schools agree that Bahu came up first and Jammu somewhat later. Both accounts merge in the reign of the great Raja Mal Dev (c. A.D. 1370).

Dr. D.C. Sharma has a totally revisionist version. Without citing authority he says that Kirpal Dev and Sangram Dev belonged to Rajasthan. According to him, these two brothers (and their clans) fled Rajasthan when India was attacked by 'Mohd. Gauri and Mohd. Gaznavi.' (The latter must be Mahmûd of Ghazna.) When they reached the Bahu area of Jammu, they found it largely uninhabited, except for a few Megh (scheduled caste) families.

Some migratory tribes would take their cattle and sheep to the pastures of Bhaderwah and Kishtwar every summer. Dr. Sharma says that every time when they returned to the plains for the winters, they would forcibly occupy the Meghs' fields. Therefore, when Rajputs from Rajasthan came over to settle in the Bahu area, the Meghs felt a sense of security. The Rajputs decided to protect the Meghs from the 'barbarities' of the migratory shepherds and cowherds. Later the tribals, too, submitted to their authority. Kirpal settled at Bahu and Sangram founded Jammu. So, no Bahu-Jambu. No tiger and no deer/goat.

Was ancient Jammu part of Madr Désh/Janpad?

Jammu was part of the region called 'Madr Janpad' by Panini and Madr Désh by other ancient writers. There is unanimity among scholars on this point. As a result we have some authentic information about the ancient Jammu region. Shagal, Sakal or Shahal (Sialkot) was the capital of this major *janpad* (region), which covered much of west Punjab and Jammu.

That Madr was somewhere near Jammu is beyond doubt. The *Nilamat Purân* says that when Jalodhbhav, the demon, terrorised the people, they fled to Uttar Madr (North Madr). The great ancient saint Kashyap had visited the Madr as well as Trigart janpads. He mentioned several rivers, including the Devika, the Irâvati (Ravi), Taushi (presumably the Tawi), the Chandrabhaga (certainly the Chenâb) and the Vipasha (the Beas?). If all these rivers had indeed been in or around Madr, then this region must certainly have been Jammu and the adjoining parts of the Punjab.

The great Pânîni divided the hills of 'outer Kashmir' into two: Pûrav (eastern) Madr and Apr ('not inside' or 'outer') Madr. Pûrav Madr was between the Râvi and Chenâb rivers. Apr Madr was between the Jehlum and the Chenâb. ('Outer Kashmir' and 'the outer hills' are expressions used by 19th century scholars and administrators—mainly British—to describe much of the present Jammu province.)

According to Dr. S.P. Shrivatsa[2], the *Vishnu Dharmothar Puran* mentions that the Devika was a popular and sacred river that flowed through the Madr region. Today there is a sacred river of that name in Jammu region. Therefore, Shrivatsa does seem to have a point. He adds that the author of the *Kashika Vritti*, another ancient text, talks about 'water flowing from the underground channel of [the] Devika.' That seems to be the Devika of Jammu, all right.

Dr. Shrivatsa says that Panini, too, lists the rivers of the region as the Devika, the Iravati, the Bhidya (probably the modern Bai), the 'Chandrabha' and the Udya (Ujh?).

However, this merely establishes that the Madr region (*janpad*) had included much of Jammu province. What after that? Do we know anything about this region? Very little, it would seem. Kunti, of the *Mahabharat* fame, had a lot of nasty things to say about the people of Madr. Prince Bharat, brother of Sri Ram, had passed through Madr, and spent three nights with its king, on his way to Raigarh. The king was called Anshuman. Prince Bharat then crossed the Chandrabhaga.

This region had apparently produced great scholars, including the wandering Charak clan of scholars. (By what simply has to be a

2. *Daily Excelsior*, Jammu, 7 and 14 January, 2001.

coincidence, there is a Rajput clan of the same name in Jammu today.) We also have the names of some kings of Madr, a description of its capital at Sialkot and a record of some royal visits to the region.

Buddhism in Madr Desh: Menander, the Greek, ruled Sakal (Sialkot). Mendhar, a town in Poonch, is said to be named after him. He converted to Buddhism and took the name Milind. Because of his efforts the region came under the influence of Buddhism. Greek-inspired artefacts have been been excavated at places like Ambaran, where the base of a grand Buddhist stupa has also been found.

We learn from the famous Allahabad pillar inscription that King Samudragupt had subjugated Madr Désh. As a result, in the fourth century the influence of the Guptas and Madhya Désh (central India) was seen in the art of Madr Désh as well. The Buddhist terracotta heads of Akhnoor are an example.

When the Gupta Empire collapsed, tiny kingdoms sprang up in this region. The *Rajatarangini* mentions several such principalities (see the section on 'Paucity of sources' in this chapter).

A somewhat more detailed history of Jammu state

Old Jammu was a state in the valleys of the Tawi and Chenâb rivers. The state included some of the neighbouring plains. The kingdom would often extend to Sakal (Sialkot) in the south. From the very beginning, from the days of Jambu Lochan, right up to the present, relations between the rulers of Jammu and Sialkot, which is just 45km. away, have often been tense. Jambu killed Chandrahas, the king of Punjab, in battle, before founding Jammu. That is why one of the four corner turrets ('watch towers') of the Bahu fort faces Sialkot (now in Pakistan).

It was in the eighteenth century that the main expansion of Jammu took place.

Even conservative British Raj historians estimate that the state originated in the first century A.D. 'or earlier'. How much earlier? No one knows. Few records are available. So the Jambu Lochan story could date to the 14th century B.C.—as claimed—or be as recent as one or two centuries before Christ.

Jammu town has no ancient, and only two mediæval, buildings. With the exception of the 15th century Peer Kho, none of Jammu's numerous temples was built before the 19th century. Not even the building that now houses the Bahu temple. However, around the 14th century Raja Mal Dev erected the Purani Mandi palace complex.

The Jamwals, the royal family of Jammu state, "are believed to be of the Surya/ Surajvanshi Rajput clan, i.e. descended from the Sun". In between in their ancestry are supposed to have been Sri Ram, the deity, and his son Kush. Jâmwâl roughly means 'Jammu wallah'.

Jambu Lochan's Successors

Purankaran succeeded Jambu Lochan. His son Dayakaran was the next ruler. According to the *Vanshawali* (genealogy), Dayakaran went to Kashmir, at the request of the people there, to restore order, He did so and stayed on. The Bhau Rajputs, whose capital used to be in Kaleeth, near Akhnoor, are descended from Dayakaran.

Jambu's descendant Shib Prakash became the king a few generations later. Raja Sala Vahan of Sialkot, whose empire extended to Gandhar (Peshawar), invaded and destroyed the town of Jammu (Bahu, to be precise). As a result, for a few generations, Shib and his successors had to hide in the mountains, before being able to recapture the capital.

The Dutts of Takshashila, and the Rais

In the 5th century B.C., Raja Bodh Arjun is believed to have ruled over Jammu. His dynasty reigned for 357 years. Invaders from Gandhar/ Takshashila and Sakal (Sialkot) then annexed Jammu. Jammu was part of the Dutts' Gandhar/ Takshashila-based empire till Alexander's invasion. The Dutts were perhaps a Persian people. They, in turn, were subject to Persia's Achæmenians.

Charak and Billawaria say, 'The seventh ruler of the dynasty, Ajay Sinh, seems to have settled at Jammu. He was related to Porus who has been named Raja Puru Sen in the Jammu genealogy. It also gives the name of the capital of Porus as Goti-pani, which no other source mentions.[3] Ajay Sinh died while fighting against Alexander on [the] side of [Porus].'

Around 50 B.C. the Rai dynasty of Sakal (Sialkot) annexed Jammu to their kingdom. The Rais' empire started crumbling around the time of Jog Rai. He partitioned the kingdom between his two sons. Suraj Hans was the younger son. He received Jammu, which included Babbapura, Bahu and the present Jammu town. Some historians now call his descendants the Dhar dynasty because their names ended with a 'Dhar.' Others continue to call it the Rai dynasty.

---

3. In fact, no other Indian source has any details about King Porus either. We know of him mainly from Greek records. The Dutts have always claimed Porus as one of their own. The Jammu *Vanshawali* is the first independent corroboration of this fact.

(Archæologist Dr Mani has a slightly different take on this. He writes, 'Sindh-Rai established his kingdom at Babbapura and rulers of his line called [the] Rai dynasty ruled from about the third to [the] fifth century A.D. Rulers of the same line administered the area for [a] further about four hundred years...' Thus, Dr. Mani has shifted the dates by two and a half centuries and has a different first name of the founder.)

The next historical reference, several generations later, is to the king of Jammu being killed in a battle with the king of Nagarkot on River Ravi.

The Chamba copper-plates of around A.D. 1050-66 are the next authentic record. We learn that around A.D. 910-30 'the lord of Durgara and the ruler of Saumataka' were among the kings who assisted the Kiras (presumably, the Kashmiris) in their invasion of Chamba. Saumâtâ (Sâmbarta) was perhaps the capital of Vallapura (present Billawar). This could be the incident mentioned in the *Rajatarangini* but dated at A.D. 1028-63, when Raja Anant Dev of Kashmir defeated the king of Chamba and replaced him with his own nominee. What is clear from both is that Kashmir enjoyed suzerainty over Durgara, as well as some other hill states.

This conclusion is reinforced by the fact that Kirti Dhar, king of Babbapura (c. A.D. 1070-90), was among the eight hill chiefs who went over to Kashmir in 1087-8 to pay homage to King Kalash of Kashmir.

* * *

2

Kishtwâr

(Pre-history—A.D. 1500)

'Kishtwar was a lake'

It is believed that the entire Chandrabhaga valley was a huge lake called Gowardhansar. Then the gods drained it by cutting a passage through one of the mountains. There is indeed some geological evidence of the Kishtwar area once having been a lake.

There is an identical belief about the Valley of Kashmir. Even the Kargil-Khaltse area was supposed to have been a lake. Who knows, perhaps most of the state once was a series of lakes till, one by one, their waters got drained out.

Protagonists of Kishtwar never fail to mention that civilisation existed in Kishtwar when Kashmir was still submerged. They claim that one of the eighteen ancient Purâns of the Hindus was written at Kishtwar. They also say that the history of their land goes back to the Mahâbhârat era. (The people of most parts of the state say the same thing.)

The place has at various points of time been called Kashtvata, Kishtwarak, Kashyap, Kaligarh, Lohit Mandal and, of course, Kishtwar. Apparently, Lohit Mandal means 'the land of saffron.' The people of Kishtwar town still refer to their town as Mandal.

The old kingdom

Traditionally this kingdom has consisted of Dachhan, Kishtwar proper, Marwah, Warwan, Kountwara, Bahunjwah, the Dodâ-Siraj-Banihal area, Saroor-Sarthal, Nagseni, often Padar, and, occasionally, Zanskar. In other words, all of the present-day Dodâ district, minus the Bhaderwah kingdom.

The relatively warm 'Dodâ city' was often the winter capital of the Kishtwar kingdom.

It is believed that in 200 B.C. King Manendra invited Nagsen, the respected Buddhist scholar, to his palace at Sakla to study Buddhism from him. The story goes that the scholar so impressed the king with his teaching that the king converted to Buddhism and took on the name King Milind. Nagsen transcribed these discussions and discourses into a book that is about the basics of Buddhism and is called the '*Milind Panha a Pali*'. As mentioned above, there is a whole area called 'Nagseni' in Kishtwar. It was the seat of a minor principality.

The kingdom of Kishtwar

It is assumed that the Kishtwar state was founded in the tenth century A.D., possibly by a line descended from the Rajas of Bengal. They were related to the kings of Suket, Keonthal and Mandi (all three in HP). The earliest definite mention of Kishtwar is to a visit to Kashmir by 'Uttamaraja, the ruler of Kashthavata' to pay homage to Raja Kalasa (A.D. 1063-89) of Kashmir. The title 'Thakur' came to be used in the Chandrabhaga valley at least by the eleventh century. Two of these Thakurs helped the Kashmiri king Harsh's grandson Bhiksha Char when he attempted to recover the throne of Kashmir. (Since mediæval times the Thakurs-or Thakkars-have been Hindus as well as Muslims.)

Historian Wali Mohammad Aseer Kishtwari, however, says, "Kahan Pal or Kahan Sena was the first recognised Raja of Kishtwar State who belonged to the royal dynasty of *Ujjain* [emphasis added] and established his rule much earlier than 1087-88 A.D. He was succeeded by Raja Gandarb Sen and subsequently by 45 others in the line of succession."

The next few references to Kishtwar are all about it being a place that Kashmiris would run to whenever they got into trouble in the Valley. This aspect of Kishtwar continues almost to the present. In ancient times Hindu nobles did this. In medieval times if a (Muslim) prince fought with his father, the king of Kashmir, he would seek refuge in Kishtwar. In the 1990s Kashmiri militants (and Pakistani kidnappers with western hostages) fleeing the security forces in Kashmir would sometimes hide in Kishtwar.

Alkah was the capital of Kishtwar in mediæval times. It was at a distance of 60 *kos* from Srinagar.

* * *

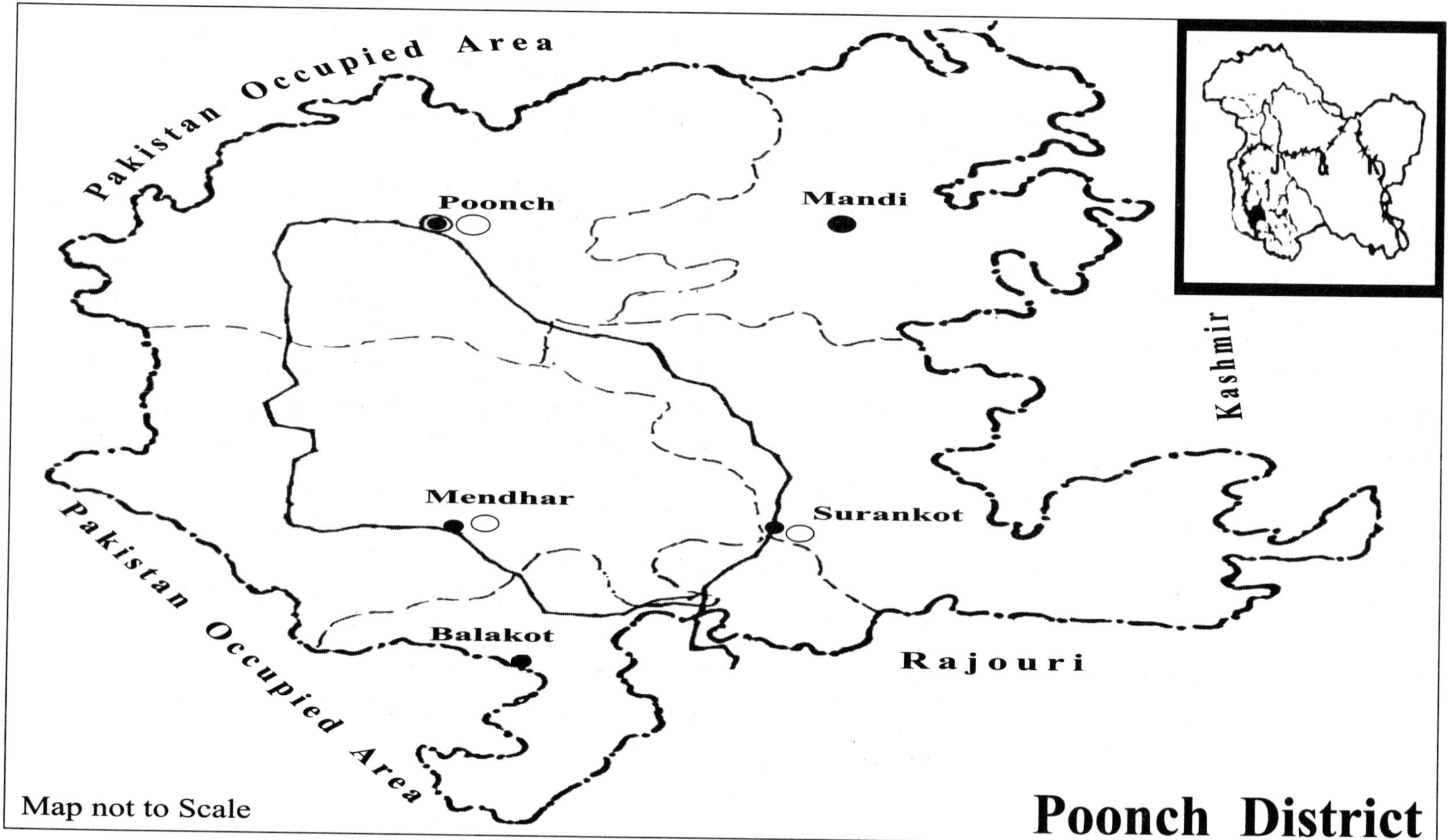

Poonch District

3

Poonch

(Pre-history—A.D. 1500)

The word Poonch is a shortening and corruption of Parnotsa, the ancient name of the region. It has been spelt Punch in British records and is pronounced poon-chh, the 'oo' being as in 'good'. The word Parnotsa is, in turn, perhaps derived from the Sanskrit *parna* (leaf). The earliest available reference to the area is in the A.D. 633 account of Hiuen Tsang, the Chinese traveller, who called it Pun-nu-tso. The Kashmiris, who have frequently ruled over Poonch, as they did in Hiuen Tsang's time, call it Punats.

These names have generally been given to the area located in the valleys of the Poonch Tohi (Tausi) and its tributaries. In the north is the Pir Panjal range, Rajouri is in the east, the plains to the south and the Jehlum in the west. Like Rajouri, it lies between the Jehlum and the Chenâb, within the hill tract called Darvabhisara. Across the mountains in the north are Baramulla and Uri in Kashmir.

Its ancient capital, Lohara, was northeast of today's Poonch town, and was the same as today's Loran (Lohrin), as Cunningham has convincingly shown. In the centre of Loran valley is a ridge on which was located the formidable Loharakotta (or Lohkot) fortress, the residence of the Lohara kings mentioned by Al Beruni (A.D. 1017–31). It was attacked twice, both times unsuccessfully, by Mahmud, the famous invader from Ghazni.

The fortunes of Poonch have always been linked—and not just geographically—with neighbouring Rajouri. Both were inhabited in ancient times by the Khasha tribe (perhaps the ancestors of today's Khakhas). The *Rajatarangini* mentions this tribe and calls the kings of Raja(p)uri and Lohara 'the lords of the Khashas.'

Hiuen Tsang says about Poonch, 'The people are true and upright. They are Buddhists. There are five sangharamas, mostly deserted. To the north of the chief town is a sangharama with a few priests. Here there is a stupa, which is celebrated for its miracles. The country has no independent ruler and is tributary to Kashmir.' From his description it seems that neighbouring Kotli was once part of Poonch.

Parnotsa was the name of the area. The kingdom was called Lohara till at least the 16th century.

A merchant called Nara founded the Lohara state around A.D. 830 and ruled it till 870 or thereabouts. The evidence indicates that his kingdom spread well beyond today's Poonch district. The *Rajatarangini* mentions that he owned 'spotless horses, as well as villages.'

It was during the reign of his son Nara Vahana (c.A.D. 870-890) that Poonch's first recorded conflict with Kashmir took place. During a journey through Lohara, King Shankar Varman of Kashmir and his army camped in that kingdom and at night killed Nara Vahana and his followers, whom they suspected of treachery.

Involvement in Kashmir's politics

Six (recorded) generations later, Didda, a princess from Lohara, was given in marriage to Kshemagupt around A.D. 950. She occupies a prominent position in the history of Kashmir because when her husband, the king, died she got rid of her son and grandsons and grabbed the throne for herself. She ruled Kashmir from 980 to 1003. Thus began the Lohara dynasty of Kashmir.

Didda chose Sangram Raja, the son of her brother Uday Raja, the ruler of Lohara, to succeed her to the Kashmir throne. Meanwhile, around A.D. 1001 Sangram's elder brother Vigrah Raja, who became the king of Lohara upon their father Uday's death in A.D. 1000, made an unsuccessful bid to capture the Kashmir throne. Didda defeated him.

By now all of India west of the Indus was under Muslim kings. Sultan Mahmud of Ghazni began knocking on the doors of the Hindu Shahi kings of the Punjab, two of whom, Anand Pal and later his son Trilochan Pal, fled the invaders and sought refuge in the valley of the Poonch Tohi (Tausi). By this time the Hindu Shahis, the Loharas and the kings of Kashmir had close relations with one another. However, in January-February 1013, despite help from the latter two, the Shahis were crushed by Mahmud's forces, in a battle at the junction of the Tohi and the Jehlum, and their dynasty was finished for ever.

Several Muslim historians of the Indian plains (e.g. Ferishta) claim that Mahmud pursued the Hindu army into 'the Kashmir valley.' However, Kashmir's own extremely detailed histories make no mention of this. Therefore perhaps areas like Lohara, which were subject to Kashmir, were meant.

After the rout of his army and those of his two allies, Tunga, the commander-in-Chief of the Kashmiri army started preparing to return home. Vigrah Raja of Lohara, who bore an enmity to him, got him and his son killed by Sangram Raja of Kashmir.

Mahmud, on his part, returned in 1015 to punish Lohara for having sided with his enemies. He spent all summer trying to capture the tall and strong Loharakotta fort. Unable to do so he retreated to Ghazni when snow began to fall in the winter and by when Lohara had received reinforcements from Kashmir. This, as Ferishta notes, was Mahmud's first 'disaster suffered in India.' In 1021, Mahmud repeated the siege, but once again Loharakotta proved too difficult for him to conquer. He was defeated a second time by the brave warriors of Lohara/ Poonch.

When Sangram Raja of Kashmir died he was succeeded by his son Hari Raja, who ruled for all of twenty-two days. After Hari came his minor brother Anant Deva. Vigrah Raja of Lohara, who had a much longer reign than his brother Sangram, had in the past been defeated in his attempt to capture Kashmir. In 1030, given the fluid situation in Kashmir, he decided to try again. After spectacular initial successes, he was killed by young Anant Deva's army.

Kshiti Raja, who succeeded his father Vigrah, reigned for thirty-five years. However, his son Bhuvan Raja tried to dethrone his father, first with the help of his uncle, Anant Deva, and then by enlisting the support of the army of Nilapura (one of Jammu's old capitals). Around now we learn that Kshiti defeated the Raja(p)uri army. The latter probably included Bhuvan's contingents.

Kshiti probably had no other sons. So, in 1065, he abdicated in favour of Utkarsh, an infant, who was the grandson of Anant Deva. Kshiti went on to become a learned saint devoted to Lord Vishnu. He spent his remaining days at Chakradhara, a shrine in Kashmir.

Utkarsh's father Kalas became the king of Kashmir after Anant Deva. Kalas' elder son Harsh was the heir apparent. But Harsh committed some crime for which his father punished him. When he was about to die Kalas got his younger son Utkarsh called over from Lohara and asked him to take over the Kashmir throne. Thus was Lohara merged with Kashmir. From that day Lohara (and, its successor, Poonch) would, from time to time be ruled by Kashmir.

Upon Kalas' death in 1089, Harsh was released from prison by his guards and accepted as the king of Kashmir by loyal courtiers. Utkarsh, who was barely twenty-four years old, committed suicide, perhaps afraid that he would be killed.

Lohara continued to loom large in the politics of Kashmir. Around 1095, Uchchala and Sussala, two young princes of Lohara origin, grew popular in Kashmir because of their bravery in a war against the Dards. Their relative and mentor, King Harsh Dev of Kashmir, suspected them of fomenting trouble in Kashmir. So, in 1101 they had to flee Kashmir. Uchchala, the elder, was given refuge by the king of Raja(p)uri. Harsh Dev paid a Raja(p)uri official to murder Uchchala. This did not work out. Instead, the brothers, backed by Kashmiri warlords (the feudal Damaras), marched on Harsh and killed his son Bhoja and him.

Thus did the first Lohara dynasty come to an end.

The victorious brothers carved up the territory between themselves. In 1101, Uchchala took over Kashmir and gave Lohara to his brother Sussala. A dissatisfied Sussala tried to wrest Kashmir for himself. His invasion of Kashmir was a failure. However, following Uchchala's assassination in 1111 by one of his own officers, Sussala was asked to take over the throne of Kashmir.

Meanwhile, Bhoja's son Bhiksha Char, who had been spirited away to Malwa as a child following Bhoja's death, came of age. In 1120, he defeated Sussala and made him retreat to Lohara. For six months the throne was back with Harsh's dynasty, but soon Sussala recovered the kingdom.

* * *

4

Rajouri

(Pre-history—A.D. 1500)

The earliest references

In mediæval times the main town was called Rajapuri or 'the town of the king.' However, in older times still, and till at least the twelfth century, the area was called Darvabhisara. The *Mahabharat,* the *Purans* and the *Brihatsamhita* use this name. The *Rajatarangini* tells us that Rajapuri was part of the Darvabhisara region. With time the whole area came to be known by the name of its capital.

The older name was derived by putting together the names of two tribes, Darva and Abhisara, which lived in the outer hills between the Jehlum and Chenâb rivers. (These rivers are referred to as the Vitasta and the Chandrabhaga respectively in old records.)

Some historians believe that the Panchal Desh of the *Mahabharat* is the region near the Peer Panchal/ Panjal mountains. Such a kingdom would naturally include Rajouri. Therefore, they argue that Draupadi, who married the Pândavs, was a princess of this region.

The *Mahâbhârat* also says that King Arjun had subjugated the Darva clan. This mention is, without doubt, about Rajouri.

The Abhisara state later broke up into Loharkot or Parnotsa (Poonch), Rajapuri (Rajouri), Kalinjar and Nilapura. The area was often subordinate to the kings of Kashmir. The Khasa tribe lived here.

Abisares and Alexander the Great

The 4th century BC: Ancient Greeks wrote of Abisares (obviously Abhisara), a king from this area, 'the king of the Indian mountaineers'. He was an ally of the legendary Porus, the ruler of the plains between the Jehlum and the Chenâb. Together they were in a state of war with the king of Takshilâ.

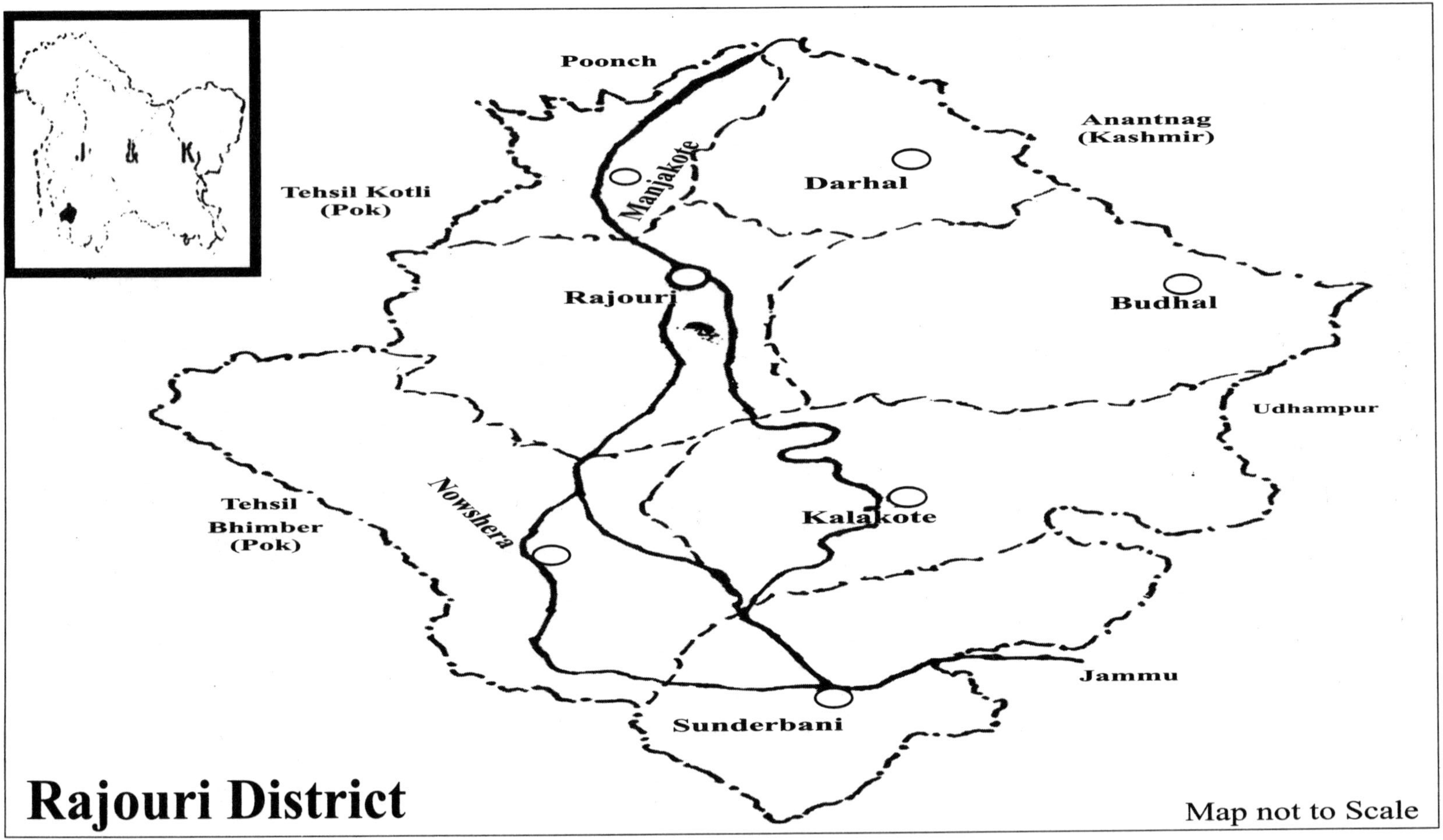

Rajouri District

Only a year before, the then king of Takshilâ had submitted to Alexander's authority at Nikaia (now Jalalabad). He died shortly thereafter. A year later, his son, the new king of Takshilâ, met Alexander at Ohind and presented the Greek with seven hundred horses, supplies for the Greek army and expensive gifts. He offered Alexander an alliance. In return he wanted the Greeks to help him against the Porus-Abisares combine.

Alexander and his army headed towards the Indus. Abisares tried to resist Alexander on the Indus. The Greeks conquered Aornos, as well as the route to the Indus. Abisares realised that there was no point in putting up a fight.

He sent his brother and a group of envoys to Takshilâ to tell Alexander that Abisares would accept his overlordship. Alexander was pleased by the news. He thought that Porus would do the same. As we all know, Porus did not. He had to be defeated in battle instead. Abisares' army did not take part in that battle.

Porus' defeat unnerved Abisares. Once again he sent word to Alexander that he was prepared to give himself up and hand over his kingdom. However, Alexander was informed, perhaps correctly, that Abisares' submission was only tactical. Porus and he had been planning to fight the Greeks at the Hydaspes (Jehlum). Because Porus' army had not arrived in time, Abisares panicked and decided to surrender.

Alexander was infuriated by what he saw as double-dealing. He commanded Abisares to appear before him, failing which he would attack his territory. Once again Abisares sent his brother and envoys over to Alexander, with forty elephants and expensive presents. The Greek was again pleased.

Arsakes, the king of Urasa (Hazara), had already tendered his submission, with presents, to Alexander, at the Chenâb. Alexander made Abisares the Viceroy of the outer hills between the Chenâb and the Indus, and put Arsakes under him.

Abisares' diplomatic skills thus saved the region from the wrath of the then invincible Alexander. He also managed to do quite well for himself in the process.

The winter capital of ancient Kashmir

King Abhimanyu I ruled over Kashmir around the second century. He used to spend his winters in Darvabhisara. Obviously the region was part of the kingdom of Kashmir as early as that.

At some stage between the 2nd and 7th centuries A.D., in the so-called Buddhist period, Rajouri was part of the Gandhar kingdom. In the Mauryan period, the town was an important trading centre.

Hiuen Tsang travelled through Rajouri in A.D. 633. He refers to the area as Ho-lo-she-pu-lo. He wrote, "The country has no independent ruler, but is subject to Kashmir. There are ten *sangharmas* [Buddhist monasteries], with a very small number of priests. There is one temple of Devas with an enormous number of unbelievers." The great Chinese pilgrim was not above making generalisations about 'national characters'. He described the people of Rajouri as 'quick and hasty'.

Apparently, the Pal dynasty administered Rajouri even in Hiuen Tsang's times.

The next reference to Rajouri relates to A.D. 850. The *Rajatarangini* says, "Nara and other merchants, who were in possession of spotless horses and owned villages, ruled Darvabhisara and the neighbouring regions, setting up [their own] thrones." This indicates that the chiefs of Rajouri 'owned villages', under the overall control of Kashmir.

A chief of the Khasha tribe is likely to have founded the Rajapuri state, freeing it from the suzerainty of Kashmir.

Al Beruni visited Rajouri around A.D. 1021. By then the name of the place had changed to Rajawari. (In the Arabic and Persian scripts 'Rajawari' and 'Rajouri' are both spelt the same way.)

Vassals of Kashmir

In the winter of 1087-88, several hill chiefs went to Kashmir to pay homage to King Kalas. Raja Sangram Pal of Rajouri was one of them.

From the *Rajatarangini* it is seen that in the 15th century the (Hindu) kings of Rajouri would send their princesses to Kashmir. This was done in the hope that the, by now Muslim, Sultan of Kashmir would marry their daughters.

One such Sultan, the great Zain-ul-Abedin, was camping near the Wular Lake when he saw a lady's palanquin pass by. He asked, 'What mother's palanquin is that?' The Sultan was told that it was Rajya Devi, daughter of King Sundar Sen of Rajouri, who had been sent to marry him. The Sultan replied, 'How can I marry her, now that I have called her 'mother'?'

Rajya Devi stayed on in the Sultan's harem anyway, though, so to speak, as the Sultan's 'mother'. She converted to Islam and built the Rajouri/ Rajwir/ Rajey Kadal bridge. Her father was not one to give up. He then sent his second daughter, Sundara Devi, to marry the Sultan, and this time the Sultan agreed.

* * *

5

Jammu

(1100–1846)

The capital shifts from Jammu to Babbapura

By A.D. 1001, India had begun to be attacked by armies from the west. Jammu (Durgara) was one of the important cities on the route of the invaders. Therefore, its rulers probably shifted their capital from Bahu to Babbapura (Babor) for a few generations, perhaps two hundred years. Lahore and the plains of the Punjab had come under kings who happened to be Muslim. However, the rulers of Lahore were unable to conquer the kingdoms in the mountains, which continued to be ruled by Rajput chiefs.

Kirti's descendants Ajay Dhar, Vijay Dhar and Vajra Dhar aka Vajral Dhar (c. 1110-1125) succeeded him.

By A.D. 1101, Uchchala and Sussala had killed Bhoja and assumed power in Kashmir. Princess Asamati spirited Bhoja's infant grandson, Bhiksha Char, away to Malwa, where he remained till 1112. He met several hill chiefs, including Vajra Dhar and the crown prince of Vallapura (Billawar), at Kurukshetra, where they had gone on a pilgrimage. The two princes from Jammu province promised to help Bhiksha Char regain the Kashmir throne.

Bhiksha Char's invasion of Kashmir was unsuccessful. So, Vajra Dhar switched his allegiance to Sussala. It is clear that Vajra Dhar was subordinate to Sussala.

There is some disagreement about the period during which the Dhar dynasty ruled over Jammu. Charak and Billawaria believe that this dynasty 'ruled at Jammu upto about A.D. 840 when its last ruler, Bajar Dhar, died.' Dr. Mani supports this view. He says that 'Surajdev became the ruler of the area in the ninth century A.D. after snatching power from Bajradhar...'

On the other hand, there is a whole body of scholarship which shows that Bajar/ Bajra Dhar (Vajra Dhar) continued to rule till around A.D. 1125. He was a contemporary of Kashmir's Sussala. (Dates pertaining to mediæval Kashmir are accurate to the month.)

The Dev dynasty

Vajra Dhar's successor, Surya Dev (c.1125-50), was the first king of Jammu to use the surname Dev. The Dev dynasty remained in power till around 1816, when the main branch of the family was expelled from Jammu. The Dogra/ Jamwal dynasty, which ruled till 1947, is an offshoot of the Dev dynasty.

Charak and Billawaria write that 'brave rulers of this dynasty put up a strong resistance to the Turk invaders and defeated even raiding armies of Mahmud and his successor Masaud on several occasions. But it is strange that the rulers of this dynasty became allies of Muhammad Ghori and fought on his side against Prithvi Raj Chauhan. At the battle field of Tarain the Raja of Jammu was found on the side of Muhammad Ghori along with Jai Chand. The Jammu contingent was commanded by Narsing Dev, son of the Raja. The *Rajadarshini* narrates that Prithvi Raj's brother, Khande Rao, was killed at the hands of Narsing Dev.'

In any case, it was the Dev dynasty that united the tiny principalities of Jammu province. This led to economic development as well. Dr. Mani credits this dynasty with having built the great temples of Kiramchi and Babbaur. He says that the temples were 'mostly located on ancient trade routes.' (I wonder about that. Now, Kiramchi was indeed on the route to Kashmir. But what about Billawar, Sukrala Devi, Sudh Mahadev and the temples of Rajouri? Babbaur itself could have been on a trade route, but the reason for its temples was that it was the capital of the kingdom.)

Bhuj Dev (c.1150-75) succeeded Surya Dev. His second son, Autar Dev (c.1175), followed. Nothing is known about the successors of Autar's son Jas Dev (c.1195), except their names. Jas Dev established the Jasrota state, as well as the clan that would rule over it for several centuries. Manak Dev, another descendant of Bhuj, founded the Mankot state and clan.

Mal Dev (c.1370) was the tenth king after Autar. (Records kept by contemporary Muslims date his reign to 749 Hijri.) According to the *Vanshawali* he represented the 63rd generation of the Agnibaran/ Jambu Lochan clan, after its migration from Oopa. From all accounts Mal Dev was a great, visionary ruler. It probably was he who brought the capital back from Babbapura, this time to the present Jammu town itself. He also conquered areas west of the Chenâb and up to Sialkot.

Bhim Dev (c.1395) came next. While he has not been mentioned by name, perhaps he is the anonymous Raja of Jammu referred to in the memoirs of Timur, the Central Asian conqueror. Some, like Charak and Billawaria, believe that the Raja who fought Amir Timur in February 1399 was the great Mal Dev. They put Mal Dev's reign at between 1360 and 1405. We can accept both assertions, but not their subsequent claim that Mal Dev's 'strong defence discouraged Timur from attacking Jammu town.'

Timur's invasion: A.D. 1398-9

Timur laid a successful ambush on the Jammu army. After that he returned to Samarqand, past the Chenâb and the Indus. He described Jammu as 'a green and fertile country' with 'arable land'.

Let us hear the story in his own words: "The castle of Jammu was near [and] connected with the Siwalik and Kuka mountains. Its inhabitants were not submissive and obedient to the Sultans of Hindustan. [On learning this, in 1398] I marched from Mansar, determined to carry my arms [against Jammu]... The people of Baila, in the territory of Jammu, had placed themselves in ambush in many places along the borders of the jungle, prepared to give battle and offer resistance... When the cries of my warriors sounded in their ears, they wavered and fled, seeking refuge in the dense jungles and thickets. I directed the Amirs... that [my] troops [should] enter the village of Baila and plunder it in security... The soldiers obtained great quantities of grain, sugar and oil. After that they set fire to the houses and destroyed the buildings... On this day Ra-Timur was wounded. [He doesn't say how—PD.]

"[Three days later] I sent my army over the river to the foot of a mountain, on the left of the town, and to the village of Manu on the right. When my forces had secured these positions, the demon-spirited Hindus sent off their wives and children from their villages to the tops of the mountains, and they fortified themselves in the village. The Raja, with his warlike gabrs, and athletic Hindus, took his post in the valley where they howled like so many jackals. I commanded that not a soldier should go towards the mountain or have anything to do with these gabrs, but they should attack and plunder the town of Jammu and village of Manu. Accordingly my forces fell to plundering, and secured an enormous booty in grain, goods of all kinds, and cattle. I returned victorious... and passed the night in pleasure and rest...

"After I had marched away, the Raja of Jammu and other devilish *gabrs* came down confidently from the tops of the hills. When they reached the plain, the Amirs rushed suddenly from their ambush upon the infidels, and killed a great number of them... The Raja of Jammu, who was ruler of the country, with fifty Raos and Rajputs, had been made prisoners...

"When my eyes fell upon the Raja of Jammu, who was wounded and a prisoner, fear took possession of his heart, and he agreed to pay certain sums of money and to become a [Muslim]... When he had thus been received into the fold of the faithful, I ordered my surgeons to attend to his wounds, and I honoured him with a robe and royal favours."

Relations with Kashmir and the Khokhars

While studying the history of Kashmir we learn that the great Zain-ul-Abedin became the king when his brother, Sultan Ali, proceeded for the Haj pilgrimage via Jammu. This happened some time between A.D. 1416 and 1420. We also know that Ali had gone to Jammu to meet his father-in-law, the king of Jammu.

It was not unusual for the Hindu kings of Kishtwar and Rajouri to give their daughters in marriage to the Muslim kings of Kashmir.[1] Therefore, I had always supposed that it must have been so even in the case of Sultan Ali's father-in-law, whose name has not been recorded anywhere. However, it is certain that the king whom Timur had converted to Islam was Ali's father-in-law. Only the name is not known. We can safely assume that the recently (in 1399) Islamised Bhim Dev was Sultan Ali's father-in-law.

Historians of the British Raj, including those whom I have relied on for this account, describe Timur's as a 'Muhammadan invasion'. Apart from the word 'Muhammadan' being unPC (politically incorrect), it is totally wrong to describe Timur's foray in terms of religion. The fact is that Punjabi Muslims opposed Timur, while Rai Bhim Dev, the Hindu king of Jammu, assisted him. Besides, Bhim was on very good terms with Mubarak Shah, the Sayyid king of Delhi.

A leading Muslim noble called Nasrat Shaikha Khokhar had been the Tughlaqs' Governor of Lahore. In 1420, he bravely, if unsuccessfully, tried to halt Timur's advance towards Delhi. Incidentally, it is from Timur's memoirs that we first hear of the Khokhar family, which looms large in the histories of both Kashmir and Jammu right up to the late 19th century.

Some time later, Jasrath Shaikha Khokhar, perhaps Nasrat's nephew, too, rose against Timur, who defeated him. Jasrath fled towards Jammu. Timur and his army followed him all the way to the Jammu kingdom. Rai Bhim visited Timur's camp and offered to be his pathfinder in the

1 Till the Mughal Emperor Jehangir forbade the practice in 1620, the Muslim girls of kingdoms like Rajouri would, in turn, marry Hindu men.

pursuit of Jasrath. He took Timur to Jasrath's fortress in Tekhar, which Timur conquered.

That Bhim was on bad terms with Jasrath Khokhar is certain. He also enlisted the support of Mubarak Shah of Delhi in his wars with the Khokhars.

In 1423, Jasrath invaded the Punjab again. Rai Bhim died defending the land. At some stage Jasrath married Bhim's daughter, who killed him to avenge her father's death.

Relations with Central Indian emperors

We know nothing about the five kings who succeeded Bhim Dev, except their names, which indicate that all of them, even Bhim Dev's son Hamir Dev[2], were Hindu. The last of the five was Kapur Dev (c.1530-70). There was a bitter dispute between his sons Jag Dev, who ruled from Bahu, and Samil Dev, whose capital was Jammu. It was these two (and not Bahu and Jambu Lochan) who started the Bahuwal and Jamwal lines.

During their time, and that of their respective sons Paras Ram Dev (c.1585) and Sangram Dev, relations between the two kingdoms were extremely tense. People from the other side of the Tawi would be robbed, physically abused and, sometimes, killed if they crossed over.

Let us, however, go back to A.D. 1009. That was when Mahmud briefly captured nearby Nagarkot (Kangra, Himachal Pradesh) and ruled it till 1043, interrupting its ancient line. By A.D. 1193, the first Muslim kings had taken Delhi. Around that time, Jammu, too, had become tributary to the various Muslim kings of the Indian plains.

The Mughal emperor Humayun exercised sway over Jammu. In 1542-43, his rival and successor, Sher Shah Sur(i), defeated Kapur Dev.

After the Mughals regained Delhi, several Kings of Jammû visited the Mughal court. These included Kapûr Dév, who went there in 1557. Later, says Dr. Sharma[ii], so did Râjâ Jav [sic] Dév (c.1570-90), the son of Smâil [or Samil] Dév. He wanted the Mughals to intercede in his favour in the dispute for the Jammû throne. (I believe this was Jag Dév, who had a dispute with his *brother* Smâil.) Then, during the reign of Emperor Jehâñgîr and perhaps also during that of his son, Shâh Jehân, Râjâ Sañgrâm Dév went over to Delhi to pay homage. About Hari Dév's close association with Aurañgzéb we shall read anon.

2 Charak and Billawaria say that Hamir Dev was an alias of Bhim Dev.

Rebellions against the Mughals and Surs

The hill states, especially Jammu, would periodically rebel against Delhi/ Agra/ Lahore and declare themselves independent. The most famous of these rebellions was against Salim Shah Sur(i) (1545-1553). Salim annexed Jammu formally in 1550. That perhaps was when Jammu first became a part of India, politically. Jammu's various Rajas had some autonomy but they were clearly subordinate to a governor, who was normally based in Lahore.

The Suris ruled India rather briefly. When they fell, Jammu reassserted its independence, also very briefly.

Akbar became the Emperor of India in 1556. He ensured that for the next almost two hundred years the hill states were part of the Mughal Empire, even if reluctantly.

In 1588-89, the hill states chalked out a joint strategy against the Mughals. Almost all of them rose as one. Apart from Paras Ram of Bahu, the other chiefs involved were Bal Bhadar of Lakhanpur, Buzurg of Jasrota, Daulat of Kot Bharta (Bhaddu), Partap of Mankot, Rai Krishan of Billawar and several chiefs of what is now Himachal Pradesh. Raja Bidhi Chand of Kangra, obviously a great leader, orchestrated this massive and widespread rebellion.

Akbar's foster-brother Zain Khan, however, proved an abler strategist. He led the Mughal forces through Pathankot, divided the forces of the hill chiefs, took them on one by one, defeated them all and took the chiefs to the Mughal court.

Dr Jerath writes, 'Most of the soldiers of [the hill] states surrendered before the Mughal army except Bhivu Dev, the feudal lord of Jasrotâ. A fierce battle took place for days together. Jasrotias harmed the Mughal forces to the extent that they had to withdraw. On the next day, Mughal forces jointly attacked the fort of Jasrota. In the evening and after overcoming a strong resistance they succeeded [in getting] into the fort. But even then Bhivu Dev did not surrender and fled towards Sâmbâ. He was seized again but he again fled towards the hills.' (*The Hindustan Times*, 21 April, 1999.)

Ultimately the chiefs submitted to Mughal authority, gave expensive gifts, left a son or other relative each as hostage at the Mughal court, were pardoned and were sent back to their principalities. (See also 'Bhaderwah' in the chapter on 'Regional Histories for an interesting take on this series of events.)

The hill chiefs were sullen in their defeat. Six years later, in 1594-95, they rose again. This time Buzurg, the Raja of Jasrota, led them. Jammu and Ramgarh were certainly among the states that rebelled. Sheikh

Farid, the Mughals' Bakhshi (paymaster), led the Imperial Army against them.

The Sheikh began by attacking Jammu. Contemporary accounts describe Jammu as 'one of the strongest forts in that country, which had once been reduced, after considerable resistance, by Salim Shah Sur'. The Mughal army overawed the chiefs. Samil's son Sangram Dev, a minor, was the Raja of Jammu. He surrendered his fort in panic. The Sheikh then captured the Ramgarh fort by force. Thereafter, he intimidated Jasruna (Jasrota) and Lakhanpur into submission.

In 1616-17, a hill chief killed Raja Man, the Mughals' governor of the Punjab, in battle. Sangram Dev could possibly have been this chief. And yet the Mughals did not hold this against Sangram.. He was either useful to them or too important among the hill chiefs to offend.

Indeed, the *Tuzuk-i-Jehangiri* (Emperor Jehangir's memoirs) speaks warmly of Sangrâm Dev. It first refers to him as a *zamindar* (landlord; feudal chief). In 1619, Jehangir conferred on him the title of Raja (king). It mentions the gifts (of money, robes, elephants and titles) that the emperor gave Sangram, on various occasions in 1618 and 1619.

Thus, Sangram was clearly a favoured subordinate of the emperor. Jehangir also gave him two major promotions. Sangram was accepted as a mansabdar with the rank of 1000 *zât* and 500 *sawâr*. This was not a high rank in the all-India hierarchy, but it was one of the best in the Punjab hill states.

In 1620, Sangram, obeying orders from the Mughals, sent his troops to Kishtwar to put down a rebellion there. Sangram acted so even though the King of Kishtwar was related to him.

Sangram ruled till 1624. His grandson, King Hari Dev (c.1656-92), impressed Emperor Aurangzeb, who made him a mansabdar. Indeed, he seems to have enjoyed the same rapport with Aurangzeb as their grandfathers had with each other.

Kripal Singh (c.1660) was the fourth king of Bahu after Paras Ram. The then Mughal Viceroy of the Punjab, Khwaja Rezia Beg, began to annex the territories of the hill chiefs through periodic raids. Kripal teamed up with King Dhiraj Pal of Basohli and some Himachal chiefs. They employed Pathan mercenaries to defeat the invaders.

Some time around 1675, the Bahuwal Rajas left Bahu, never to rule again. It is almost certain that Hari Dev, who had Aurangzeb's support, forced them out. Jammu was united again, a unity that has lasted to this day. (Dr. D.C. Sharma alone says that this merger took place under Ranjit Dev, i.e. after 1735.)

Around 1692, Aurangzeb went to the Deccan. He took Hari Dev along. The Raja of Jammu died while he was there.

Collaboration with the Afghans

The Mughal emperor Aurangzeb died in 1707. Till his death, Jammu was a faujdari (province) of the Mughals. His successors were weak. So, Mughal power began to wane. Hari's grandson, Dhrub Dev, became the king in 1703, against this backdrop.

A close relationship had always existed between Jammu, Bhaddu and Basohli. During Dhrub's time this developed into an alliance. Together they invaded Guler (HP). In turn Guler allied with Chamba to drive the intruders out.

All the same, the alliance with Bhaddu and Basohli, as well as internal unity, gave Jammu state the confidence to assert itself over its neighbours. Jammu brought most of the smaller states between the Chenâb and the Ravi under its control in the first few decades of the eighteenth century. Dhrub annexed Samba, Jasrota, Lakhanpur and Billawar.

Above all, around this time, Jammu, like other hill states, expelled Mughal officers and declared itself independent. Charak and Billawaria say that this happened during Dhrub's reign. Others give credit for this to his elder son, Ranjit Dev.

Ranjit Dev: Jammu's first empire builder

Ranjit Dev (A.D. 1733) was the most remarkable king of Jammu state ever. Zakariah Khan, the Mughals' governor of the Punjab, was told that Ranjit was not loyal to the Mughals. So, Zakariah marched to Jammu, arrested Ranjit and kept him in prison in Lahore for twelve years. Ranjit's brother, Ghansar, acted as the regent in his absence.

Adina Beg Khan, the governor of Jalandhar, pleaded on Ranjit's behalf. Accordingly, in 1747, shortly before Zakariah's death, Ranjit was released for a ransom of two lakh rupees.

Ahmad Shah Durrani, the Afghan, overran the Punjab and wrested the province in 1752. Mughal control was thus terminated. Ranjit supported Durrani and was duly rewarded. Durrani gave him a large jagir (estate) in Kashmir. Ranjit thus became the first ruler from Jammu in recorded history to possess some kind of territorial rights in Kashmir.

That same year the Afghans annexed Kashmir. In 1754, their governor, Sukh Jiwan, declared himself virtually independent. Sensing an opportunity, in 1755 Ranjit made an attempt to conquer Kashmir for himself. He failed.

Durrani invaded Kashmir in 1762, to reassert the Afghans' supremacy over their rebellious governor. This time Ranjit helped the Afghans only after considerable pressure had been exerted on him.

The Afghans' hold on the Punjab was shaky. The neighbouring hill states were under them only in theory. This was partly because of Maratha invasions. More important, the Lahore kingdom and the hill chiefs had begun to reclaim the areas that the Mughals had taken from them.

The talented Ranjit Dev declared himself independent. After that he claimed all territories between the Chenâb and the Ravi. He invaded Chamba, with the help of Amrit Pal of Basohli. For a while, his kingdom included Poonch and Rajouri in the west, Nurpur and Chamba (both HP) in the east and Sialkot and Gurdaspur (both Punjab) in the south. Kangra, Mandi and Suket (all HP) came under his sway.

However, in 1775, Raja Raj Singh of Chamba expelled Ranjit's forces, with the help of Ramgarhia Sikhs.

Ranjit was more successful in subduing Kishtwar and Bhaderwah, though.

The present royal family of Jammu, the junior branch of the Jamwal dynasty, is descended from Ranjit Dev's third brother, Surat Singh. (Gulab Singh, the first Maharaja of Jammu and Kashmir, was Surat Singh's great-grandson.)

Ranjit Dev and the rise of Jammu town

It was during the reign of the great Ranjit Dev that Jammu town suddenly grew in importance.

The 1890 Gazetteer records that Ranjit's "reputation for justice and moderation extended as far as Lahore, and numerous families of high rank and large fortune fled to his territory and stronghold. He commenced the building of the present palace [Mubarak Mandi] of Jamú, and in the year 1775, or five years before his death, the town had increased to about 3½ miles in circumference, about twice as large as the present day [1890], and boasted 150,000 inhabitants.

The Mughals' trade route to Kashmir and the north-west frontier of undivided India had become unsafe. Forster, an Englishman who travelled through Jammu in 1783, noted that this was so because of "the inroad of the Persians, Afghans and the Marhattas, but especially since the period of the Sikh conquests".

As a result, an older route from the plains, through Himachal Pradesh, which had been mentioned by Al Beruni (1017-1031), was revived. It passed through Nahan, Bilaspur, Nadaun, Guler and Basohli before reaching Jammu. (In later Dogra times the route proceeded from Jammu to Srinagar at times through Kishtwar but mostly along the present national highway.) Forster noted that "the journey [was] tedious and the expenses of merchandise increased" because the route was longer and the road worse. However, the route was safer than the Mughal route, which then fell into disuse, perhaps forever.

As in the 1990s, disorder in the neighbouring areas made people, many of them wealthy merchants, flee to Jammu for asylum. Hutchison and Vogel note, "To all alike, Hindu or Muhammadan, the Raja extended a warm welcome, and his capital grew and flourished."

Ranjit's immigration policy was as fascinating as enlightened. He encouraged merchants, artisans and displaced royalty to settle in Jammu. Forster, writing shortly after Ranjit's death, says, "[Ranjit Dev,] perceiving the benefits which would arise from the residence of Muhammadan merchants, observed towards them a disinterested i.e. impartial and honourable conduct. He protected and indulged his people, particularly the Muhammadans, to whom he allotted a certain quarter of the town, which was thence denominated Mughulpur, and, that no reserve might appear in his treatment of them, a mosque was erected in the new colony,-a liberty of disposition the more conspicuous and conferring the greater honour on his memory... He was so desirous also of acquiring their confidence and esteem, that when he has [sic] been riding through their quarter, during the time of prayer, he never failed to stop his horse until the priest Muslim had concluded his ritual exclamations."

Ranjit also overruled Hindus who complained that the water of public wells was being polluted by the Muslims' vessels. Ranjit decreed that water was pure and could not be defiled 'by the touch of any class of people'.

Among the political refugees whom Ranjit gave asylum to were Malka Zamani, a Delhi queen, members of the family of Raja Kaura Mal, the Dewan of Mir Manu, the Mughals' Viceroy of Lahore, the son of the Dewan of Yahya Khan (another Mughal Viceroy), and 'the remains of other families of the nobles of Delhi, or of the Viceregal Courts' (Hutchison and Vogel). We are told that one of Mir Manu's widows, too, found refuge in Jammu. It was because of acts like these that Ranjit's kingdom came to be known as a *Dâr ul Aman* (land of peace).

Jammu became a boomtown. Forster notes, "This made Jammu a place of extensive commercial resort, where all descriptions of men experienced in their persons and property a full security."

Braj Raj Dev was Ranjit's son and heir apparent. Ranjit wanted him to treat with honour the nobles who had sought refuge in Jammu, as well as other immigrants. Braj did not do so. Braj was also a bit of a rake. So Ranjit decided to pass the kingdom on to his younger son, Dalel Singh.

The Sikhs gain a foothold

Braj Raj appealed to his father's old enemy, Sardar Charhat Singh of the Sukarchakia Sikh *misl* (clan). He also asked Jai Singh of the Kanheya misl to help him depose his father. This was in 1774. Ranjit thus found himself compelled to seek the help of Jhanda Singh of the rival Bhangi misl. Jammu had been tributary to the Bhangi misl since around 1756, when the clan had first raided the state and plundered the town. (Their second raid took place in 1761-62.)

A six-month war between the two groups ensued. Charhat Singh was killed, either when his own matchlock burst or in a battle at Udhu Chak near River Basantar. It was clear that the Bhangis were going to win. So Jai Singh bribed a sweeper in the Jammu camp to assassinate Jhanda Singh. The sweeper did so when Jhanda was walking about (or, perhaps, riding) in his camp, unarmed.

Both misls thus lost their leaders, and returned to the Punjab. However, the Sikhs had obtained a foothold in Jammu. (Charhat Singh's grandson, the illustrious Maharaja Ranjit Singh, would later rule over it.)

Despite pinpricks from his elder son, Ranjit established Jammu as the main power among the 22 hill states. Rajouri, Akhnoor, Kiramchi, Chenaini, Bhoti and Dalpatpur were among its tributaries. Mankot, Basohli and Bhaddu were dependent on Jammu. Jasrota was still independent, but Sâmbâ had been annexed. Jammu probably controlled Kishtwar and Bhaderwah, too. However, Forster says that Kishtwar and Bhaderwah were under Chamba. He adds, "It appears that Jumbo [Jammu] continued to increase its power and commerce until the... period of Ranzeid-Dev's death."

Ranjit died a natural death in 1781 (or 1782). Braj Raj succeeded him. He asked his cousin, Mian Mota, to kill his brother and rival, Dalel. Mota did so at Charan Paduka, when Dalel was on his way up to the shrine of 'Trikota Mai' (obviously Sri Mâtâ Vaishno Devi ji). Dalel's little son, Jit Singh, escaped to the Punjab and sought help from the Sikhs, presumably the Bhangis.

Forster continues the story thus, "Pleased in having obtained so favourable a pretext for entering Jumbo, which they attempted in vain during the administration of Ranzeid-Dev, the Sicques [Sikhs] promised to espouse the fugitive's [Jit's] cause with vigour. A small sum had been annually exacted by them from Jumbo, but in a much less proportion than what was levied in the adjacent territories. The Sicques, indeed, aware of the respectable state of the Jumbo force, and the ability of the Chief, were contented with the name of tribute." Meanwhile, many of Braj Raj's subjects were "driven by [Braj's] oppressions to the party of his brother".

Jammu becomes subject to the Lahore kingdom

The Bhangis annexed Karianwala, a territory in Jammu. Braj allied with the Kanheya misl, which helped him recover Karianwala. However, the Kanheyas then abandoned Braj and made up with the Bhangis. So, Braj allied himself with the Sukarchakia misl. The Kanheyas defeated him and he agreed to pay them an annual tribute of Rs. 30,000. However, he did not actually pay up. The angry Kanheyas won over his allies, the Sukarchakias, and prepared to attack flourishing Jammu.

Maha Singh Sukarchakia led the attack. Braj Raj fled to the Trikuta hills. The Jammu elite greeted the invaders with presents, hoping to appease them. However, Maha Singh's army wanted more. "The place was plundered and sacked. The whole country around was also laid waste, which resulted in a destructive famine throughout the state," say Hutchison and Vogel. They add that the booty carried away amounted to two crore (twenty million) rupees.

Jammu became subject to the Sikhs, having to pay an annual tribute of Rs. 30,000.

The Bhangis invaded Jammu in 1786-87. Braj Raj died trying to resist them. His son and heir, Sampuran Dev, was just a year old then. Sampuran died at the age of twelve. Dalel Singh's son, Jit Singh (or Jit Dev), succeeded him.

Maharaja Ranjit Singh of the Punjab set out to conquer Jammu in 1800-1. Jit submitted to his authority and also presented a tribute. So, Ranjit withdrew. For the while.

Around then arose in the Jammu hills a man described both as 'brave and fearless' and a 'plunderer': Mian Deedo. He was related to the royal family. Deedo rebelled against the Lahore kingdom in 1809-10. So a Sikh force was sent to subdue him.

Jammu is formally annexed by the Lahore kingdom

Between 1810 and 1816 Jammu was formally incorporated into the Lahore-based Sikh kingdom. Jit was deposed and Jammu was given as a jagir (estate) to Maharaja Ranjit Singh's son, Kharak Singh. Jit's descendants were given a jagir near Dina Nagar in the Gurdaspur district of the Punjab. (That probably explains the J&K Gujjars' Dina Nagar connection. Dina Nagar is the southernmost area that they migrate to in winter, and perhaps the only place outside the state.)

However, Deedo continued to thumb his nose at Ranjit. Around 1819 baskets containing fruits were being carried to Ranjit's court in Lahore from the newly conquered Kashmir. Mian Deedo intercepted the convoy, got the fruits removed from the baskets and replaced them with cowdung.

The furious Ranjit sent another force against Deedo, which killed him in 1820.

Thus what was left of the Jammu royal family was the line of Surat Singh, whom we have mentioned before.

The rise of three talented brothers

At the beginning of the 19th century there were three brothers who would later go on to shape the destiny of the state: Gulab Singh, Dhian Singh and Suchet Singh. They were the sons of Kishore Singh, who was Surat Singh's grandson.

Gulab Singh had served the kings of Rajouri and Kishtwar as a teenaged soldier. The story of how Gulab caught Maharaja Ranjit Singh's eye says so much about the character of Ranjit Singh and his generals, and the chivalrous ethos of that era.

In 1807, a Sikh force led by Dewan Misr Chand invaded Jammu. Gulab Singh, then nineteen, engaged Sikh horsemen in hand-to-hand combat on the dry, stone-infested bed of River Tawi. The Dewan was rather impressed by the excellence of Gulab's battle skills. He mentioned them with admiration to the Maharaja. whose force defeated the Jammu army in that battle.

Gulab got to know of the Dewan's recommendation. So, around 1810 he went over to Lahore in search of a better job. He took his brother, little Dhian (born 1797) along. Gulab was accepted in the Sikh army. In time Maharaja Ranjit took a liking to this handsome, talented and principled man and promoted him to a high rank. He asked the Jamwal brothers to 'remain in attendance upon him.'

In 1813, Gulab and Dhian requested the Maharaja to be allowed to bring over their twelve-year old brother Suchet to Lahore. The Maharaja agreed. He grew so fond of the loveable little boy that, to quote a contemporary British account, 'the [Jamwal] Rajpút brothers became all in all at court'.

Jacquemont, a Frenchman, met Gulab Singh in 1831. He called the Raja a lion in courage, but with the plainest, mildest and most elegant manners. Drew (1875) described Gulab as a ruler who was extremely patient with his subjects. 'He was always accessible,' Drew wrote, 'and was patient and ready to listen to complaints. He was much given to looking into details.'

Dhian Singh, too, rose rapidly because of Maharaja Ranjit's recognition of his talents. Prinsep, the nineteenth century historian, describes his rise thus: "While Ranjit Singh was reviewing his troops he observed by the side of his elephant a common lancer breaking in a vicious horse. The beauty of the young man (then about twenty-five) as well as his skill and bold carriage struck him, and the replies made to his questions confirmed his good opinion... [This man, Dhian Singh] not only acquired Ranjit's confidence, but possessed great influence over the Sikh nation... Ranjit took Dhian into his household, made him first porter to the palace, then *deorhiwala* (lord of the privy chamber) and ultimately [in 1828-43] Prime Minister; in which capacity he amassed enormous wealth, became master of a large mountainous country on the borders of Kashmir, studded with hill forts, maintaining an army of 25,000 men and a fine artillery."

Maharaja Ranjit's munificence towards the brothers from Jammu was almost endless. In 1818, he gave each of the three brothers the title 'Raja'. Dhian Singh received Poonch as a jagir and Suchet was given Bandralta (Ramnagar). In 1819, Gulab, by now a commander in the Sikh army, first conquered Rajouri and then Kishtwar for the Lahore kingdom. The king of Mankot gave up without a fight.

So, around 1820, Maharaja Ranjit gave Raja Gulab Singh the biggest prize of them all: the government of the Jammu hills. Jammu was given on lease to the three brothers, to administer on behalf of Lahore.

In 1828, Raja Dhian's eldest son, Hira Singh, too, was made a Raja. In 1834 he was given Jasrota as a jagir.

Jammu annexes all the neighbouring hill states—and Ladakh

By the middle of the century most of the smaller neighbouring states had been brought under Jammu. Many of them had enjoyed a spell of independence or autonomy after Ranjit Dev's death in 1839. Earlier, Akhnoor had been subjugated once again in 1812, Khari Khariali in 1810, Kotli in 1815, Poonch in 1819, Chenaini and Bandralta around 1822, Jasrota in 1834 and Krimchi (Bhoti) in 1836. Bhimbar was annexed in 1840, Baltistan in 1840-41, Bhaddu around 1841 and Basohli around 1846. Reasi, Sâmbâ and Dalpatpur had been absorbed earlier. Padar was taken from Chamba in 1836.

In theory, Raja Gulab Singh annexed all these states on behalf of the Lahore kingdom. In fact he was in full control of all of them, without any interference from Lahore. In the British assessment he 'came to be considered, after Ranjit Singh, the greatest Chief in the Punjab... in reality Raja Gulab Singh was practically independent'.

The Mughals had conquered Lakhanpur, perhaps during Akbar's time. After that either Basohli or Jasrota controlled it—till the late 18th century when Nurpur annexed it. However, a few years later, in 1816, the Lahore kingdom took over Nurpur.

Rajouri was subject to the Lahore kingdom. In 1846, 'alpine Punjab' was ceded to Gulab Singh who, by then, was a Maharaja.

These takeovers were not painless for the deposed rulers. The rajas of Kishtwar and Chenaini appealed to Maharaja Ranjit about their loss of independence. The former was ignored, but the Raja of Chenaini was permitted to stay on in his erstwhile state and also granted a jagir. The Rajouri rulers chose to go over to British territory on a pension, some of them migrating to Kangra and others to Wazirabad. The royal family of Khari Khariali was given a jagir in Jammu as well as some land in Gujrat, a district in British-ruled Punjab. The family shifted its residence to the latter. Ahmad Shah, the Raja of Baltistan, was sent as a prisoner to Kishtwar, where he died.

The most spectacular military victories won in Gulab Singh's name (in turn, on behalf of Ranjit Singh) were by General Zorawar Singh in Ladakh. These successes emboldened the Dogras to go one further: to try to conquer Guge (Western Tibet) as well. Zorawar was killed in the battle that ensued, in December 1841. Many Dogra soldiers were taken prisoner. Others died because of the cold.

That was the last time that Gulab Singh undertook a major military enterprise.

Decline and change in Lahore

Meanwhile, things were evolving rapidly in Lahore.

Maharaja Ranjit Singh died in 1839. His son, Kharak Singh, could step into the great man's shoes for only a few brief months, after which he was overthrown. He died in 1840. The army became the real ruler of the Lahore kingdom.

A series of assassinations, natural and accidental deaths, and palace coups led to the Lahore throne changing hands frequently. Touchingly, the nobles from Jammu died as they had lived: with their Sikh mentors. Gulab's eldest son, Udham Singh, died in the above-mentioned accident involving Sikh royalty. In September 1843, Gulab's brother, Dhian Singh, was among those killed during the assassination of another Sikh royal.

Gulab's other brother, Suchet Singh, died in 1844, in a brief battle with a section of the Sikh army. This faction did not support Suchet's claim to becoming a minister in the Lahore kingdom, whereas a section of the Khalsa did. Suchet had no children. Therefore, his jagir, Ramnagar, was merged with Jammu.

Dhian Singh's son, Hira, too, died without a male heir, also in 1844. Of his territories, Basohli and Jasrota were merged with Jammu, while Poonch was taken over by his younger brother, Jawahir Singh.

Till then the Jamwal brothers would keep all the family jewels and treasures in the Jasrota Fort. As soon as Jawahir heard of Hira's death he went over to Jasrota and began shifting the treasury to Jammu. He even managed to move some of it.

A section of the Lahore army had the same idea. They sent a force of ten thousand to steal those valuables. Raja Gulab Singh got to know that the army from Lahore was heading towards Jammu. So he shifted all the family treasures to—um, no one is sure. The standard belief, and the one recorded by Raj historians as well, is that Gulab hid them all in Reasi, in the Bhimgarh Fort to be precise. This fort is located in what then were truly remote mountains, much too far for a force from Lahore.

Gulab's army chased the invaders back to Lahore. Indeed, many Sikh soldiers deserted the Lahore army and opted for employment in Gulab's armed forces.

From then to the partition of India, no army ever dared to march towards the state.

The Treaties of Lahore and Amritsar

By 1844, the Lahore treasury was empty. There were reports that the British were planning to invade the Punjab. Some historians suggest that the queen mother of the Punjab empire, who was also the regent, wanted to sap the Khalsa army of its strength. Therefore, she decided to send the Khalsa army to war against the British because she knew that it would be badly bruised.

In any case, a battle took place between the British and Lahore armies at Sobraon on the 10th February, 1846. The Lahore army was defeated and lost a very large number of men.

Raja Gulab Singh had not been involved in any of these events. However, after the defeat of its army, the Lahore government appointed him its chief representative for its negotiations with the British.

The British asked for the Jalandhar Doab area, as well as an indemnity of £1.5million. The Lahore government was in no position to pay the indemnity. So, in addition to the Jalandhar area, it yielded the hilly area between the Beas and Indus rivers, in lieu of the first £1m. of the indemnity. Which left £0.5million to be paid in cash.

Two treaties were signed to this effect, on the 9th and 11th March, 1846. Gulab Singh's services in restoring friendly relations between the British and the Lahore kingdom were appreciated by both powers. In return, they agreed to recognise him as independently sovereign over such territories in the hills as might be given to him.

Five days later, on the 16th March, 1846, Raja Gulab Singh signed a separate treaty with the British. He agreed to pay them £0.75million. In return they gave him 'in perpetual possession' all the hill territories between the Ravi and the Indus—including Chamba. He thus got the entire Valley of Kashmir, the outer hills between the Ravi and the Indus, as well as Ladakh (including Gilgit, Baltistan and the Indus valley up to Chilas). Poonch was not recognised as independent of Jammu.

Raja Gulab Singh, in turn, agreed to give the dispossessed chiefs of the Dugar (Dogra/ Jammu) states between the Ravi and the Jehlum allowances that added up to Rs.62,000 a year. The chiefs could either continue to live in Raja Gulab Singh's territory or leave it. Most of them elected to leave. These included the Rajas of Basohli, Bhaddu, Bhimbar, Jasrota, Khari Khariali, Kishtwar, Mankot, Rajouri and Ramnagar.

Some, like the Khakha-Bamba chiefs of the Upper Jehlum valley, agreed to serve under Raja Gulab Singh, so long as they were allowed to run their jagirs autonomously. Interestingly, almost all the chiefs who left the Jammu territory were Hindu. Those, like the Khakhas and Bambas, who were agreeable to working under Gulab were mostly Muslim. So much for Hindu vs. Muslim interpretations of history.

The British agreed to pay annual allowances to the Rajas who had migrated to British territory. Raja Gulab Singh gave the British land worth Rs.42,800 near Pathankot and on the Beas, to enable them to do so.

The Raja of Chamba protested at having been made a subject of Jammu. So, a compromise was struck. He conceded Bhaderwah to J&K and the rest of his state was absorbed into British India instead.

The Hazara chiefs had revolted against Maharaja Ranjit Singh's authority. They were not going to accept Raja (later Maharaja) Gulab Singh either. The Raja knew that it would be very difficult to bring them under his control. So he offered to return Hazara to the Sikh Darbar of Lahore, so long as he was given territory half as valuable. The Sikh Darbar agreed. The Raja was given the areas of Manawar and Garhi instead.

With these treaties, the destinies of Jammu, Kashmir and Ladakh merged with each other. So did their histories.

The period 1846-1947 is covered in the volume about 'Kashmîr.'

References

i The People of India: Jammu and Kashmir, p. 281.

ii Sharma, Dr D.C., 'Origin of Jammû school of Pahari Paintings,' *Daily Excelsior*, 30 September, 2001.

* * *

6

Kishtwâr

(1500–1800)

Relations with Kashmir

There have always been royal matrimonial alliances between Kashmir and Kishtwar. The first recorded invasion of Kishtwar by Kashmiri forces was in A.D. 1547. Later, two Thakkar tribes, Rotar and Ganai invaded the plateau where Kishtwar town is now located, and founded Ziora village and the central part of Kishtwar town respectively. ('Rotar' could possibly mean Rana *putr*, or 'the son of a Rana noble'.) Kishtwar is in Jammu province, being south of the Pir Panjal range. However, its rulers were mostly under Kashmir's sway, albeit nominal.

Sultan Shihab ud Din of Kashmir added Kishtwar to his empire.

Kishtwar's Rajas remained Hindu till Aurangzeb's time. However, centuries before that they had given their daughters in marriage to the (Muslim) sultans of Kashmir, notably Yusuf and Yaqub Shah Chak.

In 1572, Bahadur Singh, King of Kishtwar, was defeated by Sultan Ali Shah Chak of Kashmir. He then gave his sister Shankar Devi (later Fath Khatun) in marriage to the Sultan's grandson, Yaqub, and also agreed to continue to pay an annual tribute. (Big fish eat smaller fish, which had eaten fish that were smaller still. Around the same time Ali Shah was persuaded to give his niece in marriage to Mughal Emperor Akbar.) The Sultan defeated Bahadur again in 1574 when Bahadur reiterated his pledge of a tribute and also gave his son, Narain Singh, as hostage.

Both Yusuf and Yaqub would make a beeline for Kishtwar whenever they'd quarrel with their respective fathers in Kashmir. Indeed, when Yaqub Shah Chak, the last independent ruler of Kashmir, came under pressure from the forces of Akbar, he fled to Kishtwar where he died and was buried (at Sirkot on the Chaugan).

The Kishtwaris ward off the Mughals

In 1620, Dilawar Khan Kakar, the Mughal governor of Kashmir, attacked and annexed Kishtwar. Emperor Jehangir recorded the event in considerable detail in his memoirs.

The provocation came when two Chak nobles, Gauhar and Aiba, fled from Kashmir to Kishtwar to seek refuge. (The Mughals had conquered Kashmir from the Chaks in 1586. However, some Chaks continued to offer resistance from bases in neighbouring Kishtwar.) There were 10,000 foot soldiers and cavalrymen in Dilawar's army. This indicates how strong the combined Kishtwar-Chak army must have been.

The Mughals, led by Dilawar's son Jalal, first defeated the Kishtwaris at Nârkot. Aiba was killed in the battle. This demoralised Kunwar Singh, the Raja of Kishtwar, who fled to a place across the river. His forces killed several Mughal soldiers and held the invaders' army at the bridge for twenty days.

That was when Dilawar Khan decided to intervene personally. He led a bigger force to Kishtwar. The Raja knew that it was pointless to resist. He begged to be pardoned and agreed to appear at 'the refuge of the world' (i.e. the Mughal court). Dilawar rejected Kunwar Singh's request and decided to continue with the war.

The Kishtwar army destroyed the bridge to prevent Dilawar's army from crossing over. Dilawar's soldiers made a foolhardy attempt to swim across. Only ten of them managed to cross over, two of whom were taken prisoner by the Kishtwaris. Another sixty-eight Mughal soldiers drowned in the attempt.

The Kishtwaris thus managed to keep the Mughal army across the river for four months and ten days. During this while Dilawar won over the local *zamindar* (feudal chief) and did what a Kishtwari would have done. He got a *zampâ* (rope bridge) fabricated. (See the section on 'Kishtwar' in the chapter on 'Regional Histories.') At night, when the Kishtwari soldiers were sleeping, the rope-bridge was installed across the river.

The Mughals conquer Kishtwar

Two hundred Mughal soldiers, all of Afghan stock, crossed the bridge and killed the sleeping Kishtwari soldiers. They took the Raja alive, because he cried out, 'I am the Raja. Take me alive to Dilawar Khan.' The Mughals then captured Mandal Badr, the seat of the Kishtwar government.

The king of Kishtwar was married to the daughter of Sangram, king of Jammu[1]. Our polygamous friend also married a daughter of Suraj Mal, Raja of Kangra (HP). When the Mughals attacked Kishtwar, he sent his family to the Raja of Jaswal, for their protection.

Dilawar sent Kunwar Singh to the emperor's court. Jehangir took a liking to the prisoner. He wrote, "[The Raja] is not wanting in dignity. His dress is after the Indian fashion. He knows both the Hindi and the Kashmiri languages. [Thus, even in the 17th century, Kishtwar was consciously bilingual.] Contrary to the *zamindars* of these regions he looked like an inhabitant of the town."

Jehangir agreed that if the Raja were to leave his sons at the Mughal court, he would be freed. The Raja did not do so. Therefore, Jehangir imprisoned him at Gwalior.

The Kishtwaris continue to defy the Mughals

The Kishtwaris launched a resistance against the Mughals. Jehangir blamed it on the ineptitude of his own man in Kishtwar, Nasrullah Arab. Apparently, Nasrullah was harsh on the feudal chiefs of Kishtwar. Secondly, he let a large number of his soldiers go on leave.

Finding the Mughal forces somewhat depleted, the feudal chiefs got together to drive out the invader. Their biggest assets were their ferocious rivers. So they destroyed the main bridge. Now, the Mughals could no longer receive reinforcements or supplies.

The brave Kishtwaris attacked the besieged Mughals and killed Nasrullah and many of his men.

Jehangir now asked his friend Sangram, king of Jammu, to help control the rebellion in Kishtwar. Sangram obliged, and with success.

But in 1622, the Kishtwaris started attacking the Mughals again. Jehangir knew that it was difficult to control that rugged and remote region through force alone. So he released Kunwar Singh from jail and decided to rule Kishtwar through an autonomous Raja instead. He wrote, "Having brought Kunwar Singh, the Raja of Kishtwar, out of the fortress of Gwalior, where he was imprisoned, I bestowed Kishtwar on him and gave him a horse and a dress of honour, with the title of Raja."

---

1. The state of 'Jammu *and* Kashmir' has two regions, namely, Kashmir and Jammu. Dodâ and, thus, Kishtwar are in Jammu province. And yet the Muslims of Dodâ-Kishtwar often say that they belong to the 'and' province. This is their way of saying that while their district might physically be in Jammu, they share links of religion, ethnicity and language with the Kashmiris.

   Clearly, the Raja of Kishtwar had, by the 17th century, mastered the art of balancing the two regions.

Incidentally, the Raja was a very rich man. His annual income was around Rs.1,00,000. Every house paid him six *sanhasis* (Rs. 4) a year. On the other hand, he did not receive any kind of land revenue. All lands that produced the extremely expensive saffron were given to Rajput army officers and to 700 gunmen/ cannon-operators (*topchi*), who had been with the royal family for several generations.

The coming of Islam

The kings of Kishtwar converted to Islam. This was perhaps through the influence of Syed Farid-ud-Din (born c.1592 in Baghdad) and his sons, Syed Asrâr-ud-Din Saheb (died 1685) and Hazrat Akhyar-ud-Din (died 1725).

Farid-ud-Din Saheb came to Kishtwar "to preach Islam among the general masses residing in that hilly region. The present population ratio of district Doda [where the Muslims are in a majority] is proof of the success of his mission," Aseer Kishtwari writes. ('Facts about Hazrat Syed Asrâr-ud-din,' *Kashmir Times*, Jammu, 10 November, 1998.)

Through their preaching and moral example, the Syeds are said to have turned Kishtwar into 'a place like Baghdad' (Baghdad-e-Sani). Raja Muhammad Kirat Singh, the son of Raja Jai Singh, was the first king of Kishtwar to convert and this while his father was alive.

Jai Singh, too, had high respect for Farid-ud-Din Saheb. Aseer Kishtwari says that he built a "monastery out of his own funds to fulfil the requirements of the saint."

Kirat's younger brother was renamed Miyan Muhammad Khan and his sister, Bhup Dei, was married, in 1717, to the Mughal prince Farrukhsiyar.

* * *

7

Poonch

(1500–the present)

In 1596, the Mughal Emperor Jehangir put Poonch under Siraj-ud-Din, with the rank of Raja. Siraj-ud-Din's descendants ruled over Poonch till 1792. They were followed by the Sangoo Gujjar dynasty founded by Wazir Rooh Allah, which ruled for three generations. At that time the Afghans ruled Kashmir.

Meanwhile, a Lahore-based empire was rising in the south. Maharaja Ranjit Singh of Lahore coveted Kashmir. His army invaded Kashmir in 1814 and 1819. On both occasions Raja Rooh Allah supported the Afghans. He died in 1819. Ranjit succeeded in defeating the Afghans, also in 1819. Hutchison & Vogel (H&V) say that 'the Punch Raja... was [then] expelled from his State'. H&V confess that 'of the subsequent history of the family we know little'.

Other historians, however, say that Rooh Allah's son Raja Amir Khan (died 1823), and his grandson Raja Mir Baz Khan succeeded Rooh Allah as rulers. H&V mention neither. They only refer to Sher Baz Khan, 'the head of a collateral branch of the family, [who] was granted a jagir in Punch, probably by Ranjit Singh'. Mir Baz is generally accepted as the last independent ruler of Poonch. However, H&V insist that 'before 1822' Maharaja Ranjit Singh gave the Poonch territory 'in fief' to his Dogra Prime Minister, Dhian Singh, with the rank of Raja. After examining three different histories, I am of the opinion that the Dogra takeover took place in 1824 or shortly thereafter.

In any case, Lahore controlled Poonch till 1850. By then both Dhian Singh and his eldest son and successor, Raja Hira Singh, had been assassinated—in 1843 and 1844 respectively. (The Sandhianwala Sirdars had killed Dhian Singh for reasons connected with Lahore, not Poonch, politics.) Raja Jawahir Singh succeeded his brother, Hira. In March

1846, all the 'Punjab hill states,' including Poonch, were given to Jawahir's uncle, Maharaja Gulab Singh of Jammu.

Jawahir wanted to preserve the autonomy that his kingdom had enjoyed under Lahore. He began to intrigue against his uncle, Gulab, and cousin, Ranbir (later, Maharaja Ranbir). Gulab died in 1857. In 1859, Ranbir banished his cousin, Jawahir, to the Punjab, gave him a pension of Rs.1 lakh a year, and formally annexed Poonch to Jammu.

Jawahir's younger brother, Raja Moti Singh, and after him Moti's descendants, were then allowed to administer Poonch for the Dogras. This they did till April 1947. Jammu and Kashmir acceded to the Union of India a few months later. At the time of the accession, the Poonch jâgîr had an area of 1,594 square miles and an annual income of Rs.12 lakh.

Earlier, in 1901, the British Government of India had granted Poonch, thitherto a principality, the rank of state. In 1947, Poonch witnessed much bloodshed, when invaders from newly independent Pakistan overran all of Bagh and Sudhnutti tehsils and half of Haveli tehsil. Pakistan continues to be in illegal occupation of this tract.

After 1947, Poonch-Rajouri became a district of the Indian state of Jammu & Kashmir. Rajouri was separated from Poonch in 1968. In the winter of 1978-79, Poonch was rocked again. Youths from the town complained that the process of recruitment of government servants ignored academic performance and was weighted in favour of the rural areas. The agitation lasted several months and was occasionally violent.

In the 1990s, Pakistan pushed armed militants into Poonch once again. The people of Poonch as a whole remained peaceful and stayed away from militancy. However, the militants would occasionally terrorise the rural areas by killing secular and pro-India Muslim politicians, Muslim tribals and others.

Poonch has produced eminent 20th century Urdu littérateurs. Krishen Chander did not belong to the district, but he spent most of his childhood and formative years there. The Indian Prime Minister, Mrs. Indira Gandhi, drew considerable flak in the 1970s when she claimed that Chander was a better writer than Mirza Ghalib, who arguably is the greatest Urdu writer ever.

* * *

8

Rajouri

(1400–1846)

There are three theories about how the rulers of Rajouri converted to Islam.

(i) *The Cunningham/ Mirza Zafarullah Khan theory*: Sundara Devi's eldest son from the Sultan was called Adam Khan and his elder son Fath Khan. Adam's relations with his father and brother were not happy: Indeed, he once plotted a boating accident in the Wular Lake to drown his father. So Sultan Zain-ul-Abedin sent Adam away to Rajouri-Poonch as the governor of that and its neighbouring regions. (Some historians say that Adam had to flee to the plains.)

Fath Khan, had three stints as the king of Kashmir (between 1486 and 1516). His younger brother Sikandar Khan Sani's son was called Sher Afkun and his grandson was called Nur Shah or Nil Shah. Fath helped Nur/ Nil conquer Rajouri. Nur married the daughter of the Raja of Rajouri. This was around A.D. 1500.

(ii) *Vernacular histories*: The Muslim rulers of Rajouri were descended from Jira Pal, the King of Kalanaur. Jira was the younger brother of Jhet Pal, the founder of Nurpur state. Around A.D. 1193, Muhammad Ghori defeated Jira's descendant, Raja Sahib Singh, in battle. Sahib and his son Nil Singh converted to Islam, under the names Sher Afkun Khan and Nur-ud-Din Khan. They then shifted to Rajouri, after defeating the Pal rulers of that kingdom.

(iii) *Hutchison and Vogel's conclusions*: The *Rajatarangini* clearly shows that Hindu kings continued to rule Rajouri much after 1193. The *Tuzuk-e-Jehangiri* equally unambiguously says that the kings of Rajouri were converted to Islam 'by Sultan Feroz

[Shah Tughlaq (1356-88)] despite which they are still called Rajas'. H&V rightly seem to consider Jehangir's account the most accurate.

Either way, Nur-ud-Din/ Nil Shah was the first Muslim king of Rajouri. His descendants are known as the Jaral dynasty. Each Jaral king had a 'Hindu name' in addition to an 'Islamic' one. (The same was true of many kings of Kishtwar who had converted to Islam.)

The name of this pioneer could well have been Nihâl Singh. Dr. Ashok Jerath[i] believes that he was defeated by the Mughals, who later killed him. Dr. Jerath writes that Nihâl's queens committed *sati* upon his death—they burned themselves on his pyre. One queen, who was pregnant, did not. She fled to Kashmîr, along with the family priest. There she gave birth to a child called Jûrâ, whose descendants are called by the name Jarâl.

Relations with the Mughals

Jehangir's memoirs have a lot to say about the people of Rajouri, not all of it very complimentary: "[Despite accepting Islam, the people of Rajouri] still have the marks of the Age of Ignorance and Imbecility [i.e. the age before the advent of Islam]. One of them is, that just as some Hindu women burn themselves along with their husbands, so these [i.e. Rajouri Muslim] women are put into the grave along with their [dead] husbands... Also when a daughter is born to a man without means they put her to death by strangulation.

"They ally themselves with Hindus, and both give and take girls. Taking them is good, but giving them, God forbid. I gave an order that hereafter they should not do such things, and whoever was guilty of them should be given capital punishment."

Jehangir also indicated that child marriage was common in Rajouri, among the Muslims as well. Female infanticide was practised there.

In 1644, Shah Jehan's son, Aurangzeb, married Rajbai, a daughter of the Raja of Rajouri (perhaps Taj-ud-Din Khan @ Chattar Singh).

Against this backdrop it is difficult to agree with Dr. Sufi when he says that Aurangzeb's army defeated the Raja of Rajouri upon which the Raja converted to Islam and got back his kingdom. The Jaral dynasty of Rajouri had accepted Islam—and Mughal overlordship—much before. There was no need to defeat or convert them.

For several years Rajbai, now in Delhi, had to play host to a fugitive from Rajouri, her young grandnephew Raja Azmatullah Khan. Azmat was just three when his father, the Raja of Rajouri, died (around 1683). His uncle Rafiullah Khan became the de facto ruler and began looking for ways to exile the young Raja. Rafiullah's wife blurted this out to Azmat's mother, who got Ajaib Singh, the wazir, to take Azmat to the princess in Delhi.

When Azmat grew up he requested Emperor Aurangzeb to let him return to his ancestral land. Aurangzeb sent a small contingent with Azmat to Rajouri. He also sent word of this in advance to Rafiullah, who assured the emperor that Azmat was welcome to take over the kingdom. By the time Azmat reached Rajouri his uncle had shifted back to the estate allotted to him.

During his stay in Delhi Azmat had become friends with Aurangzeb and Rajbai's son, Muazzam Shah. When the emperor died Muazzam fought a war of succession with his brother Azam Shah. Azmat and his army fought for Muazzam, who won and took the name Bahadur Shah.

The Jaral dynasty ruled Rajouri till the 21st October, 1846. They had several Hindu ministers, notably Ajaib Singh and the Mehtas. Hindu Rajputs were the first choice for their army.

* * *

9

Rajouri

(1815–the present)

By 1815 Rajouri's independence was under threat. Maharaja Ranjit Singh of Lahore coveted Kashmir, which was then under the Afghans. The road to Srinagar passed through Rajouri. Raja Aggar Ullah Khan of Rajouri agreed to help the Maharaja. However, the Afghans won him over by making it an 'Islam vs. the infidels' issue. Ranjit's first attack on Kashmir was unsuccessful. He attributed this to Aggar Ullah's 'treachery'.

The outraged Ranjit's army attacked Rajouri in 1815, to punish Aggar Ullah, rather than to annex his kingdom. The Raja put up a very brave fight and held out till the Lahore army asked for guns to be brought in from the plains. When the reinforced Lahore army blasted the walls of Rajouri town, the Raja escaped to the Kotli area.

It were outside forces that sought to inject communalism (racism) into the Rajouri palace. Aggar Ullah's mother was a Hindu. Therefore some courtiers wanted his younger brother, Mirza Rahim Ullah Khan, born to a Muslim mother, to be the king instead. Aggar Ullah was quite open to allying with the Sikhs, till the Afghans put him on the defensive by appealing to religion. On the other hand, Rahim Ullah, the 'genetically pure' Muslim, actually allied with the Sikhs in 1818, on the promise that he would be made Raja of Rajouri.

In 1819, the Sikhs occupied both Rajouri and neighbouring Poonch. The rulers of both kingdoms tried to help the Afghans. Mirza Rahim Ullah guided the Lahore army to the best and easiest routes and passes into Rajouri and, thence, Kashmir. For this assistance he was made the Raja of Rajouri and also given an estate (jagir) in Kashmir. Rajouri became a province of the Lahore empire. The next year, Gulab Singh, then a general in the Lahore army, captured Aggar Ullah and imprisoned him in Lahore. (Those who view the history of the state through the prism of Rajouri say that this deed so pleased Maharaja Ranjit Singh of Lahore that, in 1822, he appointed Gulab Singh the Raja of Jammu.)

Rajouri was one of the states received by the Dogra Maharajas in 1846 as part of the Treaty of Amritsar. They changed the city's name to Rampur. Mian Hathu was the first Dogra governor of Rajouri. He got a temple built near the Thanna Nallah. The construction of the Dhanni Dhar fort is attributed to him. (Some claim that Emperor Jehangir had built the fort.) The present building is no older than the 19th century. It is possible that the old fort had fallen into disuse, or had been blasted by the Lahore army, and Hathu had built a new fort on the old site.

Around 1856, the status of Rajouri was reduced to that of a tehsil of Bhimbar district. In 1904 it was brought under Reasi district. In 1947, Pakistani forces invaded and illegally occupied some portion of Rajouri. After 1947 it became a part of the new Poonch-Rajouri district. In 1968, it became a separate district.

Despite Pakistan's best efforts, the people of Rajouri stayed away from the militancy of the 1990s. However, armed terrorists from Pakistan would periodically massacre unarmed rural people in the district.

* * *

10

Kishtwâr

(1800–the present)

Raja Muhammed Teg Singh was the last independent ruler of Kishtwar. The Dogra rulers of Jammu had to conquer Kishtwar in 1820 or 1821, on behalf of their Sikh overlords.

What had happened was that Shah Shuja, the former amir of Kabul, had escaped from Maharaja Ranjit Singh's custody in Lahore in 1815. The Raja of Kishtwar gave him asylum. This offended the Maharaja enormously. He entrusted Raja Gulab Singh of Jammu with the task of doing the needful, which was done (Gulab had earlier been in the employment of the Raja of Kishtwar.)

The Dogra era—and after

The Raja of Kishtwar was invited to Dodâ, which was a part of his kingdom. There he was made prisoner and sent to Lahore. He tried to appeal to Maharaja Ranjit Singh against Gulab's encroachment of his autonomy. The Maharaja ignored his pleas. Three years later the Raja's servant poisoned him.

In June 1823, Gulab Singh, who did not visit Kishtwar himself, appointed Zorawar Singh Kahluria the Governor of Kishtwar. Zorawar was a son of the Raja of Kahlur (Bilaspur). He attacked Ladakh (see The History of Leh) four times between 1834 and 1841. During the first of these he also conquered the Marwah area of Kishtwar.

Zorawar's control did not go uncontested. Ratru, the Palsara of Padar, organised the local people to revolt against Jammu while Zorawar was invading Zanskar. (Padar apparently was under the control of the king of neighbouring Chamba (HP). The Palsara was Chamba's highest-ranking officer in Padar.) The rebels lay siege to the Chattargarh Fort where the Dogra soldiers were garrisoned. Zorawar came back and, in

1836, personally led a 3000-strong force that 'liberated' the fort, which he got renamed Gulabgarh. Ratru darted for Chamba, only to be sent by the government of Chamba to Jammu as prisoner.

Zorawar Singh died on December 12, 1841, in the Battle of Doyo, during his fourth invasion of Ladakh. In 1846, all of present day Jammu province, the Valley of Kashmir, Chamba and some other areas officially became a part of the empire of Maharaja Gulab Singh. In 1875, when the newly formed state of Jammu and Kashmir was organised into divisions and districts in the style of the British Raj, the kingdom of Kishtwar was relegated to the status of a district, with Kishtwar as the headquarter. In 1909, its status shrank further still—it was placed under Udhampur district. In 1948, what now is the enormous Dodâ district was separated from Udhampur. The position has changed since. Kishtwar first became a mere tehsil and later a sub-division of Dodâ. In 2006-2007 it was upgrade to a full-fledged district.

* * *

11

Jammû: 1885-1947

A Composite Culture

'There was a lot of poverty but there was a contentment and a glow on the faces of people.'[i]

-Malkâ Pukhrâj, *Song Sung True.*

'It was a time of happiness and contentment.'

-Khâlid Hasan, *Memory Lane to Jammû.*

In the early 20th century, Hamîrpur Siddhar, a village in Jammû district, had a saint called Bâbâ Roti Râm. 'No one knew…whether he was a Hiñdu, a Mussalmân, a Sikh or a Christian,' the legendary classical singer Malkâ Pukhrâj writes.[ii] And, as we shall see, it didn't matter. The Râm in his name would suggest that he was a Hiñdu. However, it was the people of the village—Hiñdus and Muslims together—who had given him that name. Bâbâ, on the other hand, is an Arabic word, normally used for Muslim divines.

The Bâbâ was a follower of Kabîr, the great 15th century Central Indian bridge between Hiñduism and Islâm. Many of the religious symbols that Roti Râm used were Hiñdu-Sikh. He would call men—including Muslim men—Gobiñdâ. and women—Hiñdu as well as Muslim—by the name Pârvati. This would not only not offend the Muslims, they saw it as a form of endearment. They would take their newborn babies to the Bâbâ for his blessings. The Bâbâ would then give elegant, purely Persian-Arabic names to the Muslim children.

This, too, is a cherished Indian tradition. Ali Shér Khân Añchan, the great 15th century emperor of much of Baltistân-Ladâkh, gave a pristine Buddhist name to his grandson, because the child's father was a Buddhist. And the name that he gave the future Emperor of Leh—Sengge Namgyâl

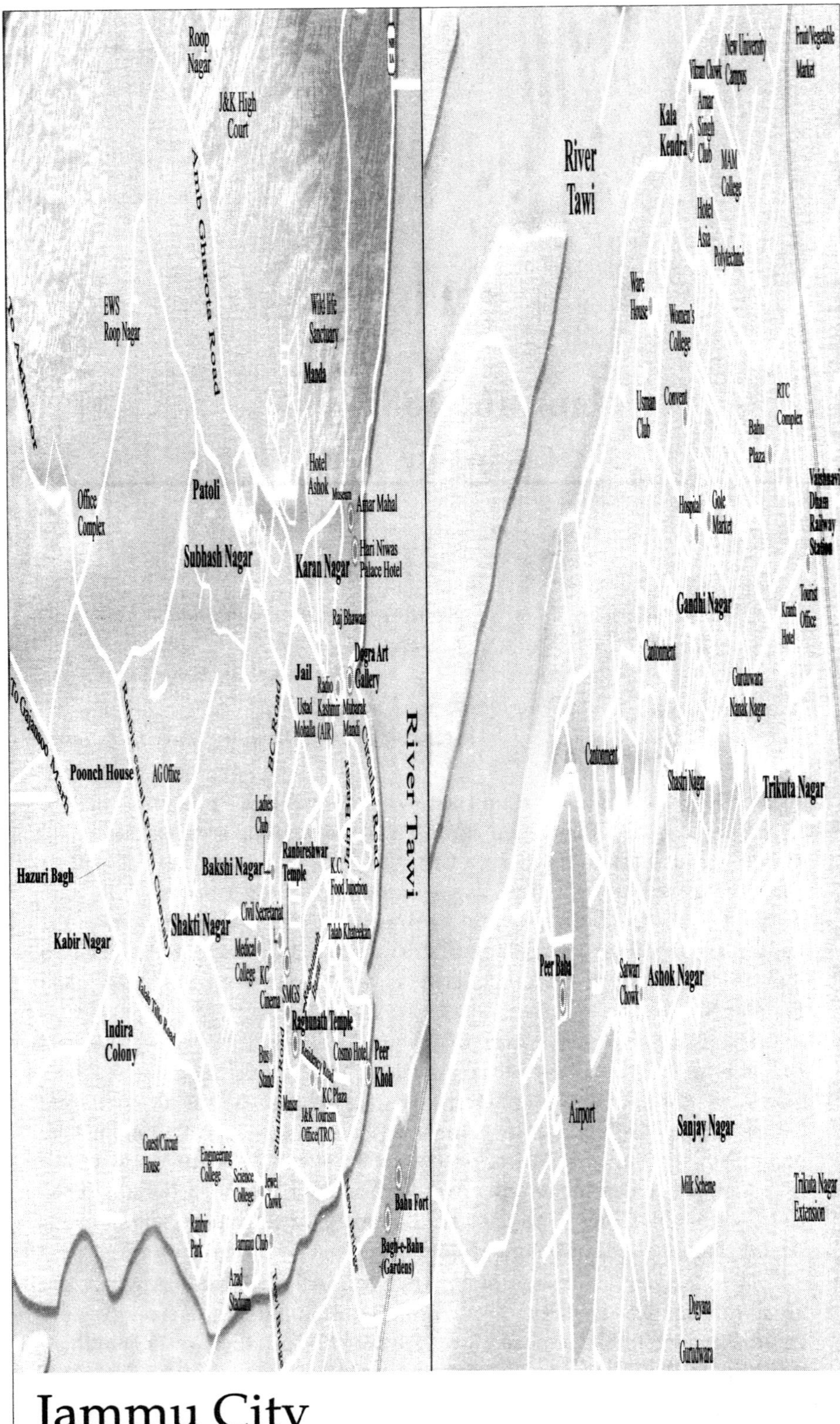

Jammu City

Map not to scale

('the lion' + 'king')—was as carefully chosen as the one that the Bâbâ would, five centuries later, give the greatest known singer in the history of Jammû, Malkâ Pukhrâj ('the empress' + 'topaz').

Malkâ Pukhrâj was born during the reign of Mahârâjâ Pratâp Singh (1885- 1925). Even before she entered her teens, she was employed as a singer by Mahârâjâ Hari Siñgh (1925-1947). In the 1940s Pukhrâj shifted base to Lahore, which later became a part of Pâkistân. Her fascinating memoirs, ably translated as *Song Sung True* by Saleem Kidwai, conjure up a Jammû where the Hiñdus and Muslims lived in harmony and where people were content despite their poverty. Her memoirs are an invaluable source of history. I have culled information from this remarkable book as well as the memoirs of Jammuites who had to flee to Sialkot in 1947 to put together a social history of Jammû from roughly 1885 to 1947.

Mahârâjâ Pratâp Singh embodied the composite religious identity of Jammû. He also personified the contradiction that many well meaning, God-fearing Hiñdus of his era suffered from. On the one hand, he allowed himself to believe that if he saw a Muslim before breakfast the purity of his piety would be compromised.

On the other, as Pukhrâj reminds us, he was as generous in his charity towards the Muslims as with his Hiñdu subjects.[iii] Miyâñ Lâl Dîn, a high-ranking Muslim official, was one of Pratâp Siñgh's closest advisors. Besides, the Maharaja 'had great faith in holy men of all types.'[iv]

So did the people of Jammû.

For instance, when the women of Pukhrâj's family wanted to travel from distant Jammû city to Hamîrpur Siddhar village (it was a full day's journey by horse) to pay respects to the Bâbâ, a Hiñdu and a Muslim insisted on escorting them—partly to protect the women and partly in the hope of receiving the Bâbâ's blessings for themselves.[1]

Bâbâ Roti Râm predicted that some deadly epidemic would strike Jammû city. Hiñdus and Muslims alike believed him. His prophecy came true. A terrible plague swept through Jammû city. Both communities started seeking the help of Dr. Râdhâ Krishan and both blessed him for helping them without charging a high fee.[v]

Bâbâ Charas (marijuana) Sâheb was the other important religion-indeterminate saint of that era. Not everyone in Jammû had faith in

1. In some parts of the world this craving for the blessings of a saint of another religion (or of no particular religion) might seem strange. However, in Jammû this has continued into the 21st century. Tens of thousands of Jammû Hiñdus would similarly travel great distances to pay their respects to Darvésh Ishâq Sâheb of Kishtwâr, till he died at the turn of the century (circa 1996).
Similarly, till their migration in 1990, the Puñjâbi and Kashmîrî Hiñdus of Srînagar would not think twice before going to the fields near the entrance to Makhdoom Sâheb to sit at the feet of the (Muslim) Goph Peer ('the saint who lives in a cave').

medical doctors. Even in the 21st century rural Jammû often prefers the local medicine man. Pukhrâj's father did not like doctors either. Like many Jammûites of both communities, he relied on the blessings of Bâbâ Charas to see him through that plague. At least in his case it worked.

The royal succession

Mahârâjâ Pratâp Siñgh's queen was called Mahârânî Chârak, after her maiden name. The royal couple did not have any children. Mahârâjâ Pratâp wanted his nephew, Hari Siñgh, to succeed him. The queen, instead, was in favour of the prince of Pooñch, whom she had adopted. Pratâp Siñgh was a drug addict and mostly oblivious to the world. His ambitious wife, therefore, wielded more power than a queen consort would normally have. She saw to it that Hari Siñgh never got to speak to his uncle except in her presence.

The loyalties of the palace staff were with the queen. She also had the British Resident on her side. This was important because the British often decided who would succeed kings who died without any children.

Hari Siñgh was married to Rânî Billaurâñ and loved her deeply. When the Rânî was with child, Mahârânî Chârak got an order passed that Hari Siñgh should not be allowed to meet the Rânî till the child was born. Hari Siñgh decided to spend those months of separation in England. The Rânî died during labour. Hari Siñgh, who later became the Mahârâjâ, always believed that Mahârânî Chârak had poisoned his wife.[vi]

Mahârâjâ Hari Siñgh then married the princess of Dharamkot. He was the first of his dynasty 'to marry the daughter of a Mahârâjâ.'[vii] His predecessors would take as wives the daughters of the nobles of Jammû.

The royal administration: The Diwâns of Jammû and Kashmîr (no relations of this author) apparently received a very substantial share (12.5 per cent) of the revenues of the state. (Don't I wish we'd been related?) Mahârâjâ Hari Siñgh put an end to this custom. He also outlawed untouchability. The so-called untouchables were allowed to enter any temple that they chose to.

Once every year, on the day after his birthday, the Mahârâjâ would invite the Râjpûts—rich as well as poor—to dinner at the palace.[viii]

Today, we think of corruption as a modern disease. However, the money that Mahârâjâ Pratâp Siñgh had kept apart for the poor and infirm—Rs.200 a day—was often pocketed by his courtiers instead. They would take advantage of the illiteracy of the people for whom the Mahârâjâ had sanctioned grants. These courtiers would give the beneficiary only a fraction of what had been authorised, but would make them sign a receipt for the full amount, pilfering the rest.

Religious rituals

Baisâkhî used to be a religion-neutral festival. These days corporations (and rich doctors and dentists who have flourishing practices) send gifts to important clients for the (Christian) New Year. In the Dogrâ era—and, perhaps, in the preceding centuries, too—rural midwives (irrespective of religion) would send garlands of dry fruits beaded together to all the children (again, regardless of religion) that they had delivered.[ix] (I often wonder how those impoverished midwives could afford to do this.)

Urban Jammû was equally liberal. It had a Séwâ Samiti ('a committee of the servants of the society'), a government-backed organisation, which had eight members—an equal number of Hiñdus and Muslims. (Some might argue that the Muslims should have had greater representation, because the kingdom was overwhelmingly Muslim. Others would say that the Samiti was meant only for Jammû town, which was mainly Hiñdu—as were the districts to the immediate north and south of Jammû. Therefore, the Hiñdus should have had more members. In the event exact parity seems to have satisfied both.)

One of the main tasks of the members was to arrange for the cremation or burial of the unclaimed bodies of members of their community. The hospital where the bodies were kept would give four rupees to the member—again regardless of religion—who took on this task. At the time, the sum was more than adequate for the last rites.[x]

For Eid, Mahârâjâ Hari Siñgh would go to the mosque where the biggest congregation offered prayers. He would take the Nawâb of Pâlampur along to the mosque, where the Nawâb would join the Muslims of Jammû in prayer. Hari Siñgh would stand respectfully for two hours[2] while prayers were being offered—a gesture greatly resented[3] by some non-Muslims.[xi] When the Eid prayers were over, the Mahârâjâ would give the Imâm (the leader of the congregation) an expensive *pashminâ* (cashmere) robe and a cash grant.[xii]

All this affection for the Muslims came at a price. A rumour, obviously spread by hardliners, swept Jammû that Hari Siñgh had converted to Islâm but was keeping that a secret lest he be deposed from his throne.

The Mahârâjâ had shifted his palace from the ornate and huge Mubârak Mañdî complex to the infinitely smaller Râmnagar palace, later known as Hari Niwâs, because he shunned ostentation. However, certain fanatics

2. The two hour figure is from Pukhrâj, op. cit., p. 94.

3. The right always asks two questions—and does so with venom—to justify its resentment: Does the other community reciprocate during our festivals? And do these bleeding hearts from our community do as much for their own festivals as they do for the festivals of the other community?
I have tried to answer both questions in this chapter.

alleged that he had done so because he did not want to hear the bells that rang in the Mañdî's temple.[xiii] Incidentally, the Hiñdu Dogrâs chose the Arabic—even Islâmic—name 'Mubârak Mañdî' for their main palace.

As a child Pukhrâj was trained, by Muslim *ustâds* (maestri), to sing *bhajans* (sacred Hiñdu songs). At the Mahârâjâ's court she sang '*Arey Râm, kaisey paar utaariye*?', "O Râm! How will you take me across to the other (river) bank?" which Mamman Khân of Delhi had taught her. She recalled this without hesitation in her old age in Pâkistân. Like countless Muslim singers throughout South Asia, her favourite râgs (Jaijaiwañti and Shañkarâ) had a 'Hiñdu origin.' She also sang *holîs* (traditional songs connected with the Hiñdu festival, Holî).[xiv]

When she entered her teens, every morning Pukhrâj would sing bhajans at the temple in Mubârak Mañdî. She did not consider this odd. On the contrary, she would later write, 'Singing bhajans there was considered a great honour.'[xv] Nor did any Hiñdu feel that the temple (or the purity of the bhajans) had been compromised because of a Muslim. Indeed, the temple priests would chant prayers, blow into the sacred fire and ring the temple bells while Pukhrâj recited bhajans.[xvi]

Sorayyâ Khurshîd, who proudly recalls that Jammû was 'called the city of temples,' was one of the countless Muslims of that era who would 'every morning hear the sweet sound of temple bells which would be rung all together. The great temple of Raghunâth was surrounded by other temples. I can still [in 2002, 55 years after I left Jammû] hear those bells, and their music reverberates in my ears.' Hâshmî reminds us that the street of this famous group of temples was then called Mañdarâñ Wâlâ Bâzar ('the market where the temples are'). Râd fondly adds, 'We recall the high golden steeples of the temples.'

Similarly, even in the early 21st century, the Hiñdus of Ustâd Mohallâ are proud of how 'their' mosque has become grander over the years. They fondly recall the voices of the better muezzins of their mosque.

Every morning before dawn during the holy month of Ramzân, an expert trumpeter would go to the roof of the Mastgarh mosque—which has been built on an elevation—and blow the trumpet loud. It could be heard for miles. (Today, Muslim youths go through all streets with a significant Muslim population playing a drum. The idea in both cases is to wake the devout up.)

Pukhrâj writes that when the people saw her, then a nine-year-old, decked in jewellery (given to her by the Mahârâjâ), 'they were convinced that [she was] a goddess.'[xvii] They did not consider it strange to think of a Muslim child as a little goddess, nor did she that they regarded her so.

Clothes, books: On occasion Pukhrâj would wear sâris, a dress that the Pâkistânî establishment would, in the 1980s, decree a 'Hiñdu dress' and therefore, not to be worn by Muslims. (Never mind that all Bâñglâdéshî Muslim women—including their Prime Ministers—wear saris.) The sari should really be associated with the region (which stretches from Central and East India to Srî Lañkâ), and not a religion. If the sari is a Hiñdu dress, then Pukhrâj was more Hiñdu than the Hiñdu women of Jammû, who still mainly wear the *shalwâr qamîz* (which the Pâkistânis and some Indians wrongly think is Islâmic) because that is the dress of the Punjāb-Jammû belt.

Reading habits, too, were eclectic. The Hiñdus were diehard fans of Iqbâl, the poet, and the Muslims avidly read the 'four large, thick volumes of *Fasânâ é Âzâd* by Rattan Nâth Sarshar'—a Hiñdu who had given himself a Persian ('Muslim') last name. Everyone in Pukhrâj's family wanted to read the series. She reminisces, 'Rarely has the Urdu idiom been used better than in this book. My world changed after I read [it]. The description of Eid is so real that it seemed I was part of the festivities of that time.'[xviii]

But things began to change. For instance, in contemporary Delhi, by the early decades of the 20th century, 'you could [no longer] make out a Hiñdu from a Muslim.'[xix] That's because everyone was wearing the same Western-style clothes. Ironically, so long as people of different communities wore clothes that proclaimed their ethnic identity, there was no tension between them, and very little (if any) prejudice. It was only after external marks started disappearing that stereotypes and generalisations about other communities—and, thus, hatred—started creeping in.

Today, perhaps the Gujjars and Bakerwâls alone can be identified by their clothes, beards and jewellery. And these are the two most integrated communities of the state. They hate no ethnic group, and no one dislikes them.

Jammû town before 1947

Till 1947 the Gumat Gate—very ornate even today, though illegal shops have obscured its old elegance—was where the town began and was its lowest end. The palace complex in the Râmnagar Rakh was the highest point and the northern extremity. All visitors from the plains in the south would enter through the Gumat Gate and start climbing up its steep stone steps.

The bridge on the Tawi was built in the early 20th century. Before that people would cross the river by boat when its waters were substantial and wade through it during the rest of the year.

To this day many villages in the *kañdi* (semi-arid) belt—Gurhâ Salâthiâ, for example—have ponds (*tâlâbs*) where they store rain- and spring-water, to drink and to wash with. Jammû's famous tâlâbs—Puccâ Tâlâb, Rânî dâ Tâlâb, Tâlâb Khatîkâñ and Tâlâb Tillo—have, like the *bâghs* (gardens and orchards) of Srînagar, since been built over and been converted into residential districts.

According to an estimate, in 1941 Jammû city had a population of around 50,000, of which roughly 16,000 were Muslims.

Sorayyâ Khurshîd's otherwise unprejudiced account very gently hints that old Jammû was ghettoised. She writes, 'Jammû city was divided into two parts, the upper and the lower. While one did not understand as a child why the city was laid out like that, years later I found many Italian cities similarly laid out. In Jammû the upper or the elevated part of the city was mostly peopled by Hiñdus—though there was a Pathân mohallâ right in the middle of it.'

This is an incredible statement. Obviously five decades of separation have blurred that gracious lady's memory, for the uppermost mohallâ in town, the one closest to the royal palace, was the overwhelmingly Muslim Ustâd Mohallâ. Forest lessee Sheikh Amîn's tony mansion—the only one with Italian marble—was also close to the palace and was perched atop a similar elevation.

On the other hand, some very rich Hiñdus—notably shopkeepers and jewellers—lived in the southern half.

The Ustâd Mohallâ: Ustâd Ghaus Muhammad Khân, who belonged to Râmpur (Uttar Pradésh), was known for his expertise with horses, bows and arrows. The Mahârâjâ of Jammû and Kashmîr, Pratap Singh, invited the *ustâd* (maestro) to the state to teach his brother, Râjâ Ram Singh, and him, as well as other royals, these arts.

The Mahârâjâ granted his tutor an enormous estate close to the palace. Râjâ Ram Singh got a grand mansion, which is still intact, built for his *ustâd*. According to Prof. Suneethi Bakshi, the raja personally supervised the construction of this *havéli* (mansion) and ensured that its ground floor was built of the same materials as the Mahârâjâ's palace, which was then being constructed. And when Râjâ Ram Singh added an upper floor to his own house, he got a similar floor made for his tutor.

(References to Prof. Suneethi Bakshi are for her article 'Mute witness to a bygone idyllic and historic time,' *The Kashmîr Times,* 23 and 30 October, 2005.)

Ghaus Muhammad—whom the Mahârâjâ gave the title Sardâr—was some kind of a modern day Arjun. Apparently, the ustâd could, with his arrows, shoot down birds flying above him without looking at them. He only needed to see their reflections in a tub of water.

The ustâd founded a very illustrious line. He married Bégum Jân, whose father General Samad Khân was the landlord of Balliâñ, a village near Udhampur. The legendary Col. Peer Muhammad was their eldest son. (The colonel was, for a while, the state president of the Hiñdu nationalist Bhâratiya Jan Sañgh—the precursor of the Bhâratiya Janatâ Party. And when Pâkistân gifted armed militancy to the state in the

1990s, Farooq Khân of the Indian Police Service—who is the colonel's grandson and the ustâd's great-grandson—became one of the foremost militancy-fighters of the state.)

Upon Bégum Jân's death, Râjâ Ram Singh persuaded the ustâd to marry again. Each time that a child was born to the ustâd—and he had five children—the royal queens would come over with gifts of gems and robes embroidered with gold.

All this royal attention encouraged other elite Muslims to build houses on the ustâd's estate—which came to be called the Ustâd Mohallâ.

A widow of Mîr Mânu, the Mughals' Viceroy of Lahore, had, in the 1770s, built the substantial Wazîrni mosque at the point where the mohallâ meets Palace Road. She also built a *havéli*—the Bégum ki Havéli—for herself.

Râjâ (General) Rão Firmân Ali Khân, another illustrious resident of the mohallâ, too, had a spacious *havéli*. If Brig. U.C. Bakshî's Edwardian house was the biggest of them all—with a row of stables and garages, lawns that stretched over half an acre and three large western-style 'halls'—it was because he had the Anglicised need for lawns and the advantage of being a latecomer to the mohallâ.

After the unfortunate exodus of 1947, Râo Firmân Ali Khân's mansion was, for a few years, converted into a refugee camp. (Details in the next chapter.)

Ghaus Muhammad Khân was a gourmand, and his *havéli* was known for its colourful soirees. The best dancing girls and female singers of the day—notably Iqub alias Ballo of the Urdû Bâzâr—would enliven things for guests, who often included the Mahârâjâ's brother.

The Urdû Bâzâr: Jammû's Urdû Bâzâr (later renamed Râjinder Bâzâr after the great military martyr of 1947) used to have a major Muslim presence. Its southern end was called Pîpalwâlâ Chowk. (The pîpal tree is still there but the square has been renamed Shahîdî Chowk.)

Urdû Bâzâr had the town's most successful bakeries, both owned by Jammû Muslims—Ghulâm Muhammad and Sâdiq—and, later, another two owned by the biggest names from Srînagar—Âhdoo and Lâlâ Sheikh. This bazar was where people went for kebabs and perfumes. (Perfumes made in Kannauj, U.P., are still sold there.)

The Tâj Hotel, owned by Dogrified Muslims from Baltistân, had already made a name for itself. It has gone to greater heights and vastly expanded since.

Indeed, only Muslim chefs made certain kinds of delicacies. Omar was known for the kebab, Masood Billâ for several kinds of sherbet, Miañ Latîf for pickles, Châcha Shammâ for the Kashmîri *tsachéroo* bagel, Qutubi for the *katlammâ* and Laloo Billâ for the *bâqar-khâni*.

The Bâzâr was best known for its sex artistes. (Sex artistes are women who, in Hindi-Urdû films, sanctimoniously proclaim, 'We sell our art [classical singing and/ or Kathak dancing], not our bodies.' And yet the world—Râd, for instance—associates them mainly with 'the world's oldest profession.')

Only Malkâ Pukhrâj, who lived for a few years on that street of talent and pleasure, was able to establish herself in Pâkistân after the maelstrom of 1947. But then she had shifted to what later became Pâkistân much before partition—and was already a superstar.

The Muslim elite—and middle class

Incidentally, how big was the Muslim elite—and middle class—of Jammû? Different writers have offered various estimates. Pukhrâj was under the impression that the Muslims did not own shops or get government jobs in the same proportion as their share of the population. I have tried to crosscheck that noble lady's gut feeling. In this book, I have listed the Muslim elite, without expressing its number as a percentage. I have also tracked down the better-known Muslim entrepreneurs and shopkeepers of that era.

Prof. Suneethi Bakshi writes, 'By 1947, there were 167 Muslim families in the [Ustâd] mohallâ of whom barely 12 per cent in all were in the upper elitist bracket.' The percentage would surely have been no different among Hiñdus in similar mohallâs.

For Jammû province—and, indeed, the state as a whole—there is another indicator. 71,667 soldiers and officers from the state served in the British Indian Army during the Second World War. Of them 60,402 (or 84.28 per cent) were Muslims. (In 1941, 77.11 per cent of the people of the state were Muslim.)

The state had a very tiny organised private sector at the time and it consisted mainly of the production of and trade in handicrafts and fruits. Forest lessees were among the richest people in the state. The civil service was small. Service in the army accounted for the biggest chunk of salaried employment. Therefore, soldiers, even the ones at the bottom of the army's food chain, constituted the bulk of the middle class. Brigadiers, on the other hand, formed the rung just below royalty.

Perceptions—of the self and of others

In South Asia the various communities began to think of themselves as belonging to the majority community or to a minority only after 1881. That was when British-administered censuses started informing Indians which community formed what part of the population in which city or state or the country as a whole. Till then people went by general impressions. That's the feeling I get from all pre-1880 Indian literature, which normally seems to assume that the Hiñdus and Muslims were roughly equal in number. (In fact, the ratio was almost 3:1.)

Even afterwards, only educated and politically aware sections of the population knew the exact figures—and cast aspersions on the accuracy of figures that did not suit them.

Pukhrâj's is a classic example. In order to justify the reaction of some Hiñdu fanatics against the Mahârâjâ because of his concern for the Muslims, she writes, 'There were more Hiñdus than Muslims in the kingdom'.[xx] Please consider this: a Pâkistânî Muslim, writing in her old age, for a readership that was entirely Muslim and Pâkistânî, was making excuses for the Hiñdu right, based on figures (and reasoning) that were widely off the mark. But why did she get this impression? Perhaps because in the belt that she lived in (the districts now called Jammû, Kathuâ and Udhampur) the Muslims were in a minority. (In Jammû province, as well as the state as a whole, the Muslims were overwhelmingly in the majority.)

The impetus arrives from the cities: Till India was partitioned along religious lines in 1947, the common man was not much concerned about religion. To a great extent things are much the same to this day in the remoter villages of all South Asian countries—villages not yet polluted by fanatics from the cities. The same is true of the urban poor.

Pukhrâj tells us that the rural Muslims of Jammû rarely knew the *kalimâ*—the two-phrase fundament of Islâm. (I get the same impression about the rural Pâkistânî Punjãbî Muslims of the 1940s from the liberal Pâkistânî literature of that era.[4]) She says that there were no mosques—or schools—in these Muslim villages. (There were countless Muslim shrines, though, and these continue to be venerated by the Hiñdus and Sikhs after the unfortunate exodus of the Muslims.)

Sâîñ Rahîmâ, a *faquîr* (Muslim mendicant) took it upon himself to correct some of this. He started reading the *azân* (call to prayer) but initially the entire rural Muslim population ignored his call. Later, Pukhrâj's grandfather and one other Muslim began to respond to it. The Sâîñ then tried to teach the *kalimâ* to rural Muslims but only a few bothered to learn from him. Most rural Muslims considered religious rituals 'useless.'[xxi]

However, because of the constant efforts of outsiders like the Sâîñ (and his Hiñdu counterparts) a thitherto indifferent rural population gradually began to become religious.[xxii] That is one reason why a people who had lived with each other like brothers for centuries slowly started drifting into two implacably hostile nations.

Contentment: From the time that it was founded, Jammû had the reputation of being a very clean city. Because it is built on the slopes of

---

4. Sabîhâ Sûmar's classic film, *Khâmosh Pânî* (Silent Waters, 2004), and Ashfaq Ahmed's *Gadariya* bring this point very powerfully.

a hill, all it took to wipe the city clean was one rainfall—and stone-lined streets and a good drainage system. Every visitor—and visiting writer—has commented on this. 'Modern' engineering has interfered with the drainage somewhat, and the streets are now made of cement or asphalt.

The Mahârâjâs' Jammû was also a particularly inexpensive place to live in—especially when compared with neighbouring Puñjâb. *Ghee* (melted butter), for instance, was almost forty per cent cheaper than in Lahore. This was mainly because the Mahârâjâ had banned the export of a very large number of local products.[5] As a result prices were kept down. Pukhrâj writes, 'This might have been the reason that people, in spite of being poor, felt content.'[xxiii]

Ustâd Khân Sâheb Ali Baksh was one such person. His musical talents—singing, as well as playing the tânpurâ—won him acclaim in Lahore and Sindh. He was supposed to be the best Hiñdustanî music singer in undivided India—a talent that was never recognised formally. (That of his son, the legendary Badé Ghulam Alî Khân, was—by fans, by the market and by the Indian State.) The Ustâd would have earned at least a living wage (if not much more) had he migrated from Jammû to where the real market for his music was. But he chose not to. Pukhrâj comments, "Lord knows what attractions, what magic, Jammû had that he did not want to leave even though he was on the verge of starvation."[xxiv]

And he was not the only Muslim who loved Jammû so intensely. Pukhrâj writes that the Hindus and Muslims would alike 'pray for their Mahârâjâ. They sincerely believed that since Allah had appointed the rulers, it was their duty to love and respect them. They loved their land so much that they did not think of moving to another city."[xxv]

In turn, when Pukhrâj was a child and unknown in the world of singing, the Jammû elite encouraged her because she was a fellow Jammûite. They did not see her as a Muslim. Thâkur Kartâr Siñgh was one such noble.[xxvi]

On his coronation, Mahârâjâ Hari Siñgh sent every family in his kingdom—Hiñdu as well as Muslim—two seers (roughly one kilogram) of sweets. Both communities were equally excited about his ascension to the throne. The Mahârânî of Jammû was a style icon even for Muslims like Pukhrâj.[xxvii]

Muslims at the royal court—and in the arts

Ustâd Ali Baksh and his first cousin, Allâh Baksh, were the great singing geniuses that Jammû city produced in the early 20th century. Unfortunately, some mental illness overwhelmed Allâh Baksh.

5. The ban on the 'export' of *râjmâ* [red beans] and Jammû's famous basmati rice to the rest of India remained in place till the mid-1990s.

There was a very large number of Muslim musicians in the Mahârâjâ's court. The king always made sure that all the best musicians were invited. Therefore, there was no discrimination. The Mahârâjâ was so impressed by Ustad Mamman Khân's singing that he gave the Ustad his own emerald necklace. The other top classical singers of his era included Miyâñ Maulâ Bakhsh Talwañdîwâlé.

When the Mahârâjâ decided that Malkâ Pukhrâj ought to go in for advanced training in music, he specified that a good 'Khân Sâheb' should train her, when he could as well have sent her to a Pañdit jî. Maulâ Bakhsh was the best available, so Hari Siñgh got his government to employ him.[xxviii]

The Mahârâjâ had a number of Muslims in his employ. Many of them were in senior positions. Among the ones mentioned by Pukhrâj are his secretary, Abdul Qayyûm Khân and Nawâb Khusrau Jung.[xxix] Pukhrâj talks about several Muslim ministers at Mahârâjâ Hari Siñgh's court. These included a poet. His name was 'Khushi Muhammad or perhaps Nazîr Ahmed,' she recalls.[xxx] (Actually, his name was both. Khushi Muhammad Nâzir was the greatest Urdu poet of undivided India at the turn of the 19th/ 20th centuries.)

Muhammad Abdullah of Chamkor Saheb (Ropar, Punjab), who graduated from the Aligarh Muslim University in the 1890s and was thus one of the few Indians with a BA at the time, joined the highest rungs of the Mahârâjâ's civil service. His son, Qudratullâh Shahâb, of the Indian Civil Service, became a great Urdu writer. Shahâb would later recall that while preparing for the ICS examination, whenever he needed pin money he would go to the Pañj Pîr shrine in Ramnagar Rakh, and pocket some of the coins placed there by devotees. He kept a meticulous account of all the money he had taken. After he got into the ICS he returned every penny.

Moulvi Hashmat Ullah Khan was another ranking civil servant who, like Muhammad Abdullah, held the highest office in Gilgit. Incidentally, the Flagstaff House in Gilgit is still called Samad House after the aforementioned Gen. Samad Khan, who had led the Gilgit Campaign on behalf of the Mahârâjâ.

Dr Noor Hussain was the Mahârâjâ's personal physician and was appointed the Director (Health Services) for the entire state in 1947. The government gave him a large, Victorian bungalow on Jammû's elite Residency Road. He 'was looked upon with favour by Mahârâni Târâ Devi,' his son, Khâlid Hasan, recalls.

Other leading doctors of the era were Dr. Abdul Karîm, Dr Azîz Kash, Dr Rehmatullâh and Dr Wazîr Ahmed Qureshi.

The highest ranking Puñjâbi/ Dogri/ Pahârhi-speaking Muslim officers who stayed on after 1947 were Chaudhary Niâz Ahmed, Chief Secretary (the highest ranking government servant in the state), Malik Muhammad Maqbook, who was the Registrar (Cooperatives), Syed Nisâr Hussain Shâh, Food Controller, and Wazîr Muhammad Khân, Senior Superintendent of Police.

Chaudhari Fazl e Haq was the deputy inspector of customs. Abdul Hai, too, was in the customs department. Malik Fazal Haq was the inspector of schools.

Though the Muslims—like the Mohyâl Brahmins—were not proportionately represented in the civil services and shop keeping, they did quite well in the army (as the reader will notice in the 'History' section), the police and professions that required specialisation—again, like the Mohyâl Brahmins.

After the state army came under the British Indian Army and was given parity of rank, Brigadier was the highest rank that an Indian could hope to rise to. There were two Brigadiers in the state at any given time: one each in Kashmîr and Jammû. In 1947, Brig. Khudâ Baksh headed the army in Jammû province. He then became the head of the state army, first as a Brigadier and then as a Major General. (Pooñch was later put under a Brigadier.)

Earlier, the state army had several Muslim generals—notably Gen. Samunder Khân and Gen. Farmân Ali Khân. Brig. Bashîr Ahmed and Col. Jamshed were among the other ranking officers.

During the troubles of October 1947 the head of the Jammu Sadr [central] Thâna [police station], which controlled the entire town and some adjacent villages, was Râjâ Sohbat Ali, sub-inspector. (Throughout South Asia, the Thâna Sadr of the state capital is the posting most sought after by policemen of the appropriate rank.)

The Superintendent of Police [SP] of Udhampur, the highest ranking police officer of that district, was Sheikh Muhammad Salîm. Muhammad Yâhyâ Qureshi was the SP of Mîrpur. Miâñ Abdul Rashîd, the Inspector General of Police, was the head of the state police. [Yusuf Saraf says that Rashîd was the SP of Jammû. According to Hasan he was the IGP.] Miâñ Saîd Ali was the district inspector of police.

Other ranking members of the tiny corps of police officers were Syed Sultân Ali Shâh, Sheikh Fazal Âlam and Durrâni.

Chaudhary Feroz Dîn Salâria was the Divisional Forest Officer. Malik Âftâb Ahmed was an engineer, Bâbu Roshan Dîn was in charge of the water works in Udhampur and Bâboo Abdul Hamîd was an overseer.

The arts: Gâmâ made the best sitars in the state, and among the best in undivided India. People from Bengal and Bombay would travel to Jammû to buy his fabled sitars.

From all accounts, Jammûites of the pre-1947 era had a very advanced knowledge of classical music. And this was not confined to the elite. Street singers would sing classical songs and teenagers would be able to identify the râg that the songs had been set in. Kashmîr and Jammû were not as insular as they later became. Most of the songs were in the Awadhi language of Eastern Uttar Pradésh. Zubaidâ, a teenaged singer from Tâlâb Khatîkañ, would sing in the Benâres style.

Râd informs us that on winter evenings at the Peer Mitthâ Chowk, Muhammad Dîn Mirâsi would often be found playing Râg Gujri Todi on the clarinet, with the legendary Allâh Rakhâ Mirâsi accompanying him on the drum. (Allâh Rakhâ went on to become India's best known and highest paid tablâ player. His grandson, a trendy tabla player and sometime film star, is better known for hawking tea on television.)

Ustâd Âshiq Ali Khân of Patiala, another music luminary of that era, would camp at Sâîñ Samiullâh's Ahâtâ (courtyard) and perform at the Kashmîr Soap Factory on Residency Road.

The Khudâ Bux Band operated at a different level. But as the city's only [military-style] 'band' it was in great demand at all weddings—and at the funerals of very old Hiñdus. Later, Bairo Sâheb, too, started a band. Ooyi Allâh, Ferojâ Mirâsi and Jânâ were the leading clowns of the era.

Ghulâm Pehelwân ran a successful wrestling pit. Hakîm Barkat Ali owned the famous Râz é Hayât Clinic. Habîb Kaifvi's shop, Hobsons, sold furniture and rented tents and other accessories for weddings and other feasts. His shop also doubled as a literary salon for all communities.

Mirzâ Jâfar Ali Khân Asar and the great litterateur Maulvi Abdul Haq were among the state's elite.

Urdû remains the official language of Jammû to this day. Till the 1950s it was the only Indian language that most Hiñdu, Sikh and Jain men knew. It was also the language of their choice. Jammû was known for its mushâirâs (soirees, where Urdu poetry is recited), Sorayyâ Khurshîd notes.

Qais Sherwâni permanently headed the Bazm e Urdû. He was also its founder. Sherwâni later joined the Mahârâjâ's civil service.

Col. Adâlat Khân had served as the Mahârâjâ's ADC.

Just before partition, two of the Mahârâjâ's *aides de camp* (ADCs)—Sâhebzâdâ Nûr Muhammad and Malik—were Muslim, as were his head chef, head-waiter and several orderlies. (Fundamentalist Indians, especially before 1947, would rather appoint people of the other community as Prime Ministers than eat food cooked by them or have them in the immediate household staff.)

Under Hari Siñgh the royal kitchens cooked only *halâl* (kosher) meat, because his Muslim officials and other subjects would eat no other. The Hiñdus of Punjãb-Jammû—including Hari Siñgh's own clan, the Râjpûts—

on the other hand, did not eat *halâl* meat. Forced to choose between the two, Hari Siñgh went with the majority community of his state.[xxxi]

Then why the impression in Kashmîr that the Dogrâ Mahârâjâs did not employ Muslims? Perhaps what is meant is that they were not employed in proportion to their share of the population. Some of the Muslims in the Dogrâ Mahârâjâs' government were from outside the state. Khusrau Jung, for instance, was Hyderâbâdî royalty.

However, when one reads about the Mahârâjâ's army—in the volume about 'Ladâkh' as well as in this volume, in the next chapter—one can not fail to note the preponderance of Muslim names, among officers as well as soldiers.[6] Perhaps they were mostly from old Pooñch-Rajourî.

Patronising Kashmîrî crafts: The Dogrâ Mahârâjâs used the culture of Kashmîr to represent not just the Valley but also the state as a whole. The Mubârak Mañdî of Jammû, for instance, 'was a brilliant example of Kashmîrî craftsmanship.'[xxxii] In particular, the doors of the large hall in that royal campus showcased the best of Kashmîrî art.[xxxiii]

The hallmark of the architecture of the Dogrâ Mahârâjâs—especially Hari Siñgh—was elegance in simplicity. The quality of construction was uniformly good. The location of the Dogrâ palaces—whether in Jammû, Udhampur, Srînagar or Gulmarg—was always outstanding. These palaces were built overlooking the best views in town.

Simplicity pervaded every aspect of Hari Siñgh's character. His palaces had none of the ornate curves and flourishes of, say, Râjasthânî palaces. Hari Siñgh would often say that he felt 'uneasy with the priceless things around [him].' He preferred rooms with 'plain walls and ceilings, which had no embellishments on them.'[xxxiv]

So, he left the elaborate Mubârak Mañdî palace and shifted to spartan Râmnagar (where his descendants now stay and also run a hotel). His advisors tried to dissuade him on the ground that a mahârâjâ ought to live in a palace that befitted his status. However, Hari Siñgh persisted with his decision. While this saved the contemporary taxpayer some money, the maintenance of the Mubârak Mañdî palace suffered. So much so that most Jammûites born after 1947 do not realise that the Mubârak Mañdî was once a palace.

One Kashmîrî craft that grew further during the Dogrâ era was that of building houseboats. Some three- and four-storey houseboats would be anchored near the Srînagar palace that now houses the state legislature. Considering that the traditional houseboat has only one floor, these were greatly admired by spectators.[xxxv]

6. For instance, the 6th Jammû and Kashmîr Infantry Battalion, posted at Bunji (old Gilgit-Ladâkh), consisted of two companies of Pooñch Muslims, one Dogrâ Hiñdu company and one Sikh company.

In order to promote Kashmîrî handicrafts, Mahârâjâ Hari Siñgh got an exhibition ground—with permanent stalls—constructed in Srînagar. Private dealers could display their goods there. This triggered off a wave of creativity.[xxxvi] Kashmîrî craftsmen started thinking up new designs and products now that they, for the first time in history, had rival shops next to each other, each exhibiting its products. (The traditional way of selling goods—which continues to this day—is from the workshop or factory itself. Displaying goods in a show window is a western concept that dates, in J&K, to the 1930s and was perhaps introduced to Kashmîr by this exhibition.)

Travelling to Kashmîr: Before the era of automobiles, travelling from Jammû to Kashmîr (or back) was a hazardous and time-consuming affair. Those who could afford to hire a horse or mule would do so. Others took almost a fortnight on foot. The Jawâhar Tunnel at Banihâl was built only in the 1960s. Before that whether on foot or in a car, people had to go all the way up to the Banihâl Pass, which received snowfall in spring and autumn as well. People would freeze to death there. Which is why those who weıe about to embark on that journey would first go to all their friends and relatives and ask them to forgive them their trespasses. (This custom probably has its origin in the Islâmic Haj. People seek to be forgiven for fear that they might not come back alive.)

The Mahârâjâ of Kashmîr, like his Mughal precursors, would be carried in a palanquin. A staff of around twelve hundred people of varying ranks accompanied him. Their first halt in Kashmîr would be at an elegant rest house in Qâzigund which was burnt down by militants in the early 1990s.

Friends and counsellors: The first prince to arrive in Jammû for Hari Siñgh's coronation as mahârâjâ was the Nawâb of Pâlampur, a Muslim. He was, arguably, Hari Siñgh's closest friend. 'They behaved as if they were brothers.'[xxxvii] Such was the depth of their friendship that the Mahârâjâ got a palace called Tâleh Mañzil in Urdu (and Karan Mahal in Hiñdî) specially built for him near his own palace in Srînagar. He wanted to ensure that the Nawâb had a place appropriate to his status to stay in when he came visiting in the summer. This honour was extended to no other visitor.

Tâleh Mañzil was built at the highest point of Gupkâr Road, where the Mahârâjâ's nobility lived. I used to, half a century later, stay at the bottom of the road. Except for the house allotted to me, which was built as the official residence of the Governor of Kashmîr, and perhaps two other houses, all the vast mansions on Gupkâr (with names like Effendi Villa) housed Muslim nobles. Almost all of them migrated to Pâkistân after 1947, because they did not hail from the state.

Another regular and favourite guest was Maulânâ Sâheb. He belonged to central Indian royalty and lived in Lucknow. Whenever he came to the state the Mahârâjâ would insist on the Maulânâ spending at least two or three months with him. Even though other Muslims would (unfairly, as it turned out) warn the Mahârâjâ that the Maulânâ was not the good-natured simpleton that he appeared to be, Hari Siñgh always stood by his guest.[xxxviii]

The rulers and the ruled—an informal relationship: The Mahârâjâ does not seem to have been the 'oriental despot' of Western imagination. His employees and subjects—including Muslims—felt free to take certain liberties without being victimised. When the Mahârâjâ's secretary, Abdul Qayyûm Khân, came to summon Pukhrâj, then a child, to the court, she was asleep. Her mother refused to wake her up, saying, "If they want to listen to her singing they can send the car tomorrow."[xxxix] There seems to have been no fear of the Mahârâjâ's wrath.

In nearby Chenainî, relations with the king (who was subordinate to Jammû) were even more informal. If a person (accused, normally, of a minor crime) was summoned to the court of the king (who doubled as a judge), and if it was not convenient for him to attend the king's court that day, the accused would say so to the king. The king of Chenainî would then fix the next hearing according to the pleasure of the accused.

And if the person was found guilty and imprisoned, he could still move about freely during the day—he could till his fields, tend his flock or keep shop. He was required to report to the jail only in the evening, to spend the night there. This idyllic state of affairs continued in Chenainî till 1947. Malkâ Pukhrâj comments, 'There were no restrictions on them, and therefore the prisoners broke no rules.'[xl]

Crime was virtually unknown in the hills of Jammû—as it is to this day in Leh, Kargil and the 'Northern Areas' of occupied Kashmîr. People in these areas are simple and content with their lot—and isolation from the world of the plains.

Jammû and Kashmîr—especially the 'Northern Areas'—was an exceptionally peaceful place at the time. (Unlike, say, the Punjâb or UP, which were not.) The Mahârâjâ of Jammû and Kashmîr would move around in his state without any bodyguards or other security—and so would visiting kings, while in the state. Nor would the mahârâjâ keep guards around his chambers at night when he went to sleep.[xli] Murder and violent attacks on people continued to be rare—till, in 1989, a generous neighbour changed all that, and exported its own culture (and weapons) to this uniquely serene state.

References

i Pukhraj, Malka, *Song Sung True*, trans. and ed. by Saleem Kidwai (2002), Zubaan, Kali for Women, Hauz Khas Enclave, New Delhi 110016, page 154.

ii Ibid, page 1.

iii Ibid, page 88.

iv Ibid, page 2.

v Ibid, page 37.

vi Ibid, pp. 191-194.

vii Ibid, page 113.

viii Ibid, page 211.

ix Ibid, page 3.

x Ibid, page 21.

xi Ibid, page 94.

xii Ibid, page 93.

xiii Ibid, page 94.

xiv Ibid, page 136.

xv Ibid, page 76.

xvi Ibid, page 87.

xvii Ibid, page 84.

xviii Ibid, page 42.

xix Ibid, page 48.

xx Ibid, page 94.

xxi Ibid, page 95.

xxii Ibid, page 96.

xxiii Ibid, page 19.

xxiv Ibid, page 25.

xxv Ibid, page 66.

xxvi Ibid, page 62.

xxvii Ibid, page 140.

xxviii Ibid, page 131.

xxix Ibid, page 92.

xxx Ibid, page 83.

xxxi Ibid, page 89.

xxxii Ibid, page 67.

xxxiii Ibid, page 90.

xxxiv Ibid, page 78.

xxxv Ibid, page 115.

xxxvi Ibid, pages 146-7.

xxxvii Ibid, page 70.

xxxviii Ibid, page 133.

xxxix Ibid, page 62.

xl Ibid, page 81.

xli Ibid, page 77.

Note: This chapter first appeared as a book-review.

All references (and there are many) to

Khurshîd, Sorayyâ
Hasan, Khâlid
Hâshmî, Muharram
Râd, Rehmatullâh, and
Saraf, Mr. (Justice) Yusuf, are from

Râd, Rehmatullâh, and Hasan, Khâlid, eds., *Memory Lane to Jammu* (2004), Sang e Meel Publications, 25, Shâhrâh e Pâkistân (Lower Mall), Lahore (Pâkistân), Rs.395, a priceless volume that Gulalai Khan very kindly brought for me after this book had been composed for printing. Therefore, it has not been technically possible to put reference notes after the innumerable facts about Jammû that I have obtained from *Memory Lane*. Five wonderful people from Jammû, who were compelled to go to Pâkistân in 1947, have written it.

* * *

12

The Muslims of Jammû Province[1]

(1750–1947)

'What was it about that city that still draws us back?...Maybe it was that great fellow-feeling. It did not matter what caste, family, tribe or clan one belonged to: we treated one another as if we were members of the same family. We were together when it was time to mourn or celebrate. The people of Jammû were genuinely nice and did not say what they did not mean.'

Rehmat Ullâh Râd, *Memory Lane to Jammû*

King Rañjît Dév (1723-83) set into motion an admirable trend of inviting Muslims to come and settle in Jammû. This continued till almost 1947, when the demand of some central Indian Muslims for an all-Muslim country called Pâkistân gravely affected the living conditions of Muslims elsewhere in India.

Ajmal's is a case in point. He writes,[i] 'My great-grandfather, after getting fed up with [the] high handedness of the British rulers of India, took refuge in the state of Jammû and Kashmîr [and migrated to that state] from Qila Sobha Siñgh, District Sialkot [which is in the Puñjâb and very close to Jammû]. His father and grand father were Zamindars (land owner/ cultivators). The Mahârâjâ, based on [the] background of the family, granted him provisional citizenship of the state. He purchased a house in Jammû Tawi (the winter capital of the state) and settled there.'

This happened around the 1870s. Jammû was still a haven to which Muslims from all neighbouring states could shift if things got bad for

1. The districts now known as Jammû, Samba, Reasi, Kathuâ and Udhampur (plus Leh, in Ladâkh) were the only districts in the state where the Muslims were—and still are—in a minority.

them in their own state. And Ajmal's forefather hardly moved to an underclass existence in Jammû. That he could buy a house shows that he was welcomed into the middle-class of Jammû.

And that was how things remained. The Muslims and Hiñdus of Jammû lived together, thought the same thoughts ('ours is a very clean city'), had exactly the same love for the ice-cold waters of the Canal and the Chenâb, visited the same shrines every Thursday, celebrated each other's festivals, ate almost identical food and had identical reactions to all situations.

Whether it was big-hearted liberals like Malkâ Pukhrâj, Rehmatullâh Râd, Sorayyâ Khurshîd, Muharram Hâshmî and Khâlid Hasan, or right-wing Muslims like 'Ajmal,' they all loved Jammû as much as their Hiñdu-Sikh brethren did, and for the same reasons. Râd, Khurshîd, Hâshmî and Hasan are generous, singularly unbiased scholars, who had to migrate to Pâkistân in 1947. Despite what they went through in November 1947, they have only the nicest of things to say about Jammû, Jammûites and even Hiñdu ceremonies.

'Our clean Jammû'—a shared regional identity: Pukhrâj and Ajmal have separately recorded, "Jammû Tawi was a beautiful and clean town.[ii] It was built on the slopes of a mountain. Rains were common and after every rainfall the roads and streets used to glitter, because the rains had washed them clean. The town of Jammû had a specialty. It had flowing waters on its three and a half sides. On two and a half sides was River Tawi and on one side was a Canal fed by River Chenab. The waters of the Canal were ice cold, because they consisted of freshly melted snow. The Canal passed under River Tawi—the Tawi went over the canal through a man-made aqueduct.

"The inhabitants of Jammû were fond of picnics on the waterside or in the hills. They were also good swimmers. We used to have picnics on the banks of the Canal in summer. We did not go to the Canal on holidays because a large number of people used to come from Punjâb on holidays. During picnics at the Canal, we used to place baskets filled with mangoes, melons, watermelons or milk bottles in the canal and tether the basket to a tree with a rope. This used to 'refrigerate' the mangoes and other fruits and when we pulled the basket out, its contents would be as cold as ice." (And that was how Jammû remained till the 1970s, when 'modernisation' began to sweep away old traditions.)

All lanes in the Mahârâjâs' Jammû were paved with cobbled stones, as in old Europe. This made them easy to clean with a single rainfall. 'You could not find, even if you looked, any mud in Jammû,' Hâshmî recalls. 'This city of clean, stone-paved streets surrounded by hills had a story-like quality as if it were a tale out of Arabian Nights...I found many Italian cities similarly laid out,' Sorayyâ Khurshîd adds. Râd says, 'I do not recall ever seeing garbage piled on the street in Jammû...or puddles of standing water...Municipal water wagons kept [the roads] showered both morning and evening...Those who never knew Jammû would find it hard to imagine what a clean and beautiful city it was.'

Indeed they would, because around 1991 a few greedy engineers made crores of rupees by removing all those hand-chiselled stones and replacing them with ugly cement tiles, which will wear out in no time.

All well-to-do Jammû Muslims, like their Hiñdu brethren, recall that "we used to spend our summer vacations in Srînagar, the summer capital of the state. There we used to live in a house-boat which had two bedrooms with attached bathrooms and a large drawing-cum-dining room. A cook-boat was attached to it which housed the kitchen and residence of servants."[iii]

And yet Hasan says what Pukhrâj echoes, "Somehow Srînagar, where I was born and where I lived more than I lived in Jammû, has never had the same fascination for me that I felt for Jammû. Even today [in 2004], I would gladly return to Jammû.'

The Muslim population increases: During the Dogrâ era (roughly 1820-1947), as now, there were very few Shiâs (Shiites) in the province—or in the state as a whole. However, 'because of the efforts of [Ustâd Ghulâm Hussain] the number of Shiâs grew.'[iv] This says something about the freedom of religion in the state—that a Muslim sect could increase its numbers in a kingdom ruled by a Hiñdu.

And it wasn't just the Shiâs. Every census revealed that the Muslims formed a greater percentage of the population than a decade before—in every district, including the Hiñdu-majority districts of Jammû, Udhampur and Kathuâ. In Udhampur, for instance, the Muslim proportion increased from 28.66 per cent in 1911 to 33.37 per cent in 1931. In Dodâ, the Muslim share rose from 53.33 per cent in 1911 to 57.35 per cent in 1941. In Pooñch, the Muslims' ratio went up from 80.27 per cent in 1911 to 85.59 per cent in 1941.

Part of this increase was the result of migration from Muslim-majority areas like Gujrât (West Puñjâb).[iv]

That was how secure the Muslims felt in Jammû.

Shared festivals and customs: Malkâ Pukhrâj was secular because almost all Jammû Muslims of that era, like the Hiñdu-Sikhs, were secular. The only identity that the people accepted was regional, not religious. The Muslims and Hiñdus of Jammû thought of themselves as Jammûites, and not as Muslims or Hiñdus.

For instance, during the spring festival called Basañt the people of both communities put on identical clothes. The men wore yellow turbans while the women wore clothes that were entirely yellow.[v] The Hiñdu festival of Holî became a sore point between the Hiñdus and Muslims in some parts of India in the 1930s. But in Jammû, till 1946 or so the Muslims would not only celebrate it, they would also throw colours on their Hiñdu friends and get smeared in turn.[vi]

Dussehrâ was another festival that the Muslims—who thoroughly enjoyed the nine days of Râm Leelâ before it—celebrated with the Hiñdus. Malkâ Pukhrâj, who says that the Râm Leelâ was enacted for a month, goes into raptures about the beauty of the *bhajans* sung at those performances. Master *ustâds* had composed them, she writes.[vii] (*Ustâds* are normally Muslims.[2] In turn, Hiñdu theatre directors like Master Labhu Râm would stage plays on 'Muslim' themes such as Shîrîñ-Farhâd.)

Master Ghulâm Haider was the other leading theatre director of the era. He would, in turn, stage Punjâbî classics like Sassi Punnu.

Most Hiñdu youths of today might not know that Dussehrâ is celebrated in the month of Bhâdoñ but Râd, writing 57 years after he had to leave Jammû, has not forgotten this fact. Like most Muslims of his generation he knew the story of *The Râmâyan*, which he has summarised with obvious affection in his Urdû book published in Pâkistân, for Pâkistânîs, in 2004. He adds, 'After Dussehrâ, pilgrims would begin their annual march to pay homage to Vaishno Dévî.'

Râd also describes in detail the two Baisâkhi fairs of Jammû. His heart, and those of his family and friends in Pâkistân, still 'begin to dance with joy when we think of the Thâkur's pâlki [palanquin] being taken out on Janam Ashtami, Krishna's birthday, the festival of Holi with the colour-drenched clothes of the celebrants…We recall the festival at Pîr Khoh [a Hiñdu shrine] during Baisâkhi and Jharri.'

Jammû city's annual Muharram tableau was known for its beauty. Hiñdus as well as Muslims would stand on either side of the road when the procession went through the town. People of both communities would set up little stalls (booths) at which *sherbet* and drinking water would be served—free—to the Shiites. 'Indeed,' Pukhrâj writes, 'the Hiñdus put up more booths for they were given to praying for miracles.'[viii]

---

2. Not that it made a difference. Malkâ Pukhrâj's first teacher was a Muslim but his guru had been a Hiñdu. Whenever the diva heard a particularly good thumri being sung by a pañdit, she would hire him for a month or two—'at a generous salary'—and get him to teach her the thumri as well as the body movements associated with it.

Hâshmî adds, '[Before the 1940s] Hiñdu-Muslim unity was exemplary. Hiñdus and Sikhs would join the *ta'azia* procession...[and] would set up water points (sabeels) for the marchers.'

Syed Gulzâr Hasan Shâh, a shopkeeper and the patron saint of the idle chess players of Jammû, would lead the procession.

One of the grandest festivals of the year was the Eid é Mîlâd un Nabi. All Muslims and Hiñdus who remember that era still talk of its magnificence. A major procession would be taken through the streets of Jammû, which would begin and end at the Muslim Hall on Residency Road. The Hall was one of Jammû's major landmarks.

On average, the royal court celebrated one festival a month—and Hiñdus and Muslims took part in them all in equal measure. (See the chapter 'Jammu: 1885-1947' for more about the Dogrâ Mahârâjâs' patronage of Eid and Baisâkhî.)

The people also shared a common vocabulary. Hiñdus would spontaneously use Islâmic expressions like 'that child of Muharram' (which has pejorative implications). Leave alone Punjãbî Muslims, even Baltîs settled in Jammû tell their grandchildren exactly the same folk-tales as do their Hiñdu compatriots.

Among the Hiñdus there is a rule that when a wife's relatives look her up at her husband's home they don't eat or drink a thing there. The idea is not to be a financial burden on the husband, because traditionally the wife does not have an independent income of her own. To this day, the Muslims of Jammû treat Hiñdu women born in their neighbourhood like their own daughters and sisters. If a Muslim woman calls on her Hiñdu girlfriend at the latter's in-laws' home, the Muslim will refuse to eat or drink anything, saying, 'She is our girl. How can we accept food from her husband's family?'

Shared political views: Their political reactions, too, were identical. Balrâj Purî reminds us that 'when Kashmîrî Muslims led by Sheikh Abdullâh and supported by national leaders like Gandhi and Nehru were fighting against the rule of the Dogrâ mahârâjâ, they did not get much support from Muslims—as also Hindus—of Jammû; which [then] was [the] most populated region of the state.

'And when Sheikh Abdullâh and his National Conference had indicated their tilt towards accession to the Indian Union, the Jammû-based Muslim Conference and the Hindu Sabha supported the Mahârâjâ's desire to remain independent. One of the reasons for this decision, cited by the then president of the Muslim Conference, Chaudhary Hameed Ullah, was that "the Muslims of Jammû have never been lacking in showing loyalty and respect for the Mahârâjâ and it is because of this attachment that we did not support the Quit Kashmîr movement (launched by the National Conference for an end to Dogrâ rule)."[ix]

Significantly, as Balraj Puri and Ershad Mahmud have separately pointed out,[x] 'militancy which started in the Kashmîr region in 1989, did not extend to Jammû.'

The Muslims' impact: Even though the Muslims were in a minority in Jammû town—as well as in what are now the Jammû, Kathuâ and Udhampur districts, they had a very significant impact of the social life of the area.

Within Jammû town the Muslims were concentrated in the Khalkâ ('lower') Mohallâh, Ustâd Mohallâh (named after the Mahârâjâ's Muslim teacher) and Pathânâñ dâ Mohallâh. The Urdû Bâzâr (now called Rajinder Bâzâr), Talâb Khatîkâñ and Dalpatiâñ remain predominantly Muslim to this day. The quiet Vazârat Road was where the very substantial Muslim elite lived—right next to the palatial house of the British Resident. And it was hardly as if the people of Jammû were ghettoised into Hiñdu and Muslim areas. The toniest house in Julâha kâ Mohallâh belonged to a Puñjâbi Muslim. Several rich Hiñdus lived in Talâb Khatîkâñ and the Ustâd Mohallâh. The elite family of Air Marshal Asghar Khan [Chief of the Pâkistân Air Force and a politician in later years] lived in the Pathânâñ dâ Mohallâh.[xi]

The Muslims of Dârûgeerâñ Mohallâ, near Residency Road, had been invited by a seventeenth or eighteenth century king of Jammû to settle in his kingdom and make gunpowder (dârû) for the Jammû army.

The other neighbourhoods with a substantial Muslim population were Jatkatiâñ, Afghânâñ and what is now called Mastgarh.

Jogi Darwâzâ (now Jogi Gate) was one of the last Muslim-majority neighbourhoods to come up before 1947.

Mughalâni Begum, the widow of Mîr Moin-ul-Mulk, who was the Mughals' Governor, was among those who fled to Jammû during King Rañjît Dév's era. She built 'a grand residence in Gañdum [now Kanak] Mañdi. [Till the 1940s] this neighbourhood [was] known as Mohallâ Bégum ki Havéli.' (Râd)

Sardâr Muhammad Akram Khân's havéli in Talâb Khatîkâñ was the other major mansion. Green Gates on Vazârat Road, which this author was allotted as his official residence, was another.

The Muslims, in particular, were very cosmopolitan. Part of the reason was that many of their teachers were (Muslims) from the Punjâb. This had a profound impact on the language that they spoke (Punjâbî at home and Dogri with their Hiñdu friends), their dress and, later, the politics of some young, educated and middle-class urban people. Muslims from places as far apart as Bannu in the NWFP continued to migrate to

Jammû as late as in the 1930s. (Non-Muslim teachers, Hiñdu as well as Christian, too, came from distant lands like Shikârpur in Sind.)

Pooñch had a huge martial tradition. Employment in the army would help many Pooñch Muslims serve in foreign lands, rise in status and then settle in the winter capital of the state.

The bow-makers of Mastgarh had migrated from Batâlâ (Punjâb). After guns made bows and arrows redundant as weapons, the only patrons left were children, who would play with scaled down versions. Jammû's (Muslim) bow-makers would also make kites, especially for the (Hiñdu) festival of Janamashtami. This tradition came to an end in 1947.

I revived the kite festival in 1993, with the help of India's foremost experts (who, too, happened to be Muslim) from the walled cities of Delhi and Gujarât. However, under pressure from an influential local newspaper, my department abandoned the festival after my transfer.

The traditional vegetarian Hiñdu way of life does not enable the same kind of familiarity with animals (other than cows and buffaloes) to develop as the Muslim lifestyle does. Small wonder then that Gâmi (Ghulâm Muhammad) Qalander, the barber, owned the city's main pet shop. The majority of tongâs (horse driven carriages) in the province were owned and driven by Muslims.

Jeerâ, another barber, operated a hammâm, a tradition that was more or less lost to India after 1947.

The Muslims also had a monopoly on the very difficult art of making sword sheaths that were neither a millimetre too loose nor too tight. (Ceremonial swords were used by the Mahârâjâ's army and police till 1947, and by the upper rungs of the Indian police and army even in the 21st century.)

Shams Dîn was one of the most successful tailors of his time: the others in his bracket also being Muslim.

The Muslims took to newfangled machines with greater ease than the rest. Mistri Abdul Hamid operated a saw machine. Mistri Nazar Muhammad of Ustâd Mohallâ was a sought after motor mechanic.

Chhinj (wrestling contests) are held all over Jammû province after the monsoons. As would happen before 1947, even in the early 21st century wrestlers who happen to be Muslim win at least half of all championships.

Illiteracy and unemployment: Literacy in Jammû and Kashmîr was, and remains, the second worst in India. From all accounts, the Muslims were even more illiterate than the Hiñdus. According to Pukhrâj only half a dozen or so Muslim families were well educated and in senior jobs in the government. All of them were Pathâns. One of them had been the governor of Gilgit—which was one of the highest positions in the state. His sons were colonels and generals in the Mahârâjâ's army.

One reason why Muslim literacy was lower than that of the Hiñdus was that most Muslim women were illiterate. Even in the year 2001, female literacy in Kashmîr and Pâkistân was just a little more than half of that of the men.

Hâshmî notes, 'In those days no Muslim girl was sent to college. He adds, 'Initially, the Muslims had declared any Western education [even for men] as apostasy. It was this attitude that gave non-Muslims the opportunity to get into higher civil service posts. It was difficult for a Muslim in those days to even get hired as a peon.'

Only a few Muslims managed to receive some education, and the best that the majority of them could hope to do was to join the government as clerks or become ill-paid assistants to some unsuccessful (and normally Muslim) lawyer. Many young Muslims joined the lower ranks of the police and army.

The rural Muslims of the Dogrâ belt of Jammû-Kathuâ-Udhampur were mostly barbers, carpenters, ironsmiths and weavers. In the cities Muslims were not able to get salaried jobs. So, the youths would either become carpenters, masons and ironsmiths or set up tea stalls. Pukhrâj estimates that only half a dozen or so large shops were owned by Muslims. The Gujjars, of course, sold milk.

Unemployment among educated Muslim youths was rife during Mahârâjâ Pratâp's time. Pukhrâj writes that these educated young men were now too posh to become masons. So, they would idle away their days playing cards or chess, gossiping and ogling pretty flower sellers. At an age when they should have been supporting their parents, they would instead depend on their working-class parents for every rupee that they spent.

When other Muslims saw that even Muslim youths with Masters' degrees were unemployed, they concluded that there was no point in getting an education. They stopped sending their children to school. These children would, instead, spend their time swimming in what used to be the Khatîkâñ pond (it has been built over since) or play other street games. The few Muslim children whose parents forced them to go to school often played truant, perhaps because they found that the majority of their friends did not go to school at all. In any case, Muslim children would begin their schooling a few years later than their Hiñdu peers.[xii]

Mahârâjâ Hari Siñgh tried to give government jobs to educated Muslims. However, by then one generation of educated Muslims had been lost.

Efforts towards literacy

Till the 1910s or so, Muslims and Hiñdus attended mixed schools and colleges of the Western kind. Nusrat was the Second Master of the Sâmba High School. The primary school at Mastgarh had two teachers—Master Dâûd and a 'Pandit jî.' Obviously they had no Urdû equivalent of Vere Foster, for the Pandit jî would painstakingly write all the numbers from one to a hundred on the wooden 'slate' of each student—Hiñdu as well as Muslim. The students would then run their reeds over these numerals in order to learn how to write them correctly.

Mahârâjâ Partâp Singh ensured that no citizen had to pay a fee for primary education. Then, in the 1920s, his successor Mahârâjâ Hari Singh made primary education compulsory for all children in all the important towns. Textbooks and stationery were given to all children free of charge. Because several new schools were opened, the walk to school was greatly reduced. This gave a great boost to Muslim education—and employment, for many of the teachers were Muslim. Hakîm Farîd Âlam, for instance, was the headmaster of the Pîr Mitthâ School.

Somewhere along the way—and most unfortunately—community-oriented schools began to spring up all over India. In Jammû, the Râjpût School was the best known of these. Naturally, the Muslims, too, wanted a school of their own. Nawâb Mehboob Ali Khân Khusrau Jung persuaded the Mahârâjâ to allot the old Gundoo army barracks and the surrounding land to the Anjuman e Islâmiâ. That was how the Akbar Islâmiâ High School was founded.

To begin with the school was a disaster. Hardly any student from the school was able to matriculate successfully. The visionary Sheikh Abdul Azîz changed all that in 1933 when he took over as the headmaster. Within a year he ensured that hardly anyone failed.

All students who passed the school's internal pre-matriculation test were required to spend the night in the school hostel. They could go home for breakfast and, if it was close enough, lunch. After dinner they had to return to the school where teachers would coach them for the matriculation examination till midnight.

Sheikh Abdul Azîz must have dome something even more wonderful at home—or maybe it were his genes. His son, the legendary UNDP economist Mahbûb ul Haq, not only made Pakistan a success in the international financial market in the 1980s, he gave the world the Human Development Index. (Haq studied for a while at Jammû's non-denominational Ranbîr High School.)

All over the world schools compete with each other—especially for sporting glory. Sports teams during the British Râj were normally organised along religious lines. So, when they met on the sports field it inevitably became a clash between the concerned communities.

That is what began to happen every time Akbar Islâmiâ High School played the Râjpût School in the late 1930s and early 1940s. The boys would start fighting each other during the game. Things got so bad that teachers, too, began to take sides. Chaudhari Rehmat Khân, a teacher who had come over from the Punjâb, had to discipline two partisan teachers from the other side with his cane. After that the two teams needed police supervision each time they met on the playground.

The elite Prince of Wales College had students from all communities. As a result everyone was proud of it. Hâshmî points out that it had India's first geology department after Calcutta. He goes to the extent of claiming that it had the biggest campus for any college in India. (Guwahati's university-sized Cotton College, surely, holds that record?) POW College produced the only ICS (Indian Civil Service) officer from the province—and one of only two from the entire state—Qudrat Ullâh Shahâb.

Around the 1930s, young Jammû Muslims began to go to the Aligarh Muslim University for higher studies. 1943 was the year when the biggest batch of Jammûites went to the AMU. At Aligarh, Jammû was seen as the town where all the beauties came from. That reputation vanished after 1947.

Poor support for separatism: Chaudhary Ghulâm Abbâs was one of the few Jammû Muslims to support the theory that the Hiñdus and Muslims were two different 'nations.' He did so despite the fact that a (presumably Hiñdu) chief judge had given the Chaudhary's father employment as a peon in the court 'so that he would get a government salary. The judge was very generous toward Ghulâm Abbâs' father,' Pukhrâj writes. 'He [helped Ghulâm Abbâs' father get] an education for his three sons. Ghulâm Abbâs got a law degree. The second son was appointed as the SDO (Sub-Divisional Officer) in the irrigation department where he earned a great deal of money and lived in style and comfort.'[xiii]

Allâh Rakhâ 'Sâgar' and Abdul Majîd 'Karshî,' who had both received some schooling, were Ghulâm Abbâs' associates. Allâh Rakhâ's father was a wealthy property dealer. The three decided to project themselves as the leaders of Jammû's Muslims. They started asking fellow Muslims for small donations for the organisation of the community's festivals. They would plant stools in the middle of the street, climb on them and lecture passers by on political issues.

Muslims who had thitherto been perfectly at peace with the Hiñdus were, 'because of these men's leadership,' made to realise that some Hiñdus were contemptuous of them. On the positive side, the trio made the Muslims more 'conscious of their dignity and self-esteem.' They also demanded that a certain percentage of government jobs should be reserved for them. The very fact that the three leaders were organising the community along religious lines—something that had never happened before in Jammû and was part of a new phenomenon throughout urban South Asia—meant that some Muslims of Jammû city had now begun to think of themselves as a separate community. Earlier, Pukhrâj writes, 'no one had felt this way.'[xiv]

Pukhrâj was Allâh Rakhâ's neighbour and knew all three men because they would frequent her ustâd's shop. The details that she provides about their lives add up to an unflattering picture of the trio. (It is an honest picture. However, had she written about the average Hiñdu leader of Jammû of that era, the pattern would have been identical—a few years of schooling plus a habit of preying on others,)

Abdul Majîd seems to have been a man who thrived on the miseries of impoverished Muslim litigants. He would 'impose his help' on those simple people when they needed legal advice and force them to pay him for his presumed services. (Touts of that kind flourish to this day, except that they no longer presume to be the leaders of their community.)

In 1930, this group formed the Young Men's Muslim Association in Jammû. It led to the formation, in 1931, of the Muslim Conference for the entire state. (The MC, and its majority faction, the secular, pro-India, National Conference, would dominate the politics of 'AJK' and Jammû and Kashmîr respectively for the next more than seven decades.) Chaudhary Ghulâm Abbâs BA, LLB, was the founding secretary of the MC.

A chasm appears: Kashmîr has always been a shining example of Muslim-Hiñdu unity. The tiny Hiñdu minority formed a little less than five per cent of the population. But it never felt insecure because the Muslims never gave the Hiñdus any reason to.

The efforts of leaders like Chaudhary Ghulâm Abbâs changed some of that. A day before the Mahârâjâ was to meet the Chaudhary and his associates, Pukhrâj happened to be walking on the bund (embankment) that leads to Srînagar's Amîrâñ Kadal. She 'saw a Kashmîrî pundit, bleeding from his head, running for his life, followed by a Kashmîrî Muslim [who had] a stick in his hands...A Hiñdu-Muslim riot had begun.' (Pukhrâj's book mentions no dates. However, this must have been in 1931.[xv])

Pukhrâj's grandfather caught hold of the pursuer and gave the Pañdit a chance to escape. (I have a theory that liberalism—like prejudice—runs in families.) The attacker told her grandfather, 'I wanted to kill [the

Pañdit] because he was a Hiñdu, a pig and a bloodsucker. We have to get rid of these Hiñdus, these *kâfirs* [infidels].'[xvi]

Pukhrâj says that Chaudhary Ghulâm Abbâs had engineered that riot. The Chaudhary had to resort to cheap tricks like those to rally the people, because he knew that the Kashmîrîs loved Sheikh Muhammad Abdullâh and not him. He incensed the people further by alleging that the Mahârâjâ was not prepared to concede the demands of the Muslims whereas, according to Pukhrâj, this was not true.

She adds that the Mahârâjâ's Muslim aides, such as Khusrau Jung, 'lowered their eyes' when the matter was discussed in the court. They knew how the Mahârâjâ had alienated many Hiñdus—especially some 'generals and colonels of his own caste'—by his decision to concede the Muslims' demands.[xvii] The actions of Chaudhary Ghulâm Abbâs and his group seemed to vindicate the advice that these generals had given the Mahârâjâ: 'Do not trust the Muslims.' The Mahârâjâ's Muslim staff, Pukhrâj writes, 'behaved as if they were guilty even though they were in no way responsible for what had happened.'[xviii]

In the mid-1940s a chasm had begun to appear between the Hiñdus and Muslims of the British-ruled parts of India. Thanks to the movement started by men like Chaudhary Ghulâm Abbâs, it cast a shadow, albeit feeble, on the Mahârâjâ's court as well. It took the form of silence, which descended on the thitherto cheerful court. For the first time the staff got unofficially divided along religious lines. Neither group would say very much to the other. Perhaps they did not want to unwittingly say something that might cause offence. Or worse, perhaps they, too, had started believing the nasty things that the right wing of their community was saying about the other.

Festivals were the first casualty. The court still celebrated them, but now neither community seemed much inclined to take part in the festivals of the other. In the 1940s, both Hindus and Muslims started obstructing religious processions of 'the other community': the Eid Milad-ul-Nabi procession of the Muslims, and the Râm Lila procession of the Hindus.[xix]

Indeed, since 1945 or 1946 every religious festival has been a tense day for district administrations in India and Pâkistân, because in some corner or the other of these two unfortunate countries someone from the other community (in the case of Pâkistân, the other sect) might try to disrupt the festivity of the other.

A province, the citizens of which used to have heroes in common (K.L. Saigal, 'angel-face' Naseem Bano, the earlier Allâma Iqbâl, Malkâ Pukhrâj, Master Madan, Rattan Nâth Sarshar, Khurshîd, K.C. Dey and Râm Dulâri) now started drifting apart. When a group of Muslim schoolboys decided to set up a library in 1946 or early 1947, they decided to call it the Jinnâh Library. Hiñdu boys began to give their patriotic symbols a religious touch.

Such was the mistrust that the 'Pâkistân Movement' created that some Muslims employed by the Mahârâjâ's government were suspected of sedition and working for the future Pâkistân dispensation. They were dismissed from government service.[xx]

After the hijrat

More than 1.8 lakh Jammû Muslims found themselves in Siâlkot (Pâkistân) and 'AJK' in November 1947, after their tragic exodus. But only their bodies had migrated. Their hearts were still in Jammû. 'They remained strangers [in Pâkistân] and are so to this day [2004],' Hasan recorded.

Sorayyâ Khurshîd could not get herself to like the guavas, jâmuns or berries of Siâlkot because 'they do not have the taste and aroma' of their Jammû counterparts. Râd would miss the 'cool breeze [that] would rise from the east [on summer nights] at around 10p.m. which we called *dhidoo*.'

Alyâ Kebâbi used to make the best kebâbs in Jammû. It was more than mere nostalgia that made him wind up his kebab stall in Siâlkot after attempting to make Jammû-style kebabs for a year. His problem was that the sheep of the hot plains of Siâlkot did not yield the same delicious mutton, as did sheep fed on the mountain pastures of Jammû.

The *panâh-gazeen* (lit. protection- or refuge- seekers) from Jammû, who had been 'happy and well-to-do people in my city of Jammû [were now reduced to] selling odds and ends in the dark and winding streets' of Siâlkot. (Râd)

Gâmi Qalander, who once owned Jammû's main pet shop, would wonder if the monkeys of Pakki Dhakki missed their erstwhile bete noire—the only person in Jammû who could tame the most ferocious of monkeys.

The monkeys must have missed him very sorely because they no longer are as overwhelming a presence in the town as they used to be till 1947. They migrated to the Bâhu Fort area.

Siâlkot, as Râd points out, is only 22 miles from Jammû. Nostalgic Jammûites now in Siâlkot often go to the ancient Siâlkot fort from which, 'on any clear evening, the Jammû city lights can be seen glimmering in the distance like fireflies.'

The feeling is mutual. Not only the people of present Jammû but also visitors from places as far away as Bengal often go to Jammû's Bâhu Fort and the Bypass to see the lights of Siâlkot, which, through emotion-choked eyes, look like the glistening waves of an ocean and which hold a similar fascination for those who identify with all that unpartitioned Jammû stood for.

References

i From 'My Life In Kashmîr,' a series of articles posted on the Internet by a right-wing Jammû Muslim who later migrated to Pâkistân.

ii This passage is a composite of the identical memories of Malkâ Pukhrâj and 'Ajmal,'

iii Again, both Malkâ Pukhrâj and 'Ajmal' have recorded this.

iv Ibid, page 31, first paragraph.

v Pukhrâj, Malka, *Song Sung True*, trans. and ed. by Saleem Kidwai (2002), Zubaan, Kali for Women, Hauz Khas Enclave, New Delhi 110016, p. 116.

vi Ibid, page 136.

vii Ibid, page 153.

viii Ibid, page 29. The point about the increase in the Shia population is also made on page 30.

ix Puri, Balraj, *Indian Express*, Wednesday 25, February 2004.

x Ibid and *The News*, July 25, 2001.

xi This passage is based on the memories of Malkâ Pukhrâj and 'Ajmal,'

xii Pukhrâj, op. cit., pp. 98-99.

xiii Pukhrâj, op. cit., p. 100.

xiv Pukhrâj, op. cit., p. 103.

xv *Kashmîr in the Crossfire* (London: I.B.Tauris, 1996) p102-3

xvi Ibid, page 200.

xvii Ibid, page 201.

xviii Ibid, page 203.

xix Alexander Evans, quoting Muharram Hashmi, in Rehmatullah Rad and Khalid Hasan (eds), *Memory Lane to Jammû* (Lahore: Sang-e-Meel Publications 2004) p. 87.

xx See Pukhrâj, op. cit., p. 213.

* * *

13

Sikhs in Jammû and Kashmir

(1750–1947)

Sukh Jîwan was the Afghâns' Governor of Kashmîr from 1751 to 1762. (For a brief while he ruled Kashmîr independently.) He gave jobs in the Kashmîr army to a number of Brâhmins from the Pathohâr and Kohistân Malth areas of the Punjãb. These Brâhmins included Sikhs as well as non-Sikhs. When they retired they stayed on in Kashmîr.[i]

Sukh Jîwan had provided refuge in Kashmîr to a fugitive prince from Balkh (Afghânistân), as well as his followers. However, the prince was not altogether satisfied with his host. So, one day, he went up to Sukh Jîwan, pulled out a dagger and stabbed him. Contemporary histories tell us that some of Sukh Jîwan's Sikh soldiers rushed in, saw what had happened and killed the prince and his followers on the spot. Fauq writes, "They then went on a rampage in that stretch of Srînagar which lies between Zâldaggar (Nawâb Bâzâr) and Pândân."

During the Afghân period, the Sikhs, like the Kashmîrî Pañdits, rose to high positions in the army as well the civil administration. For example, in 1766 when Nûr ud Dîn Bamzaî was the governor of Kashmîr, the (Afghân) Emperor summoned him to Kâbul for a while. Bamzaî constituted a two-man council to look after the government while he was away. It consisted of Bamzaî's nephew, Jân Muhammad Khân, and Sardâr Gurmukh Siñgh. It is said that Bamzaî had faith in the Sardâr's administrative abilities.

The next that we learn about Sikhs in Kashmîr dates to 1781. Hâjî Karîmdâd Khân was the Governor of Kashmîr at the time. He sent Sardâr Dîwân Siñgh as the head of an army contingent against Bahâwar Khân Khakhâ. The Sardâr was killed in that battle.

In 1819 Mahârâjâ Rañjît Siñgh's army defeated the Afghâns. The brief Sikh era of Kashmîr's history (1819-46) began. Punjãbî Brâhmins—

again, Sikh as well as non-Sikh—were employed in the army as well as civil service. However, instead of getting a salary, they were paid in kind (*jins*). These Brâhmins, writes Fauq, were Mohyâls of the Dutt and Bâlî clans. They belonged to the Râwalpiñdî and Jehlum districts of the Punjãb. Those of them who made the transition to Sikhism came to be known as Jinsî Sikhs. In Kashmîr they settled in the Trâl, Karohan, Hamal, Mattan and Budgâm *pargânâs* (mediæval-era districts).

The Sikhs of Kashmîr—*jinsî* as well as others—are landowners and farmers. The Kashmîrî that they speak is not quite the same as that of, say, the Kashmîrî Pañdits or the Muslims.

As mentioned, some Sikhs held high offices during the Afghân and Sikh periods. Then, due to a low level of literacy, came an era of decline. Fauq, who published his book in 1934, when the Dogrâs ruled the state, noted that by his time the Sikhs had once again begun to be employed in the upper rungs of the government, 'thanks to education.' He added, 'In Bârâmullâ and Srînagar they have large *dîwâns* [assembly halls] and Siñgh Sabhâs [fraternities]...There are Sikh *zaildârs* [chiefs of a group of villages] and *numberdârs* [village headmen]. The Kashmîrî Sikhs might not be as sturdy as Punjãbî Sikhs but they are not weak either. Their complexion and the quality of their skin is much like that of the Kashmîrîs...*Zamîndâr* [landlord] Sikhs came to Kashmîr during the Sikh era and have settled in Mattan (South Kashmîr) and Chogal (North Kashmîr).'

The customs of Zamîndâr Sikhs are quite different from those of Jinsî Sikhs. Normally, the two do not inter-marry. The Zamîndârs prefer to marry their children to their counterparts in the Punjãb. They speak Punjãbî at home and dress like the Punjãbîs.

Jinsî women, on the other hand, had, by the late 1800s, given up Punjãbî clothes and taken to Kashmîrî *pheran* cloaks.

The Sikh population in 1891, 1911 and 1931

Recent population figures have been given elsewhere in this trilogy of books. However, historical population figures reveal sub-castes that the more recent censuses have stopped recording.

In 1891 there were 11,399 Sikhs in the state. Of them 5,956 were in Jammû province and 5,273 in Kashmîr. This included 31 Chamâr Sikhs and 12 Dûm Sikhs.

In 1911 the break up of the Sikh sub-castes was: 14 Arorâ, 2,019 Dutt and Bâlî Brâhmins, 369 other Mohyâl Brâhmins, 99 Khatrî, 88 Mazhabî, 44 Râjpût, 38 Sâñsî, 2 Tarkhân, 6 Zargar and 12,067 other castes. Total: 14,894.

The 1931 break up was as follows: 635 Râjpût, 2,069 Kâyasth, 5,232 Labânâ, 42 Kumhâr, 1 Mazhabî, 142 Mégh, 221 Lohâr, 104 Mahâjan, 11,723 Brâhmin, 321 Basîth and 3 Batwâl. Total: 21,453.

Interestingly, the sub-castes of 1931 are quite different from the ones enumerated in 1911. Of the ones that have the same names in both censuses 'prestigious' castes like Brâhmin and Râjpût grew hugely, severalfold, while less fashionable ones declined equally rapidly. The total number of Sikhs, however, grew at a pace similar to the national average. So, obviously thousands of families claimed to be from a different caste in the latter census.

Reference

i Fauq, Muhammad ud Dîn, *Târîkh Aqwâm é Kashmîr* (Lahore, 1934). Reprinted in 1996 by Chinar Publishing House, Srînagar. Pages 113-17. Translated from the Urdu by the author.

* * *

14

Jammu: A Blood-soaked Independence[1]

I believe the tragedy of divided families is much [more] grave [in Jammû] than that [in] the Valley [of Kashmîr]. A massive migration occurred in 1947-48 due to communal riots in Jammû. Over 80,000 migrants entered Pâkistân due to 1965 and 1971 wars... The Hindus living in Mîrpur, Pooñch and Muzaffarâbâd had to leave their homes as well in 1947-48.

Ershad Mahmud, *The News* (Pâkistân) July 25, 2001[i]

By December 1946 two things were clear: i) India was about to become independent of the British, and ii) India would be divided into two countries when the British left: avowedly Muslim Pâkistân and an India that aspired to be secular.

Pâkistân was to become independent on the 14th August, 1947 and India, acting on astrological advice, a day later.

At the time India consisted of eleven provinces administered directly by the British ('British India') and 565 princely states that accepted British overlordship ('Indian India'). While the British government would decide on how to partition the eleven provinces, the princes could join either of the two successor states. The India Independence Act, 1947, did not give them a third option (such as joining neither or becoming independent).

All the same, Mahârâjâ Hari Siñgh and his Prime Minister (Râm Chandra Kâk) toyed with the idea of independence. The Mahârâjâ's guru, Swâmi Sañt Dév, had reportedly predicted that Hari Siñgh would be the monarch of a large, independent country.

Till as late as September 1946, the Muslim Conference, which had some hold on the Muslims of Jammu and Poonch, was saying that its goal was responsible government under the Maharaja, without association with India or Pakistan, author Andrew Whitehead points out. (More than 60% of Jammu province was Muslim.)

1. The political events of 1947-49, which cover the state as a whole, have been dealt with in greater detail in the previuos chapter ('Kashmîr.')

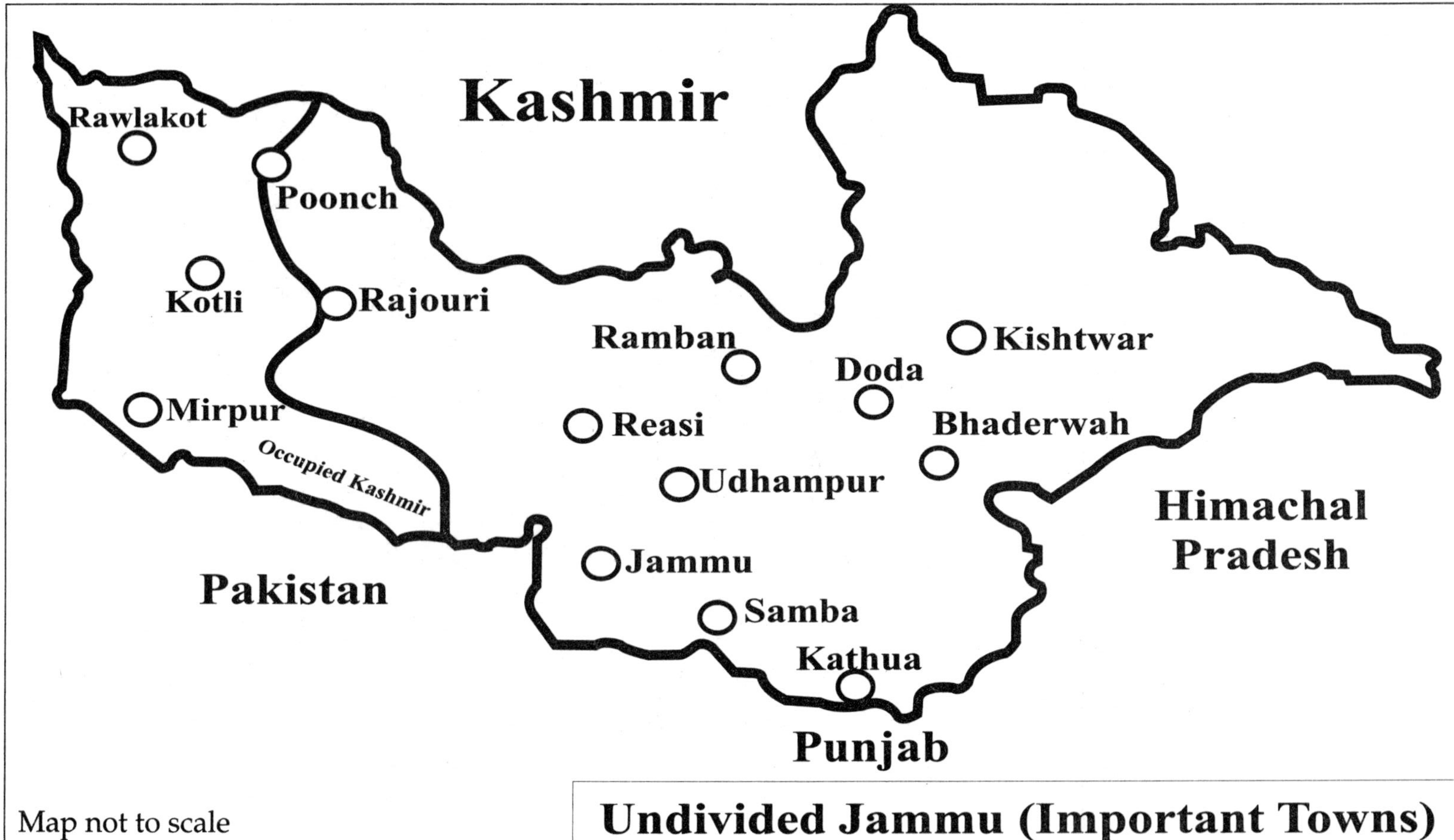

Undivided Jammu (Important Towns)

Kashmîr's most popular leader, Sheikh Muhammad Abdullâh, favoured secular India. However, labour leaders like Pt. Prém Nâth Bazâz wanted Kashmîr to accede to Pâkistân.

As a result, the Mahârâjâ was not able to decide either way. So, on the 14th/15th August, 1947, when Pâkistân and India became independent, Jammû and Kashmîr was one of only three princely states that had joined neither India nor Pâkistân.

The pro-democracy Indian National Congress wanted the people of the princely states to determine which country their state should join. The aristocratic Muslim League (ML), which spearheaded the Pâkistân Movement (and bequeathed Pâkistân that country's later propensity for unelected rulers), wanted the monarch of each state to decide about this as he fancied. 'The British supported [the ML] view using the legalistic argument that their relationship with the Princely States was based on their treaties with them. After the lapse of [British] paramountcy the rulers should be free to decide the future of their States.'[ii]

In the specific context of Kashmîr, the Congress was confident that, because of the support of Sheikh Muhammad Abdullâh and the National Conference, the people of Kashmîr would opt for India. The Muslim League, on the other hand, had excellent relations with the Hiñdu king of Kashmîr—because cordiality and affection stem from shared interests, experiences and ideas, not from a shared religion.

The perceptive Quâid é Âzam, Mr. Mohammed Ali Jinnâh, knew that. 'He even tried to persuade the Hiñdu rulers of Jodhpur and Jaisalmér [in Western India] to accede to Pâkistân and gave them a blank sheet of paper to list their demands, which he would accept. This did not work.'[iii] (Mr. Jinnâh was the founder and first Governor-General of Pâkistân [1947-48].)

The threefold strategy of the Pâkistân Army

Soon Pâkistân grew impatient with the impasse in Jammû and Kashmîr. It assumed that Jammû and Kashmîr belonged to Pâkistân because of the state's Muslim-majority.

Pâkistân's army drew up a threefold plan to annex the state.

i) The border areas: Pâkistân first sent armed soldiers—perhaps four thousand[iv]—to sneak into Jammû province, all the way from Mîrpur in the north/west to Kathuâ in the south/east.

ii) Pooñch: Undivided Pooñch, has a martial history unlike that of any other district of undivided India. So, Pâkistân persuaded Sardâr Mohammad Ibrâhim Khân of Pooñch (see 'A history of 'AJK'') to organise a force of veterans from the British Army and deserters from the Mahârâjâ's forces. The veterans alone numbered sixty thousand.[2] Pâkistân launched this part of its plan on the 23rd August, 1947, when terrorists under its command killed Jagat Râm, the magistrate of Râwlâkot (Pooñch).

iii) The Valley of Kashmîr: On the 22nd October, 1947,[v] Pâkistân sent thousands of Âfrîdî tribesmen—thirty thousand according to Mr. Maini[3]—into the state. They were led by Maj. (Retd.) Khurshîd Anwar.

Lt. Col. (later Maj. Gen.) Akbar Khân headed this three-pronged operation. His nom de guerre was Gen. Târiq. (Details later in this chapter.)

As with its similar misadventures in 1965 and after 1989, Pâkistân peaked too early in October 1947, and played its cards very badly. 'Had Pâkistân waited for 15 days or so,' Lt. Gen. Sinha points out, 'it could have... secure[d] the Kashmîr Valley without any intervention by the Indian Army.'[vi]

It would have been so because there were (and still are) only two ways by which the Indian Army could reach the Valley: by road or by air. At the time there was no tunnel through the Banihâl Pass. By mid-November the motorable road to Kashmîr would have been blocked by snow at Banihâl—only to reopen in mid-May, 1948, by when Pâkistân and its army would have settled very comfortably in Kashmîr. The Srînagar airfield operated only in 'fair weather' in 1947. Between mid-November and mid-May it would have been too unreliable for the Indian Army to depend upon.

Sorayyâ Khurshîd, a Jammûite who migrated to Pâkistân, has a similar assessment. She writes, 'Had there been no tribal invasion, the history of Kashmîr might have been different and the state may have become part of Pâkistân.'

The Instrument of Accession

In the event, on the 15th October the Pâkistânî 'irregulars' overran Fort Owen, seized Muzaffarâbâd on the 21st October and were in Bârâmullâ on the twentysixth. The Mahârâjâ had thitherto been trying to keep the state independent of both India and Pâkistân. Now he realised that this 'third option' was no longer available. He asked his Deputy Prime Minister, Mr. Batrâ, to rush to Delhi to ask India to send in its army. The Government of India did not oblige. It wanted some kind of a constitutional link with Kashmîr before it sent in its troops.

2. Mr Maini, Maj. Amîn and just about everyone else agrees on this figure.

3. In this case Mr. Maini's is a conservative estimate. India officially put the number of the raiders at 1,00,000. Even writers like Brian Cloughley agree that there were at least between fifteen and twenty thousand.)

It was on the 26th October, 1947, that Mahârâjâ Hari Siñgh signed the Instrument of Accession. This Instrument gave the 'dominion legislature' (later, the Parliament of India) the power to 'make laws for this state' only with respect to matters concerning defence, external affairs, communications and some ancillary matters. There was a proviso that the final disposition of the state of Jammu and Kashmir would be made by the free will of the people, as soon as law and order was restored.

The law and order situation in October 1947: In the weeks before Mahârâjâ Hari Siñgh signed the Instrument of Accession, the State of Jammû and Kashmîr had been caught in a pincer.

On the one hand, as we have seen, Pâkistân had sent 'irregular' forces (commanded by officers of the Pâkistân Army) to invade the Muslim-majority areas of Kashmîr, Jammû and Ladâkh. Section commander upwards, all the raiders were regular Pâkistân Army personnel. The soldiers who manned machine guns and heavy weapons certainly were. The so called 'irregulars,' in any case, were demobilised British Army soldiers.

On the other hand 'militant wings of political parties of India (Sevak Sang [sic], Maha Sabha and Akali Dal) started entering [the Hiñdu-majority areas of] Jammû in large numbers with balums, daggers, swords, rifles, etc.'[vii]

It is not clear which group came first, because both stormed the state in October 1947. Of course, there was a difference. The former was an armed force, which had come to annex land. The latter were revenge-seeking Hiñdu-Sikh youths who had come to brutalise the innocent Muslims of Jammû for what some Muslims of the Puñjâb and NWFP (North West Frontier Province) had done to their families.

The events that led to all this needless bloodshed began in the spring of 1947.

April and August 1947: Trouble in Pooñch

Till early 1947 a relative of the Mahârâjâ ruled Pooñch. According to Prof. Rashid, trouble began in April 1947 when the Mahârâjâ of Jammû and Kashmîr dethroned the Raja of Pooñch.[viii]

Though a Hiñdu, the Raja was much loved by the Muslims. Mîr Pooñchi[ix] recalls that the Mahârâjâ's government placed the newly widowed Râni of Pooñch under house arrest. Loyal Muslims, led by Maulvi Ghulâm Haidar Jandâlvi, whisked the Rani away to Lahore, in a palanquin. The delicate lady, who had never known any discomfort or physical exertion before, had to cover much of the distance on foot, because of the terrain. In Lahore her loyalists filed a case against the Mahârâjâ of Jammû and Kashmîr--and won.

The Mahârâjâ of J&K 'imposed heavy taxes on the people of Pooñch, who hesitated to pay. The Mahârâjâ's government ordered its troops to realize the taxes from the people forcibly. There was great resentment [among] the people against the Mahârâjâ's government,' Prof. Rashid adds.

After Pâkistân was born, some leaders managed to turn this resentment into a pro-Pâkistân sentiment. Pakistani terrorirsts killed magistrate Jagat Ram on the 23rd August. On the 25th August, there was a public meeting at Neelâ Butt (Dherkote) at which some people spoke in favour of Pâkistân. Some soldiers of the Mahârâjâ started shooting at the people assembled there.

By the 27th August, Sardâr Abdul Qaiyûm Khân, a former army sepoy, had assembled a band of militants.

Sardâr Ibrâhim, who was one of the main anti-India leaders, crossed over to Pâkistân and sought the support of the Pâkistân Army to sustain the rebellion, which, Maj. Amîn points out, 'had little chance of success at least in the valley [of Kashmîr] in case the Hindu ruler was able to secure Indian Army's assistance by virtue of acceding to India.'[x] Considering that the Mahârâjâ had no such plans at the time, Sardâr Ibrâhim only succeeded in forcing the Mahârâjâ's hand.

Prof. Rashid writes that the people of Pooñch 'were supported by their kith and kin and Muslims from across the border [in] Pâkistân who supplied them arms to fight against the Mahârâjâ's government and troops. On this issue relations between the government of J&K and Pâkistân started to deteriorate and [grew] bitter' by the day.

Writers like Rasal say that Sardâr Abdul Qaiyûm's fighters were defectors from the Mahârâjâ's forces. Maini implies that some of them were retired army personnel. Maj. Âghâ Humâyun Amîn, as we shall see, confirms both accounts. However, the majority of the fighters, as he also corroborates, were Pâkistânî tribals. These tribals were each given a rifle, a hundred rupees and the licence to loot whatever they could lay their hands on. (Maj. (retd.) Âghâ Humâyun Amîn, who is from Pâkistân or POK, is the foremost authority on this era. Of all South Asian military historians he is singularly free of prejudice or bias.)

In Kashmîr, most notably in Gulmarg, the tribals ransacked considerable Muslim-owned property for which reason they are remembered with hatred to this day. In 1947, the fields of Rajourî-Pooñch were often dotted with safes that had been broken open, emptied and left behind. Maj. Amîn writes, 'The tribesmen's sole motive was not the liberation of Kashmir, and they started looting [Bârâmullâ] town.'

Sept. 1947: Pâkistân plans its first invasion of Jammû and Kashmîr

Mr Jinnâh asked Prime Minister Liaquat Alî Khân to handle 'the Kashmir business.'[xi] Mr. Liaquat Alî Khân and Pâkistân's ruling Muslim League ordered Miañ Iftikhâr ud Din, Pâkistân's Minister for Refugees, to draw up a plan to bring Jammu and Kashmîr into Pâkistân. Miañ Iftikhâr delegated this task to Brigadier Akbar Khân of the Pâkistâni General Headquarters. He also consulted Sardâr Shaukat Hayât Khân, a Muslim League leader. Brig. Khân was a Burma DSO (Distinguished Service Order) and was the Director of the newly formed Weapons and Equipment Directorate.[4]

Brig. Khân authored an 'appreciation' entitled 'Armed revolt inside Kashmir' and gave it to Iftikhâr ud Din who, in turn, submitted it to Mr. Liaquat Ali Khân.

To work out Pâkistân's Kashmîr strategy, the Pâkistânî Prime Minister convened a conference at Lahore in September 1947. Finance Minister Ghulam Mohammad and Brig. Akbar Khân were among those who attended.

Sardâr Shaukat Hayât was placed at the head of the operations to annex Jammu and Kashmîr. Mr. Ghulam Mohammad persuaded his mentor and old Aligarh college friend, Mr. Liaquat Ali, to appoint Major Khurshîd Anwar (retd.) the commander of the northern tribal force.[xii]

Sardâr Shaukat, who had been a Major in the Army, opposed Anwar's appointment on the ground that the latter was not from the 'fighting forces' of the Army. (Anwar had been the commander of the Muslim League's para-military National Guard.) In the event, Brig. Akbar gave Anwar the task of attacking the Abbottâbâd-Garhi Habibullah-Muzaffarâbâd-Srînagar axis.

Major Zamân Kiâni of the anti-British Indian National Army was given the command of the southern force, which attacked the Kathua area. The Government of Pâkistân asked Brigadier Akbar Khân 'to support the tribal raiders logistically, using all resources at his disposal in GHQ as Director, Weapons and Equipment, without letting the Britishers controlling the Pâkistân Army know!' The exclamation mark is as in Maj. Amin's original.

Why Pakistan had to resort to subterfuge

Why did Pâkistân have to resort to this elaborate subterfuge? Why did it send in raiders in civilian clothes rather than in army uniform? The obvious reason, of course, was deniability—as in 1965 and after 1989. But in 1947 Pâkistân had no option either. At the time Britons were the Commanders in Chief of the Indian and Pâkistânî armies. Field Marshal Auchinleck was the Supreme Commander of both armies.

On the evening of 27 October 1947, Mr Jinnâh ordered General Gracey, who was the Acting C-in-C of the Pâkistân Army, to attack Kashmir.

---

4 Maj. Amîn writes that Akbar Khân was a Lieutenant Colonel when he met the tribals at Uri on the 8th November. However, it seems that at some stage during those operations Khân got promoted as Brigadier because many records of that period refer to him as one.

Gracey was asked to deploy two brigades of the PâkistânArmy, one from Siâlkot to invade Jammû and the other from Râwalpiñdî to annex Kashmîr.

Gracey refused because his superior, Auchinleck, denied him the permission to do so. (Gracey had called Auchinleck, who was in Delhi, at 1 o'clock that night.[xiii]) Indeed, Auchinleck flew to Lahore the very next morning and asked Mr Jinnâh to withdraw his order. Auchinleck added that if Mr. Jinnâh did not do so he would remove all British officers from the Pâkistân Army.

That would have crippled the newborn Pâkistân Army, which was the Quâid é Âzam's (Great Leader's) fond creation. Mr. Jinnâh had no choice but to call off the planned Army invasion of Jammû and Kashmîr.[xiv]

Meanwhile, Gen. Messervy, the actual C-in-C of the Pâkistân Army, returned from leave. He convened a meeting of GHQ officers and warned them against going to war with India because, he felt, the Indian Army would overrun Pâkistân within ten days. Messervy's Pâkistânî colleagues secretly disagreed with his assessment. They refused to believe that the Indian weaklings had it in them to take on the brave Pâkistânîs.

That was why an irregular force outside the control of the generals Messervy and Gracey had to be created. Its soldiers were Âfrîdi and other tribesmen from the NWFP and its officers were serving and retired officers of the Pâkistân Army.

Major Aslam Khân of the Mahârâjâ's Kashmir State Force, who had won an MC (Military Cross) in the Second World War, was one of these officers. His father, Brigadier Tor Gul, had risen to the highest rank that a career soldier could in the Mahârâjâ's Army, and had been, as Maj. Amîn points out, 'a loyal subject of the Hindu Dogra ruler of Kashmir before 1947!' (Maj. Amîn has put that exclamation mark there because of the irony of the situation.)

The Pâkistânî invasion

Khushdil Khân of Mardân (NWFP) collected the 'lashkar' (armed force) of tribesmen. The Pâkistân Army put them in trucks and took them to Batrasi, north-east of Abbottâbâd, which is on the Kashmîr border.

Andrew Whitehead, who is working on a book on the tribal raid on Jammû and Kashmîr, has an interesting insight. He has reason to believe that there was 'increasing pressure in the tribal areas for a raid on Kashmîr.' Later, he adds, 'an organizing committee was established at Abbottâbâd [by the Government of Pâkistân, for the raiders].'[xv]

By the 15th October the tribals had driven the Mahârâjâ's forces out of Fort Owen. Maj. Amin adds that 'around the same time the Dogra communication between Kotli and Pooñch was severed and the state forces' Muslim troops had almost deserted and joined the rebels while the non-Muslim units were besieged at Bhimber, Mîrpur and Mañglâ.' The Dogrâ force was also besieged at Bâgh, Méndhar and Pooñch in Jammû province and at Skardu and Leh in Gilgit-Ladâkh.

The Mahârâjâ sent in more troops to put the rebellion down. His force 'was also assisted by volunteers of the [Hiñdu nationalist Râshtriya Swayamsévak Sañgh].'[xvi] That alarmed several Muslim families of Pooñch. Elite families of the Sûdhan, Abbâsî-Râjpût and Dânyâl clans sent their women and children to the Pâkistânî part of the Punjāb. The men stayed behind.[5]

The Mahârâjâ's forces had a miniscule, and mostly ceremonial, presence in these areas. (His *entire* force consisted of nine infantry battalions.) Most of the Mahârâjâ's soldiers had never seen a war—only the few who had volunteered to assist the Allies in the Second World War had. On the other side was the army of the fourth biggest country in the world—with many distinguished veterans of the Second World War. The Mahârâjâ's soldiers started fleeing the villages for the towns. As Maj. Amin puts it, the anti-India militias 'started harassing the dispersed state forces and harassing the various roads and bridges in the state.'

A band of two thousand 'tribesmen captured the bridge spanning the Neelam river on the Hazara Trunk Road linking Muzaffarabad with Abbottâbâd *without a fight* [on the night of 20/21 October], since the all-Muslim guard platoon of 4 Jammû and Kashmir Infantry joined the tribesmen.'[xvii] (Emphasis added.)

By the next morning the raiders and the deserters had, together, captured the first major town, Muzaffarabad. Amîn points out that 'In terms of odds and comparative forces this was a predictable affair since the Hindu Dogra elements of the 4 Jammû and Kashmir Battalion, approximately two companies or about 350 men were dispersed in penny packets over an area of thirty miles, and were further internally weakened by having a 50 per cent Muslim strength or two companies... The crucial bridge over the otherwise impassable river Neelum (Kishanganga) was handed over to them [i.e. to the Pâkistânî invaders] by the Muslim guard of the 4 Jammû and Kashmir infantry, and all that they had to deal [with] were isolated Dogra platoons dispersed in various localities separated by many miles.'

The remaining Dogrâ soldiers of 4 Jammû and Kashmir Infantry defended Domel and Kohala till October 23.

---

5 The Hindus of Jammû, likewise, sent their daughters to cities like Jâlandhar (in the Punjâb) and Delhi. The troubles lasted so long that many Hiñdu families, which had hoped to return to Jammû a few weeks later, struck roots in the cities that had given their families refuge and never returned to Jammû.

Oct.-Nov. 1947: Pâkistân annexes considerable territory in Jammû

Major Boston[6] and Capt. Feroz of the Pâkistân Army were the heroes of their side. They soon annexed Trâr Khail, Dévi Galî and Hijayr. Pâkistân then seized Mîrpur, Bhimber and Dévâ Batâlâ.

The anti-India militia assaulted camps of the Mahârâjâ's forces and police at Dherkote/ Dhirkot and killed a number of Dogrâ personnel.

On the 24th (and not on the 26th) October, 1947, a 'government' was constituted for the areas occupied by Pâkistân. Trâr Khail (Palañdri) was its first 'capital.' Sardâr Mohammad Ibrâhim Khân was installed as its 'President.'

Meanwhile, the Pâkistânî forces annexed Kotlî, Méndhar, Nausherâ and Rajourî. (The Indian Army liberated the last three areas later.)

The Dogràs lost because only 'numerically small forces' (Maj. Amîn's words) defended the besieged Dogrâ garrisons. These tiny forces began to surrender to the Pâkistânî attackers. The defenders of Bhimber and Méndhar gave up on the 3rd November. The Dogrâ force left Bâgh on the 9th November—and Râwlâkot two or three days later—and fled to the Poonch Garrison. The invaders captured Rajourî on the 12th November. Chhamb, too, fell to the Pâkistânîs.

By the 14 November, 1947, almost all of Poonch-Rajourî had been occupied by Pâkistân—except the 1.5 square kilometre Poonch town itself. Pâkistânî forces were just five kilometres away from the town, which they besieged. There were just three battalions of the Mahârâjâ's forces to defend the town.

Depleted Dogrâs and squabbling invaders

Dr Ravindra Rasal alleges that '[t]he Muslim components of the regiments of the State forces of J&K murdered their Hindu colleagues by the hundreds while they were asleep on the D Day and after. At other places they treacherously sent false SOS messages to the Hindu Companies to come for their help and massacred the un-suspecting Hindu troops when they arrived answering the call from their comrades in arms in all innocence. After that the Muslim troops of the J&K State forces, traitors to their home State and the King, either handed over the area under their control to Pâkistân or marched into Pâkistân and joined them. Such information was not given due publicity by the then government of India in order to safeguard the sentiments of the minority community."[xviii]

Rasal's account is as alarmingly exaggerated and jaundiced as similar accounts by Pâkistânîs and writers from 'AJK.' This thing about

6 In the volumes about 'Kashmîr' and 'Ladâkh' we saw how British officers seized huge chunks of the state and handed them over to Pâkistân.

'murder[ing] colleagues while they were asleep' has not been corroborated by any other source. Indeed, what the establishment has buried is information about the full extent of the massacre of those who had to flee Jammû. However, in the section 'The Liberation of Rajourî' below we will see that defecting soldiers did kill their erstwhile colleagues—though perhaps not while they were sleeping.

An Indian Army officer who later investigated the killings says that the defectors killed their colleagues thus: First, the loyalists were disarmed. Then all senior officers were murdered. The 'other ranks' were killed next. The only loyalists from those units who survived were those who were away from their units at the time: on 'temporary duty' or leave. All loyalists present were killed.

What happened at Domél (lit. 'the crossroad') typifies this trend. Two thousand Pâkistânî 'irregular soldiers' reached the Hazâra-Muzaffarâbâd crossroad on the 21st October. As we have noted above, they pressurised the thitherto loyal and disciplined Muslim soldiers of the 4th Infantry Batallion to mutiny. (In general, the 'irregulars' belonged to the Âfrîdî, Mahsûd, Mohmañd and Wazîr tribes.)

On the 23rd October, they 'killed [the] commander [Lt.Col.] Nârâin Siñgh and [the] majority of Dogrâ soldiers but some of [the Dogrâ soldiers] managed to board jeeps to flee to Muzaffarâbâd and Urî.' (These are the words of Miâñ Mañzoor Ahmed, who is an executive member of the secessionist APHC [All Party Hurriyat Conference]. See *Greater Kashmîr*, 31 October 2005.)

Many Indian writers believe that '[t]he capture of Domél and Muzaffarâbâd [by the Indian Army] could have been effected easily at that time, as the raiders were in complete disarray. Pâkistân neither had their regular army build-up nor [did it have any] built up defences in that area. [Pâkistân, on the advice] of [its] British Commanders was, at that early stage of war, reluctant to deploy her regular units for back up.'[xix]

Sober Indian military historians and senior Army officers who know the area have no time for such jingoistic hindsights. They believe that Pâkistân had moved its troops into Domél and Muzaffarâbâd very soon after the conquest of these towns. After all, Pâkistân needed to defend them not for the sake of 'AJK' but in order to secure Râwalpiñdi, which is almost next door. For India to regain Domél and Muzaffarâbâd would have meant sacrificing a very large number of its soldiers and definitely losing Pooñch in the process. Therefore, India did the wise thing by concentrating on Pooñch—which could still be salvaged, and was.

But why were the raiders in disarray? Because, as Maj. Amîn wryly notes, the tribesmen were hardly there to 'fight just for [the] two nation theory.' The spoils of war were the main issue for them.

Sardâr Shaukat Hayât would later recall[xx] that the raiders had looted Rs.300,000 from the Kashmir State Treasury. Maj. Khurshîd Anwar, like a good Pâkistânî, insisted that the money should be deposited with the Government of Pâkistân. His soldiers had a 'finders-keepers' view. By the time this was sorted out, it was time for the Eid festival, which the tribals celebrated over three days (24-26 October).

Nov. 1947: The Indian Army steps in

India had, by the 2nd November, flown the 161 Infantry Brigade, one of its best, to Srinagar. 161 Brigade had a little less than four battalions. Major General Kalwañt Singh was posted as the commander of the Headquarters, Jammû and Kashmir Force, based in Srînagar. He was the head of all Indian Army operations in Jammû and Kashmir.

While the raiders were squabbling, the Force Commander, Major General Kalwañt Siñgh, relieved the competent Colonel Harbaksh of his command of 161 Brigade and, on the 2nd November, replaced him with Brigadier Sen instead.

The gallant Maj. Amîn writes, 'Brigadier L.P Sen [was] a Bengali Hindu with an excellent Second World War record (unlike the first Muslim C-in-C of the Pâkistân Army) in Burma where he had won a Distinguished Service Order.'

But Dr. Ravindra Rasal believes that 'Brigadier Sen proved incomplete for [i.e. unequal to] the task....[He] wasted a few days at Uri in regrouping all the elements of his Brigade... Even the army commander (British) Lt. General Douglas Russell, a friend of India[7] and proud of the Indian army, had advised a thrust onto Domél-Muzaffarâbâd axis.'[xxi]

Colonel Harbaksh was an outstanding officer and had won a major victory only a few days before. However, from all accounts, in the event

---

7 Lieutenant General Russell was the General Officer Commanding in Chief of the Indian Army's Delhi and Punjab Command. He was Maj. Gen. Kalwant's immediate superior and, at the next higher level, in charge of India's operations in Kashmîr. The Pâkistânîs enviously say that Russell guided India so ably while the two British generals seconded to Pâkistân, Messervy and Gracey, did not. Russell was a man of high principles and true to the country he had been sent to serve—India. Russell wanted to go to Jammû and Kashmîr to guide India's operations from close quarters. However, the British government ordered him not to enter Kashmîr—in keeping with its policy of neutrality in the matter, which it had conveyed to Messervy and Gracey as well.

This hurt Russell so badly that he asked his new masters, the Government of India, to either get the British to take back their orders or relieve him of his command. Because the Indians were not able to prevail on Britain, they had no choice but to replace Russell. Lieutenant General Cariappa took over from Russell on the 20th January 1948.

Brig. 'Bogey' Sen commanded quite well. Maj Gen Chibber, who has high praise for both, points out that Brig. 'Bogey' Sen was chosen because he was readily available and because he had been organising the airlifting of troops to Srînagar.

The Indian Army captured Uri on the 13th November. All of Kashmîr Valley was back with India. So, the war in Kashmîr Valley was over. Now the Indian Army could turn its attention to liberating what Pâkistân had captured in Jammû and Gilgit-Ladâkh, as well as Muzaffarabad district. It could also relieve the various besieged garrisons of the state forces. As we will see, there were some decisions that are regretted to this day—and some delays. (See 'Hindsight and regrets' later in this chapter.)

The Pâkistânîs, who thought that all was lost for them and that India would soon liberate Muzaffarabad, were surprised that India did not. Their assessment is that 'the Indians were too psychologically shattered to do so. Instead they wasted their strength in various relief operations.'[xxii]

However, after that initial delay, Brigadier Sen started moving his forces towards Domél.

Mid-October—6 November 1947: a blot on Jammû province[8]

By October 1947, almost the entire non-Muslim population of Pâkistân's Punjãb, Sindh, Frontier (NWFP) and Balochistân provinces—certainly the Hiñdus, Sikhs and Jains—had been forced to migrate to India. Around 20% of the Muslim population of what was left of India similarly sought refuge in Pâkistân, leaving behind the lands and houses that their forefathers had lived in for the better part of the millennium. More than ninetyfive per cent of the Muslims of Indian Punjãb, Haryânâ and Himâchal Pradésh were compelled to go to Pâkistân—just because some intellectuals[9] had decided that the Hiñdus and Muslims were two separate nations.

This wretched exchange of population, which has no precedent in human history, involved the sudden uprooting of almost two crore (twenty million) people. Most people had less than a week in August to leave their

8 That a bloody massacre took place that week is not in doubt. Most accounts indicate that it happened on the 6th November. However, historians in Pâkistân and 'AJK' believe that the correct date is November 5.

9 The theory that the Muslims and non-Muslims of India belonged to two separate nations is generally credited to Chaudhary Rehmat Ali, an Indian who was studying at Cambridge (UK) in the 1930s. Indeed, it was he who developed and popularised this theory that has caused so much avoidable suffering. However, a few years before, a Hiñdu nationalist from what is now Mahârâshtra had, in one of his influential essays, referred to the Hiñdu and Muslim nations. Part of the problem arose from the fact that in Hiñdî-Urdû the word qaum means 'nation' as well as 'community' (i.e. ethnic group).

ancestral lands forever. People who were perfectly comfortable with neighbours from the other community were told to leave because, according to the intellectuals' theory, they belonged to another nation.

The people of Jammû and Kashmîr were spared having to make this choice—till October. Riots in neighbouring Siâlkot, the 15th October, 1947 Pâkistânî 'tribal' attack on Kashmîr and the state's shotgun accession to India changed all that. The raiders' shotgun forced the wavering Mahârâjâ to seek the protective cover of the Indian Union.

The belt that runs from Kâhnâ Chak to Sambâ has traditionally been the state's border with the Punjãb. On the night of the 14th August it suddenly became an international border. There had always been a sizeable number of Muslims—Gujjars as well as others—on both sides of the border. They were related to each other. Those who found themselves in Pâkistân persuaded their brethren on the Jammû side of the border to cross over to their side.

A ranking Jammû Muslim recalls that a very large number of Muslims of this border belt shifted to Pâkistân on that fateful night. I have reason to assume that these Muslims numbered more than two thousand.

The Muslims of the rest of Jammû continued with their lives, exactly as before. Till, one day, goings on beyond the state's borders suddenly became more than just unpleasant items in the morning's newspapers.

A truck full of injured people came rushing from Siâlkot (in Pâkistânî Punjãb) to Jammû's SMGS hospital. The same ranking Muslim seems to recall that the victims were from the minuscule, pacifist Jain community. This was in September or October. The incident made some people in Jammû want to avenge what the Pâkistânîs had done to their brethren. But Jammû remained peaceful.

A few days later a Muslim peon from Ustâd Mohallâ took his goats to the forests near the Pañj Pîr shrine. Someone killed him there. This was the first murder in Jammû in ages, and the first ever suspected communal killing in its entire history.

The next to be killed—this time somewhere between Kachchi Chhâwni and Puccâ Dañgâ in the main town—was a Muslim labourer.

Hâshmî, a Jammuite, is extremely bitter about the role played by some 'Jammû leaders [who] had already moved to Pâkistân and taken possession of some of the grand bungalows left behind by non-Muslims who had gone to India. These leaders were using Radio Pâkistân to issue devastating statements against the State government, which might have contributed to the killing of the Muslims [in Jammû]. Every time one of these leaders issued a sharp statement from Pâkistân radio, firing on Muslim neighbourhoods started.'

He points out that till the 'middle of October 1947, there was complete peace in Jammû city.' The honest head of the city police station, Râjâ Sohbat Ali, contributed to this. Sohbat once heard some women and children scream. He rushed to protect them from a group of gunmen. The attackers started firing on Râjâ Sohbat instead. His deformed body was recovered from River Tawi. Râjâ Sohbat became 'the first warrior and first martyr from Jammû,' Hâshmî adds, for Sohbat died while protecting the people.

Some youths from Mîrpur then killed a couple of Hiñdus, notably Col. Dûbéy, in order to avenge the killing of their fellow Mîrpuri. Râjâ Sohbat.

Thâkur Nathâ Singh, also a sub-inspector, was extremely upset by the murder of his friend Sohbat, and other innocent Muslims. When Sohbat's assassins got to know this—and the Thâkur was probably on their trail—they killed him as well, on the 23rd October.

By then the Pâkistânî invaders had entered Kashmîr province, had captured Muzaffarâbâd and were on their way to Baramullâ.

The next day—the 24th October—they martyred Brig. Rajinder Singh of the state forces, together with his soldiers, at Boniyâr, which is only twenty kilometres short of Baramullâ. They also took control of the nearby Mohurâ power station—which was the only source of electricity for the entire Valley of Kashmîr.

Earlier that day, a 'government' had been constituted for the areas occupied by Pâkistân (and later named 'Âzâd' Jammû and Kashmîr). This formalised the secession of those areas from the Mahârâjâ's state.

It was a chilly Dussehrâ night and Mahârâjâ Hari Siñgh was in his palace with his nobles. The lights suddenly went out at nine o'clock. This was enough to cause panic in Kashmîr. This is also said to have been the trigger that made the Mahârâjâ finally decide that he needed the Indian Army to repulse the aggressors. (All of Srînagar—and much of the rest of the Valley—had to make do without electricity for the next several days, till the Pâkistânîs were evicted from Mohurâ.)

Moti Lâl Panditâ, a resident of Watlab, near Bâñdiporâ, recalls that 'it was for the first time that he had seen these men [the Pâkistânîs] in his village and after they entered, his village [was] never the same [again].'

(Like many other children of that era—Muslim as well as Hiñdu, Kashmîri as well as Jammuite— Moti Lâl was unable to attend school during the next two years, for his family fled Watlab for a relief camp set up by the Indian Army.

(Dévkî Ârigâmî spent a year and a half in a similar relief camp. When she returned home to Ajer Kharporâ, also near Bâñdiporâ, where the raiders had killed seventeen of her clansmen, she found that the Pâkistânî invasion had 'changed the social fabric of the village. [She] was stunned to see the change in the behaviour of the two communities towards each other.')

A Muslim saint, known by the generic title Peer Sâheb, found the Péshin family of Pañdits from Bâñdiporâ hiding from the Pâkistânîs in a nearby forest. He gave them shelter in his house. However, his goodness did not go down well with the invaders' allies. They threatened him with physical harm if he continued to harbour the Péshins.

Finding themselves internally displaced once again, the Péshins, like a few dozen other clansmen, changed their names for a while to buy peace with the ruthless invaders. (All three accounts—of the Ârigâmîs, the Panditâs and the Péshins—are based on Yâmini Kaul, 'Qabâili [tribal] attacks: Those who faced the brunt of it,' *The Kashmîr Times*, October 30, 2005.)

Word of these atrocities had reached Srînagar a few hours before the snapping of the power lines. Ethnic Dogrâ- and Puñjâbi- (but not Kashmîri-) Hiñdus started packing all their worldly goods. They got into trucks and most of them left Srînagar for Jammû before the dawn of the 25th October.

As elsewhere in the state, the threat was from anonymous invaders, not neighbours. Jyoteeshwar Pathik Gandotra notes, 'Our Muslim neighbours, who had been protecting us during the night, patrolling, were disappointed [to watch us flee] but they were quite helpless.'

The migration to Jammû continued into the middle of November. (From JP Gandotra, 'October 26, 1947: Some reminiscences,' *The Kashmîr Times*, October 26, 2005.)

This fresh wave of internal refugees worsened things in Jammû.

Kashmîri Muslim tongâ drivers and porters ferried the fleeing Dogrâs and Puñjâbis to Jammû—at enormous risk to themselves. Some of them were killed near Udhampur, when they were returning to Kashmîr in their tongas.

Jammû city was getting choked with internal refugees: Muslims from the villages of Jammû district, Hiñdus from Kashmîr, Hiñdus and Sikhs from Mîrpur-Kotli (not to mention West Puñjâb) and, soon, Hiñdus and Sikhs from the countless Jammû villages that were within four (in some cases, as much as six) kilometres of the Indo-Pâkistân border.

Sahâran was one such border village. Things got so tense on the border—but not within the village—that the Muslims decided to cross over to the other side, where houses and land had been vacated by Hiñdus and Sikhs a few months before. They assumed that they were going across for only a few weeks and that they would return when things cooled down.

Sat Pâl 'Kavârhiyâ,' who later earned a name for helping Muslims against stone-throwing mobs, was then in his teens. He remembers the tearful and emotional farewell that the village gave its departing Muslim members. Little did they know that soon the rest of them, too, would have to leave—for one-room cubby-holes in Jammû's Puccâ Dañgâ.

People, like Sat Pâl's family, with established businesses in their native villages, were reduced to pavement vendors in Jammû—an existence that they had to put up with for around a decade, before they could afford to buy shops.

Sahâran is sixteen miles (25km.) from Jammû—no mean distance for a daily commute even today, when roads and buses are available. In the years that followed their internal migration, farmers would get up early every morning, trek from Jammu to the village, till the fields and walk (or cycle) back to the city late in the evening.

With so many surcharged newcomers—many of them idle—in the town and its suburbs, a disaster was waiting to happen.

Well meaning Jammû Hiñdus began to fear for the safety of their Muslim friends. Mr Justice Yûsuf Sarâf singles out Bâñkay Béhâri, Nañd Lâl Pâhwâ, Charan Dâs and Dr. Séthi for praise. Other Muslims remember Shrî Girdhâri Lâl Dogrâ with gratitude, for it was he who ensured that the supply of water to Muslim neighbourhoods was restored after a few days' disconnection.

A Jammû Muslim,[xxiii] probably called Ajmal, who migrated to Pâkistân writes, '[In October] it was announced in Jammû that all people must deposit everything that could be used as a weapon. After a few days, a search of houses of Muslims was conducted and even domestic knives of over 4 inch blade were confiscated while Hindus and Sikhs wandered around carrying all types of weapons. With the start of October 1947, killing of Muslims in the villages had started...The number of villages on fire increased as the days passed.' Terrified Muslims fled the villages all through October and early November and sought the relative security of Jammû city.

Muslims from the villages closest to Jammû—especially Sidhrâ, Rehkâ and Nagrotâ—were among the first to flee to the city. Within the city, Muslims left pockets like Ban Tâlâb, where they were few, and gravitated towards Ustâd Mohallâ.

A unit of Gurkhâs was given the task of mopping up all weapons owned by the Muslims—which, for a while, made that unit somewhat unpopular with the latter. Among the Muslims who stayed on (The more influential ones) were able to get their weapons back after things settled down.

'Ajmal' adds, 'A few days later, curfew was imposed on the city. [The curfew was] supervised by the army.' This brought things under control. During the next three weeks, as the otherwise bitter 'Ajmal' notes, "Only a few Muslims got killed... the rioters did not dare to come near the Muslim areas." Ideally, no one should have got killed. However, but for the Army (which, on the Indian side, had a fairly large number of Muslims at the time) the death toll would have been much higher.

Col. Peer Muhammad, who had recently retired from the army, used his influence to get the army to guard all the main entrances into Ustâd Mohallâ. As a result, among the predominantly Muslim neighbourhoods, Ustâd Mohallâ had the lowest proportion of people who later migrated to Pâkistân or 'AJK.'

However, Julâhâ kâ Mohallâ, where the patriotic colonel's brother Saleem lived, could not be protected similarly. Saleem was killed.

Around the same time there were riots in some other towns of the province, too. The talented calico printers of Sâmbâ, whose ancestors had, a century before, turned down material inducements to migrate to the Punjãb were now forced to do so. (All that remains of their art is what can be seen in museums.)

In Udhampur, a group herded some Muslims and killed many of them near River Devika. The next morning a pious Hiñdu went to the temple there to pray. He found a little child near the corpses, bleeding but alive. The good man nursed the boy back to health. The boy said that his father, Col. Abdul Rehmân Khân, too, had survived the massacre. A search was launched and the colonel was found hiding in the holy Trikutâ Mountains.

(The boy was called Obaidullâh. He later migrated to Pâkistân where he joined the Navy and rose to the rank of Admiral.)

On Baqr Eid day (25 Oct), while the Muslim men of Udhampur town were offering collective prayers, a mob surrounded the congregation and killed many of the men. Among those killed were Habîbullâh, both his sons (including the noted poet, Abdul Kareem), his son in law and two young grandsons—in all, seven male members of this prominent family alone.

One of the surviving grandsons recalls that i) all the killers were from outside the Jammû-Udhampur region, ii) the only role that some local fanatics played was to act as guides for the mob, and iii) this massacre was a reaction to the Pâkistânî 'tribal' raid on Kashmîr and the killings in Kotli and Mîrpur.

Habîbullâh's extended family was now headed by women. They requested various scheduled caste Hiñdu families to each protect one young girl from the family. The elderly and middle aged women started walking toward Jammû.

Lâlâ Amarnâth of Udhampur, who had been a minister in the Mahârâjâ's cabinet and a friend of Habîbullâh, took them to his house in Jagânoo village, where he sheltered them till things got better. The mob never found out about the Lâlâ's generosity. However, they killed one of the Hindu men who had given protection to a girl from the family.[10]

A liberal Hiñdu, who was a college student in 1947, remembers with horror how Muslims were forced to assemble at Réâsî's Parade Ground (which has since been built over). Mob-leaders gave them the option of being 'purified' of their immediate religion and returning to that of some distant ancestor. The ones who refused were taken into a room and shot. 'The state did nothing to curb these riotous mobs, who were seeking revenge for the riots in Siâlkot [Punjãb]', the eye-witness recalls.

Disarmed and insecure, the Muslims of Jammû city felt that the safest thing to do was to stay at home till the storm blew over, which they assumed would be in a week or two. They also decided against venturing into the streets. Traditional urban Indian neighbourhoods consist of unbroken rows of houses and shops, with no gaps in between. The Muslims of Jammû demolished portions of the boundary walls that separated them from their neighbours on the left and right. They thus created a passage through which the beleaguered community could move from one end of the mohallâ [neighbourhood] to the other.

Till then there had been no exclusively Hiñdu or Muslim mohallâ or village in Jammû, However, it seems that during those fateful weeks the two communities drifted into separate ghettos, with little contact with erstwhile friends from the other community. An oral source says that for several days there was no electricity in the Muslim mohallâs. Many Muslims were unable to get any food or drinking water for several days.[xxiv]

'Ajmal' continues, 'Then one morning, it was announced, on a loudspeaker fitted on a *tonga* [horse carriage], "This is a message from

---

10 The four widows of Habîbullâh's family had to struggle hard to bring their children up. Twenty years later fate took a kindly turn and the surviving grandson got a job in the higher rungs of the state civil service. He also distinguished himself as a writer.

However, the massacre of 1947 continued to rankle. In 1990, when Pâkistân decided to unleash violence on the people of the state, one of Habîbullâh's great-grandsons, an educated young man who had led a life of relative privilege, became one of Pâkistân's ranking militants in Jammû province.

With good reason, it can be argued.

No. Had the young man, who was born more than twenty years after that carnage, made friends with the great-grandsons of the survivors of Kotli-Mîrpur, and listened to what their ancestors had gone through, he might have begun to think differently.

And that is what this chapter—indeed, this book—attempts to do.

Colonel Peer Muhammad. Pâkistân has sent buses to evacuate Muslims to Siâlkot. All people desirous of going to Pâkistân should gather in the Police Lines." The Police Lines were on [the] south edge of Jammû city [at Jogi Gate] near river Tawi, about two kilometres from the farthest end of Khalkâ Mohallâh. Though Col (Retd) Peer Muhammad was a leader of National Conference yet people believed in the message because of his name, but that was a trap.'

The Muslims thus had one or two days to pack up all the material goods that their ancestors and they had acquired over the last century or two—and snap all ties with their businesses, lands and houses, schools and non-Muslim friends—and leave for a canvas tent in an unknown land, because of a weird theory that said that the Muslims and non-Muslims belonged to separate nations.

'Ajmal' alleges that the Muslims who went to the Police Lines were often waylaid, robbed and beaten up. 'A lot of Muslims reached the Police Lines where they saw buses lined up with Pâkistân flags on top. On the 5th November 1947, people were asked to board the buses and the first caravan started. There was another caravan on 6th November, 1947.'

Jammû Muslims who were then in their teens are surprised by this mention of Pâkistân flags atop the buses. Their impression was that the Jammû administration, then headed by Mr Choprâ, the Governor, had arranged those buses: which were to transport the Muslims to the Suchétgarh border post and then return to Jammû City to fetch more migrating Muslims.

The second caravan was attacked in a forest near a canal when it was on its way to Pâkistân. Ajmal writes, "The passengers of the buses noticed Indian army personnel at a distance on both sides. They thought it was for their protection. Soon they heard slogans of *Jai Hind* and *Sat Siri Akâl*. Then appeared hundreds of Hindus and Sikhs carrying swords, Balums and daggers. The rioters passed through the Indian army line and headed towards buses. Seeing this, Muslims started jumping out of the buses. At that moment rifle fire was opened by the army on both sides of buses. Men, women and children started running for their life."

Good looking migrating girls jumped into the Chenab River at Akhnoor and committed suicide so that they were not abducted.[11] One of the worst massacres of the emigrating Muslims is said to have taken place at Saubha[?]. The girls kidnapped from Jammû city included 'a lovely

11 Absolutely true. And, as the classic Pâkistânî film *Khâmosh Pânî* (2003) shows, Hiñdu-Sikh women did the same in what is now Pâkistân.

daughter of Chaudhary Ghulâm Abbâs,[12] who himself was languishing in Central Jail, Srînagar.'[xxv]

(Munni Lâl, a Jammû Hiñdu and one of the Chaudhary's closest friends, helped recover the traumatised girl. He informed Muharram Hâshmî, a Jammuite whom we have quoted extensively in this book and who, by then, was in Pâkistân. Hâshmî got in touch with the Prime Minister of Pâkistân, who, in turn, spoke to Pandit Nehru. The Chaudhary's British sister in law and niece came over to India to take the girl with them. Munni Lâl would regularly meet not only Chaudhary Ghulâm Abbâs but also Sheikh Abdullâh while they were in jail and help them in whatever way he could.)

Col. Peer Muhammad's sister, brother, cousins and son in law, Anwar Khân, were among those killed, while fleeing to Pakistan.

The bloodiest attacks took place near what is now the Digiânâ Âshram and near Sâmbâ. [Could the latter be the aforementioned Saubha?] Now, Sâmbâ is nowhere near the Jammû-Suchétgarh road that leads into Pâkistân. So, how did a Pâkistân-bound bus happen to be on that road?

Some survivors of that carnage allege that the driver of their bus was misled into travelling towards Sâmbâ, instead of Suchétgarh.

Every account confirms this. But was the motive behind diverting the buses malign? Hâshmî, who was in that convoy on the 5th November, says that the bus leading the convoy developed engine trouble. A young Dogrâ army captain who was passing that way informed Hâshmî that the killers were heading towards the convoy. The 'frail captain' helped push the stalled bus off the road so that the other buses could pass. In the process the convoy took the wrong road.

Some Gurkhâ (Hiñdu) soldiers volunteered to be with the convoy. They even fetched water from the river for the parched—and terrified—passengers, who were expecting the savages to be upon them any moment.

Near Sâmbâ, half a dozen fanatics advanced towards Hâshmî's bus. A teenaged village boy—presumably a Hiñdu—broke one of the thorny branches of a cactus bush with his bare hands, injuring himself badly in the process, and successfully warded off the would-be attackers.

The convoy then came upon some Râjpût soldiers from the State Cavalry. The encounter with them was pleasant enough, though the passengers were apprehensive about the soldiers' intentions. The soldiers informed the migrants that Pâkistân was two and a half miles further south.

12 Similarly, a large number of Hiñdu girls were abducted to Pâkistân in 1947—and sent back a few years later with newly conceived children. Such was the stigma attached to raped women on both sides that when they returned to their countries, their relatives would sometimes refuse to take them back. In Jammû city such women were lodged in the Néhâ Ghar of Kachhi Chhâwnî.

Hâshmî's group reached Pâkistân safe but not sound, for many of them left their valuables behind and ran towards the border when a group of fanatics began to chase them.

A few days later, Sheikh Abdullâh, who had been the executive head of the Government of Jammû and Kashmîr since the 30th October, arranged an armed escort for such Muslims of Jammû province as had decided to migrate to Pâkistân. On the 16th November he also set up a camp at Ustâd Mohallâ for Muslims who had been left behind by their migrating families.

Hâshmî notes that Mahârâni Târâ Devi probably accompanied the Sheikh to the camp at the Police Lines. From his account it seems that the convoys to Pâkistân were attacked only on the 6th November and after that 'not a single Muslim life was lost.' Mr. Justice Sarâf, who was injured on the 6th November, has a similar take.

India's Brig. Usmân sent many of those who were wounded during the 6th November massacre to Jammû's Civil Hospital. There, Dr. Pratâp Singh, the superintendent of the hospital, admitted Mr. Sarâf and his family to the hospital 'as a special case'. Dr. Singh did this at some risk to his career, because apparently some members of the administration had stopped treating the would-be migrants as citizens of the state. But, Mr. Sarâf says, 'the Matron and many kind-hearted Hiñdu and Sikh colleagues and friends helped us in many ways' while they were in the hospital.

For the remaining wounded Muslims, Justice Sarâf recalls that 'an improvised hospital was set up at the initiative of as well as under the care of Dr. Abdul Karîm and Dr. Rehmatullâh in the havéli of Sardâr Muhammad Akram Khân at Talâb Khatîkâñ.'

Sheikh Abdullâh and Mrs Vijaylakshmi Pañdit, who was Pt. Nehru's sister, called on the wounded to inquire if they were receiving due medical treatment.

The Jammû of King Rañjît Dév and his successors had, for almost two hundred years, encouraged talented and/ or persecuted Muslims from all over North India to settle on its sacred soil. It was thus that Jammû district lost most of its Muslim population.

Pâkistân, on the other hand, wanted as complete an interchange of the population, along religious lines, as possible. So, when the nationalist Col. Peer Muhammad tried to persuade the Muslims of Jammû to stay on (and in the case of Ustâd Mohallâ he succeeded substantially), Radio Pâkistân started a campaign against him.

Oct-Nov 1947: The tragedy of Rajourî and fall of Jhañgar

Col. Rehmatullâh Khân was the commanding officer of 9 JAK Company at Jhañgar in late October 1947. Maj. Nasrullâh, the head of 3 JAK, and he decided to defect from the Jammû and Kashmîr Forces, with their men, rather than recover the Sensâ area of Mîrpur, which the rebels had seized in October 1947. K.D. Maini writes that they 'killed the Gurkhâ sepoys of their own companies at Junâ and marched towards Throachi Fort which was 22 miles from Jhañgar and was held by the Gurkhâs.'[xxvi]

This group killed most of the Gurkhâs, including their commander, Capt. Raghbîr Siñgh Thâpâ. On October 28, 1947, they reached Chhachhérâ and set up camp there. As one of the top officers of the state forces,[13] Col. Khân knew that only two platoons defended Rajourî town. He sent word to the newly formed 'government' of 'AJK' for reinforcements. Sardâr Ibrâhim, the leader of 'AJK,' sent a contingent headed by Sakhi Dilér, which reached Chhachhérâ a fortnight later.

On the 9th November, Col. Khân and his men surrounded Rajourî town and started firing on the Gurkhâs and local volunteers defending the town, killing most of them by the next day. In a replay of what happened in many parts of North India and Pâkistân in 1947, the young women of the town begged a respected city elder, Dînâ Nâth Kélâ in this case, to obtain poison for them, which many of them consumed and died. They did not want to be taken alive by soldiers of the other community.

The Muslims of the town were upset by the agony of their Hiñdu brothers and sisters, with whom they had shared centuries of brotherhood. Maulvi Walî Shâh, Mufti Âzam Pahâr and Maulvi Salah Muhammad begged the victorious raiders to leave Hiñdu civilians alone. Maini writes that Sakhi Dilér and Col. Khân ignored their pleas and 'on 12th November, 1947, they killed at least 4,000 people.'

Rajourî became a ghost town. According to Rasal, a contemporary writer called it 'the city of the dead and dying, so cruel [was] the treatment the populace had received at the hands of the raiders.' Rasal adds, 'Subject to plunder and looting day in and day out, not a building there was left undamaged. Maurice Cohen, an independent [British] observer to the carnage, has written: Over 30,000 men, women and children were killed brutally. All the young women and girls, who looked more dead than alive, were ravaged, often by more than 30 men at a time, one after another and scores were abducted and dragged away screaming or unconscious.'[xxvii]

I have quoted Rasal because I have cited equally rabid Pâkistânî sources in this chapter. Both sides (as well as their British partisans) add so many digits to their figures that both sets of allegations obviously lack precision—and thus credibility. Gupta's estimate of the death toll is a

13 Typically, career soldiers from the state could expect to rise only to the rank of Brigadier. Colonel, thus, was the second-highest rank that they could aspire to.

Mirpur (Pok), Poonch, Rajouri and Reasi (Udhampur)

3 of 4

Map not to scale

seventh of Rasal's—and even Gupta's figure has clearly been rounded off to the higher side. Because balanced accounts of that era are not available (the gracious Âghâ Humâyun Amin has restricted himself to the military aspect) we have no choice but to read what extremists from both sides have written and try to sift the truth from it.

Col. Khân made an attempt to revive the monarchy of Rajourî. On the 13th November he declared that Mîrzâ Muhammad Hussain, a descendant of the Jarâls, would be the ruler of Rajourî.

Significantly, the 'Government of Rajourî' was not a part of 'Âzâd' Jammû and Kashmîr', partly because considerable India-administered land lay between the two. Or perhaps the concept of 'AJK' did not exist in the minds of the people of Rajourî at the time.

When Sardâr Ibrâhim presumed to post civil servants from Mîrpur to man government offices in Rajourî, the Mîrzâ bluntly asked them to go back to wherever they had come from.

25 November, 1947: The Shame of Mîrpur

The Pâkistân Army reached the outskirts of Mîrpur on the 5th or 6th November, 1947. Neither the Indian Army nor the Jammû and Kashmîr forces could be sent over to rescue the twenty-five thousand people of Mîrpur who were trapped in that town.

C.P. Gupta writes, 'At that time there were only 800 soldiers of J&K Government [stationed in Mîrpur], of whom about fifty per cent were Muslims. The Muslim soldiers, along with their arms and ammunition, joined the raiders and gave them full information about [places of] strategic importance from the military point of view.'[xxviii]

The besieged residents of this frontier town locked themselves in nervously. Their youths joined the four hundred-odd soldiers who remained with the state forces. Together they tried to defend their town against the better trained and better armed invaders. Gupta adds, '[They] repulsed many attacks, causing heavy losses to the enemy on 6th, 10th and 11th November, 1947.'

The citizens formed Mohallâ Committees, which would send cooked food to the young defenders. It was their misfortune that the wireless set (Morse code transmitter and receiver) of the state police developed a snag. As a result they lost their only link with Jammû and the outside world.

Mîrpur town has been built on a fairly tall, flat hillock perched above a vast *khad* (plain; rhymes with 'cud') and a seasonal (*barsâtî*) stream. Six sets of steps, each at a considerable distance from the other, have been cut into the slope that leads from the plain to the hilltop town. Each such series of steps is called a *dhakkî* (or *takkî*).

The Pâkistân Army captured the undefended plain and, on the night of the 23rd November, attacked the town with grenades and heavy artillery. The poorly armed defenders of the city fought back as best as they could, but they were outgunned. Under the 'thick' cover of Pâkistânî shells, 'seven Pathâns [managed to enter] the city at midnight,' Gupta writes.

The local volunteers intercepted the infiltrators and took them on in 'hand to hand combat' (scuffles that involve body contact). Five of the outnumbered Pathâns were killed. The other two scampered back. Many local youths were killed in that fight.

Meanwhile, the head of the district administration, the Wazîr é Wazârat (district magistrate), Râo Rattan Siñgh, panicked. At three in the morning, on the 25th November, senior police officers and he mounted their horses and sneaked away to Jammû.

That the military equation was stacked against the besieged city is a fact. However, observers believe that had these senior officers showed greater sagacity, fewer Mîrpurîs would have died in the subsequent massacre. The officers could have either asked the citizens to follow them to Jammû or led them to the army camp at Jhañgar which, as Gupta points out, was only twenty miles (32km.) away.

Some Hiñdu-Sikh soldiers saw this group leave. They decided to follow the example of their spineless seniors. Within an hour or so word about this desertion spread to the Pâkistâni camp. At eighty-thirty on the same morning the Pâkistân Army stormed the city and started burning the houses of the local residents.

Gupta writes, 'The [armed raiders] pushed the population into one corner of the city. The terrified men, women and children...marched [through the chaos and] the choking atmosphere due to smoke coming out from the burning houses, to an unknown destination to take shelter. They were intercepted at many points by the [Pâkistânîs who] killed more than 18,000 [people], which included [senior citizens], children and women who either jumped into deep wells or forced their male persons to kill them on the spot to save their modesty rather than going into the hands of cruel raiders. [Around] 3,500 wounded and half-dead persons were made prisoners [by the Pâkistânîs] and taken to Alîbég Camp wherein they were physically tortured and given hellish treatment.'

Even if Mr. Gupta's figures are exaggerated,[14] the fact is that a major massacre did take place on that fateful 25th of November. Six hundred and fifty years of brotherly bonds and friendly relations between

---

14 And they almost certainly are. According to the only available figures for that era, based on the 1941 census, Mîrpur had an urban population of 16,703. However, it is true that after that bloodbath no Hiñdu-Sikh remained in Mîrpur town.

the Hiñdus and Muslims of Mîrpur thus came to an end. The entire Hiñdu population of that town was either killed or forced to flee to Jammû city. Gupta tells us that around 3500 Mîrpuri Hiñdus managed to reach Jammû alive. Wali Mohd. Aseer Kishtwâri adds that Hiñdu refugees from 'other border areas,' too, fled to Jammû city.[xxix]

Nov-Dec 1947: Reinforcements, ups and downs

From the end of October to the middle of November, India's 50 Para Brigade alone defended Jammû-Akhnoor. A squadron of armoured cars of the 7th Light Cavalry joined it at Jammû on the 9th November. A week or so later the Indian Army sent in its 268 Infantry Brigade. The idea was to relieve the garrisons at Mîrpur, Pooñch and Kotli.

161 Brigade, which had two battalions, was to be shifted from Uri to Pooñch.

50 Para Brigade and the armoured cars were to move from Jammû to Akhnoor, Nausherâ, Jhañgar, Kotli and finally Mîrpur. The force at Mîrpur was to be reinforced by the 20th November.

Things did not quite work out that way. The terrain was hostile and the Pakistanis proved to be very good fighters.

161 Brigade could not relieve the force at Pooñch. However, one of its battalions was able to reach the garrison at Pooñch and add to the force there.

50 Para Brigade liberated Nausherâ and, on the 26th November, relieved the Kotli garrison. Just then they learnt that Mîrpur had fallen to Pâkistân the previous day—the 25th November. With Mîrpur gone it was pointless to hold on to Kotli, which was further ahead. Therefore, the Indian forces abandoned Kotli.

India's 80 Infantry Brigade was brought into the Chhamb-Akhnoor area in December. It liberated Chhamb on the 10th December.

With the Valley cleared of all raiders, it was essential to secure the winter capital, Jammû, where the government then was. So, in December 1947, the Indian Army posted two squadrons of Stuart Light Tanks at Jammû—with one squadron each from the 7th Light Cavalry and the Central India Horse. In January 1948, Deccan Horse, which had a squadron of Sherman Tanks, was posted at Samba to defend what would soon become the national highway. The squadron was later shifted to Jammû.

Jhañgar: Brig. Pûran Jappî and his men re-established Indian authority in Jhañgar on the 26th November, 1947—for a little more than a month.

The Bhimber-Jhañgar-Mîrpur area now became the focus of intense fighting, even though the forces involved were quite small.

Meanwhile, Brig. Usmân led his brigade into Nausherâ. They followed Brig. Jappî to Jhañgar. The Pâkistânîs brought Jhañgar back under their control on the 24th (or 27th) December, 1947. According to Maini, the Indian forces were now 'compelled to retreat to Nausherâ.'[xxx]

Around the middle of February, 1948, the Indian 19 Brigade, which had three infantry battalions, was brought into the Nausherâ area.

March-April, 1948: The liberation of Rajourî and Jhañgar

The battle of Taindhar-How Nausherâ was saved: The Pâkistâni forces next decided to capture Nausherâ—and thus a huge chunk of Jammû province. That was when the dashing, 35 year old, Brig. Usmân (born in Uttar Pradésh) of the 5/10 Balûch Regt. was brought in to command the elite 50 (Independent) Parachute Brigade.

His colleague L S Lehl (who later became a Major General) would later recall that Usmân "took a vow to recapture Jhañgar—a feat he accomplished in three months."

Early on the morning of 6 February, 1948, the Pâkistânis attacked the Taindhar position. Had they succeeded they would have won Nausherâ.

Brig. Usmân directed the C Company to defend Taindhar with all its might. On the other side was a 1500-strong force of tribal irregulars and some Pâkistâni servicemen. They attacked in six groups of 200-300 men each. When they were within thirty metres of the Indian position and hand to hand combat had begun, Havildar Daya Râm decided to bomb the attackers with mortars. Daya Râm was wounded and his gunner was killed in the action, but the invaders lost a very large number of men. Naik Jadunath Siñgh charged at the invaders, lobbing grenades at them and firing with his bren gun. He died, but the actions of these brave men compelled the Pâkistânis to withdraw. Lt. Kishan Siñgh Rathore, the acting commander of C Company, was the other hero of the battle of Taindhar.

This victory, achieved under Brig Usmân's leadership, enabled the 1 and 3 Râjpût units of the Indian army to consolidate their position in Nausherâ and finally recapture Jhañgar on March 15/18, 1948. In the process India lost thirty-three of its men, with another 102 wounded. However, according to Rasal, Usmân and his men managed to kill around a thousand Pâkistânî soldiers and wound another thousand.[xxxi]

The liberation of Rajourî: Rajourî had been under Pâkistânî occupation for almost six months now. India's 19 Brigade and 50 Para Brigade were asked to recover the town as part of Operation Rescue.

Maj. Gen. Kalwañt Siñgh ordered the launch of an offensive operation, which Brig. Yadunâth Siñgh would command. On the 8th April, 1948, the Dogrâs moved from Nausherâ to the Barwali Hill and captured it within a few hours. They now controlled the road, on which they could ply their tanks. They brought historic Chiñgas back under Indian control on the 10th or 12th April—perhaps the latter.

Col. Muhammad Aslam and a few hundred soldiers of the Pâkistânî/ 'AJK' forces, as well as Mîrzâ Muhammad Hussain, fled from Rajourî on the 10th or 12th April, when they heard of the liberation of Chiñgas, because from that roadside village it is a short, straight road to Rajourî.

That, however, did not help the Indian Army any. The Pâkistânî forces had mined the road between Chiñgas and Rajourî, and had also set up a number of roadblocks. The Pâkistânî soldiers who did not flee Rajourî had laid ambushes at periodic intervals.

For that reason, Lt Col Zorâwar Siñgh of Central India Horse decided to avoid the road altogether. He took the brilliant decision of taking his men down to the riverbed instead. It wasn't much easier that way, but it was slightly faster and much less irritating. They had to wade across that very cold river and back eight times in the course of fourteen miles.

Meanwhile, the Indian Air Force prepared the ground by strafing the Pâkistânî and 'AJK' soldiers who were holding Rajourî town. When the last 'plane had flown back, Zorâwar and his men made a sudden appearance outside the besieged town on the 12th (or 13th) April. A fierce battle followed, because the occupying army held all the heights and vantage points. Soon they realised that they could not take on a more powerful adversary, so they slid away and left Rajourî.

Maini writes, 'This operation cost the enemy a huge loss (500 dead) and it was the biggest success of the Indian forces.' Rajourî was the most important town liberated by the Indian forces.)

When the Mîrzâ, Cdr. Aslam and their soldiers reached 'AJK,' Sardâr Ibrâhim was, naturally, quite underjoyed to see them, especially the Mîrzâ. The Sardâr lodged his uninvited guests in the Junâ camp, from which the Mîrzâ and his colleagues were sent to Râwalpiñdî (Pâkistân), where the Pâkistânî authorities arrested them.

Pâkistân was even more merciless with Commander Muhammad Aslam whom they 'discharged from [his] duties.'[xxxii] That macho nation had no room for losers.

July 1948: Brigadier Usmân and the Battle of Nausherâ

Brigadier Mohammed Usmân had been posted as the Commander of the 50th Para Brigade. He was asked to ensure that Pâkistânî forces did not cross the 'line' that ran from Akhnoor to Beripattan, Jhañgar and Nausherâ. This was a very difficult job because the terrain favoured the Pâkistân Army. (As we shall see, India and Pâkistân would in later years fight some very bitter battles over Nausherâ, Pooñch and Rajourî.)

Pâkistân wanted to annex Nausherâ firstly to defend Mîrpur, which it had taken, and then to launch an attack on Pooñch from. Besides, Palañdri, where the capital of 'AJK' had just been established, is very close to Nausherâ. Pâkistân did not want to risk letting India recapture Palañdri.

With so much at stake, both armies fought with all that they had.

The Pâkistânîs now knew that the only way out for them was to target the great military leader on the opposite side. On Radio Pâkistân they announced a reward of Rs.50,000 for anyone who brought Brig. Usmân, dead or alive.[xxxiii] (Accounting for inflation, this was like Rs.30,00,000 in the year 2005.) On the night of 3/4 July 1948, the Pâkistânîs targeted Usmân's command post at Matlasi (Jhañgar) and hit it with an artillery shell. In all they fired six hundred shells on Indian positions that night. It was thus that India lost one of its greatest heroes. Brig. Usmân was the highest ranking Indian officer to die in that war till then.

Brig. Usmân's leadership was not limited to the battlefield. He assumed command when savages on both sides were killing defenceless people from the other community. Usmân asked his men to look for all the children in the Nausherâ area who had been orphaned in those massacres. Usmân found 158 such children, all of who had been starving since the day their parents were killed or forced to flee. Usmân started feeding them from his own rations. In order to give these children a living wage, the noble Brigadier began using them as couriers. This band of 158 orphans came to be known as the Bâlak Sénâ (Children's Army).[xxxiv]

Oct. 1947- Nov. 1948: The Siege of Pooñch

The longest siege of that war took place at Pooñch—the biggest city that the Pâkistânî raiders had attacked. Refugees fleeing Pâkistân and the parts of Kashmîr occupied by Pâkistân collected here by the thousand. Brigadier Kishen Siñgh and three battalions of the Jammû and Kashmîr forces were the only ones left to defend the town. (One battalion of the Indian Army's 161 Brigade had managed to reach the besieged town on the 19th November 1947.)

According to oral histories collected by me (thanks mainly to Mîr Pooñchi), in 1947-48 the population of Pooñch town suddenly swelled from around 7,000 to 40,000. This was because of the Hiñdu-Sikhs who had fled the brutalities of 'AJK' and sought temporary refuge in Pooñch town.

These refugees started killing the Muslims of Pooñch town. Most of the Muslims of the town fled to the villages (most of which were and still are almost entirely Muslim), instead of migrating to AJK. The Indian army airlifted senior Muslim civil servants to Jammû (in which town many of these officers later settled). The only Muslims who remained in the town were the poorest ones.

The Mir's family, too, fled to a village. He was twelve at the time. His studies were interrupted and pushed back by a full year. (As were the studies of countless Jammû Hiñdus and Muslims whom I have interviewed. Jammû Hiñdus studying in Delhi lost touch with their families in Jammû for several months, ran out of money and opted for careers that they would normally have frowned on.)

There was no food left to eat in Pooñch town: partly because its population had increased sixfold and partly because Pâkistânî troops surrounded the town. The townspeople began to starve. Many of them, especially the newly arrived, rootless refugees, started going to the villages in hordes. They would ransack the villages and come back with sacks full of grains. It is alleged that some uniformed Indian personnel supported the looters. This made some terrified rural people flee to 'AJK.'

Thousands of poor villagers in Rajourî and Pooñch were caught in the crossfire between the two forces. An Indian Army Major (he later became a Maj. Gen.) who took part in those operations estimates that several dozen villages got burnt in the process. This led to another wave of migration to 'AJK.'

The mass exodus of Muslims from several areas, especially Pooñch town, alarmed the secular elements of the Indian establishment. Col. (later Brig.) Prîtam Siñgh of the Indian Army, whom the Muslims recall very fondly, went from village to village and asked the people not to migrate to 'AJK.' It worked and migration came to an end—for a while.[15]

Col. Prîtam Siñgh and his men also took charge of Pooñch town and protected the few remaining Muslims.

Things stabilised a few months later and the Indian Army recaptured many areas that Pâkistân had annexed. The Indian government appointed a Martial Law Administrator, Brig. U.C. Bakshi, to administer all such liberated areas. Under Brig. Bakshi's leadership between twenty and thirty thousand Muslims returned to their ancestral villages.

15 In 1965 Pâkistân imposed yet another war on India. It sent thousands of infiltrators to villages living under the Indian flag. The Army launched operations to flush these Pâkistânî infiltrators out. Once again people began to flee to AJK. These included some of Mîr Pooñchi's family.

Entire villages were depopulated. According to some estimates, around eighty thousand people from Pooñch-Rajourî went across to 'AJK' temporarily—because there was no route that they could take to Kashmir or Jammû. Some, like the Mir's family, returned later.

However, by the time all this happened, considerable damage had been done. It was much after Pâkistân laid siege to Pooñch town that 161 Brigade came in from Uri and, on the 19th November, Col. Prîtam Siñgh brought the Pooñch Relief Column—which was a battalion of the Kumaon Regiment—from Jammû.

On the other hand, Pâkistân fielded its regular army units and heavy artillery in Pooñch. The tribal irregulars under its control were trained in guerrilla warfare. Besieging Pooñch town were a Pâkistânî brigade at Râwlâkot, under Brig. Saad-ud-dîn, and another Pâkistânî brigade at Méndhar, under Brig. Rehmatullâh.

The Indian Air Force, under Air Commodore Bâbâ Meher Siñgh, bombed Pâkistânî positions on several occasions. It is to the credit of the small force defending Pooñch that it did not let the combined strength of these two Pâkistânî brigades capture the town.

Defending the town was one thing, but the tiny force was in no position to expel either of the two Pâkistânî brigades from Râwlâkot or Méndhar.

So, the Indian Prime Minister, Pt. Nehru, convened an emergent meeting of the Defence Committee of the (national) Cabinet in Delhi on the 4th December, 1947, to see what best could be done. The generals, including Gen. Lockhart, felt that the Indian Army should give Pooñch up, shift the civilian population to refugee camps and move the army contingent to Urî, where it would have been deployed more usefully—for reasons that we will discuss later in this section.

At the time Mahârâjâ Hari Siñgh's clansman, Brigadier Kishan Siñgh, was facing the Pâkistânî onslaught in Pooñch. It is said that the Mahârâjâ had been leaning on Maj. Gen. Kalwañt Siñgh, the force commander, to divert two battalions as well as the armoured cars of Brig. Sen's 161 Brigade to Pooñch for that reason.

Pt. Nehru did not agree with the generals either. A retreat from the most important town of the province—next only to Jammû itself—was unthinkable for the entire civilian establishment.

The Indian Prime Minister rushed to Jammû and, on the 6th December, convened a meeting with Mahârâjâ Hari Siñgh, Bakhshi Ghulâm Muhammad, who was the Law & Order (i.e. Home/ Interior) Minister of the state, Lt. Gen. Russell, and Maj. General Kalwañt Siñgh.

Rasal writes that after that meeting '[Maj.] General Kalwañt Siñgh is known to have verbally quoted the highest authority from Delhi [i.e. Pt. Nehru,] ...[and] diverted the major part of [Brigadier Sen's 161] Brigade to Pooñch.' Apparently, Pt. Nehru's orders were, 'Hold Pooñch at all costs.'

Major General Âtmâ Siñgh then collected the Raj Brigade, 19 Infantry Brigade and 5 Infantry Brigade and created a force that was almost as big as an army division. A major battle, described by some as the first 'division-level battle in the history of India and Pâkistân,' followed. The Indian Army defeated the Pâkistânîs at Méndhar, Surankote, Thannâ Mañdî and Budhal (in addition, as we have seen, to Rajourî).

The Pâkistânîs were comprehensively defeated under Âtmâ Siñgh's mature leadership. The siege of Pooñch was lifted on the 28th November, 1948,[16] a month before the cease fire. (The cease-fire has been covered in some detail in the volume about 'Kashmîr.')

The role of the Pâkistân Army

Many Pâkistân army officers who took part in the action of 1947-48 later wrote military histories and memoirs. These make it clear that Pâkistân's armed forces were guiding the operations of the 'irregulars'/ '*mujâhids'* at every stage, taking part in the fighting and even laying down their lives in the process.

Some Pâkistâni officers, like Brig. Amjad Ali Khân Chaudhry, HJ, try to suggest (in his book *September '65*, Ferozsons, Lahore 1977) that 'with the exception of one senior Pâkistân army officer who was sent to advise the Mujâhids,' the Pâkistân army stepped in only after the Indian defence forces did.

That 'exception' was given the code name 'Gen. Tariq.' Brigadier Akbar Khân used this nom de guerre for a while. So, Brig. Chaudhry reveals, did other senior Pâkistâni officers, in turns. (Chaudhry, Page 5.)

One 'exception' is enough to prove that the Pâkistân army was involved *before* the Indian Army was called in. But here we are told that more than one officer acted as 'Gen. Tariq' and that the '*mujâhids'* reported to him.

While officially Pâkistân insists that its army did not get involved even after the Indian Army came in, writers like Brig. Chaudhry are much too honest to maintain that pretence. At the time, he was the brigade major of the Artillery H.Q. of Pâkistân's 7 Infantry Division 'which was responsible for advising the Mujâhid forces and controlling the limited operations which had to be undertaken by elements of the regular army due to compelling strategic circumstances.' (Page 7.)

That is as clear an admission of the Pâkistân Army's involvement as possible.

And as far as the 'irregulars' or the so-called 'Azâd' Kashmîr forces are concerned, they consisted of more than just men from NWFP tribes. As on the Indian side, enraged refugees (Muslims, in this case) vent their anger on the other community.

16 The 22nd November, 1948, according to Maini, K.D., 'A decision that changed the fate of Pooñch,' *Daily Excelsior*.

As Pâkistân's Maj. Gen. Shaukat Rizâ would later recall, 'During the course of fighting in Kashmîr, a motley crowd of such diverse elements as ex-servicemen, ex-INA [Indian National Army] personnel, Muslims from Kashmîr State Forces, refugees, civilian volunteers mostly from Punjab and NWFP, and unattached adventurers, were given the generic name of Azâd Kashmîr Forces. By October 1948 [by when most of the NWFP tribesmen had left] they had been organised into eight brigades with a total of 33 battalions.'

This was over and above the 'regular army' that Brig. Chaudhry mentions. In this section I have tried to mention by name a few units of the Pâkistân Army that took part in those operations, as well as the names of their officers, and what they did.

The battle of Pâñdû: Pâkistân's 1 Balûch infantry battalion scored a major victory at Pâñdû, which is opposite Chakothi on the present LoC. Brig. Akbar Khân was the Brigade Commander and Lt. Col. Shér Bahâdur the Commanding Officer. Pâkistân's 2 Field Artillery Regiment and a section of two guns of 8 Medium Regiment were brought in 'to give support to Mujâhids *and elements of regular troops* who were to carry out this operation.' (Chaudhry, Page 8, italics mine.)

Indian soldiers had secured themselves in a series of terraced concrete trenches atop Pâñdû Hill. They defended their post bravely and a very fierce and bloody battle followed. However, that night the fearless Balûch soldiers decided to put their lives at stake by marching straight towards the bottom of that hill, though they could have been shot from above. In the Indian firing that followed, 'Captain Khâlid Mahmûd Butt laid down his life *while leading a contingent of Mujâhids*.' (Page 9, italics mine.) The idealistic young captain, who was from Pâkistân's elite infantry battalion, the Guides, had volunteered to fight on the Kashmîr front.

The Indian soldiers were surrounded and outnumbered. They needed reinforcements, which did not arrive. So, they left the post and slipped away in the dark of the night. By dawn the Pâkistân army had occupied all of Pâñdû.

This changed the shape of the LoC. Had Pâñdû not fallen, the Indian Army would have been on the other side of the nallah, and Muzaffarabâd would have been that much more vulnerable.

'Gen. Tariq' loses Pooñch for Pâkistân: As we have seen in this chapter, the Mahârâjâ's Army was in a desperate situation in Pooñch. The siege of Pooñch lasted almost thirteen months (Oct. 1947- Nov. 1948). Had Pâkistân played its cards well, it could have occupied Pooñch town. The Pooñch airfield was under fire from Pâkistâni field guns. ('Irregulars' do not have field guns.) However, 'Gen. Tariq' (and not some 'irregular soldier') decided not to do anything to seize the town.

He wanted to wait until winter, so that all the passes would be blocked by snow, Pooñch would be even more cut off from the rest of India than it already was and would be much easier to capture.

In November 1948 the Indian Army was able to enter Poonch through Méñdhar Valley. Pâkistân failed to check the Indian advance partly because it was not able to shift 7/1 Punjab Battalion, which had been assigned to this task, from its peace location in Jehlum. Major Abdul Rehman, the Battery Commander of Pâkistân's 1 Mountain Regiment, and his battery, did not reach in time either. This changed the balance and Pooñch was saved for India.

Kotli, Mîrpur and Khuirattâ: Had the Indian Army regained Khuirattâ valley, it would have been possible to liberate Kotli as well. Lt. Col. Ghulâm Mohammad, the Battalion Commander at Khuirattâ, got the impression (incorrect, as it turned out) that the Indian Army was planning to attack with armour, in November 1948.

Pâkistân's Commander Artillery, who was British, rushed anti-tank guns to Khuirattâ all the same.

British officers: It is impossible to generalise about the role of individual British civil and military officers in the blood-soaked partitioning of India, in which people, who had lived like brothers for almost a millennium, started butchering each other and 'abducted' a few thousand women from the other community.

If Viceroy Lord Mountbatten is seen as having been soft on India, his predecessor, Lord Wavell was the one who made sure that India was partitioned. If some British officers sliced off the 'Northern Areas' of Gilgit-Baltistan and handed them over to Pâkistân, Radcliffe gave Gurdaspur (Punjab) to India—and thus a road link to Jammû and Kashmîr. And if some British generals acted in a manner to temper Pâkistân's moves in Kashmîr, *all* British officers who had opted for the Pâkistân Army fought on behalf of Pâkistân, and against India. At one stage, till late 1947, a number of units and formations of the Pâkistân army were commanded by British officers.

Lieut. Blaker controlled the medium guns that were used against India at Pâñdû. His men and he bombarded the Indian soldiers and made sure that Indian gunners could not give effective support to their garrison at Pâñdû.

During the entire operations of 1947-49, the only Pâkistân-controlled bridge that the Indian Air Force could hit was Domél (near Muzaffarabâd) —and that only once, without causing major damage. Pâkistâni analysts credit the fact that their vital installations were not hit to the first-rate protection given by their lone battery of anti-aircraft gunners. Major Peter O'Reilly was the commander of these gunners.

Hindsight and regrets

Many Indians believe that the Indian Army could have 'easily' regained Kotlî, had senior Army officers not botched things up.

The diversion of the 161 Brigade allowed the Pâkistânî raiders to consolidate their gains in Muzaffarâbâd. They received fresh reinforcements and excellent military leaders. Two bridges would decide who would rule the Muzaffarâbâd region. These were a bridge on River Sindh near Domél and the Kohala bridge on River Jehlum. Whichever army controlled them would be able to move its men, trucks and guns to the other side of these mighty rivers. India had to capture both if it wanted to get the occupied areas (i.e. what is now called AJK) back.

It was because of India's inability to seize those two bridges that there is an 'Âzâd' Jammû and Kashmîr (AJK) in Pâkistân's occupation today. But then, it was also because of that decision that Pooñch remained with India.[17] Also because of this decision the massacre of the people of Pooñch town was prevented.

Could India have retained both Pooñch and Muzaffarâbâd-Mîrpur? Apparently Lt. Gen. Russell felt that India should have vacated Poonch and concentrated on the Domél-Muzaffarâbâd-Mîrpur belt. India would have trapped the Pâkistânîs in Pooñch and thus kept both regions. The evacuation of Pooñch would have only been temporary.

Makes eminent sense, especially with hindsight.

The horror of 1947: an attempt to assess the magnitude

The 1947 massacre of the Muslims of Jammû city, its neighbouring areas and the farther reaches of the province, remains one of the most poorly documented of the human tragedies with which the sub-continent's major religious communities greeted independence.

'Jammû 1947: gone but not forgotten,' Khalid Hasan, *Friday Times*, Pâkistân, 2005.[xxxv]

Brutal riots forced the Hiñdus, Sikhs and Jaìns of Mîrpur, Muzaffarâbâd, Bhimber, Sudh Nutti, Kotlî, Bâgh and some other parts of Pooñch to flee the homes that their forefathers had lived in for centuries. The widely respected leader Mîr Pooñchi recalls that several Hiñdu-Sikh women jumped into the Kishen Gañgã with their children to escape dishonour.

---

17 A veteran, patriotic Muslim leader of the area adds: Some units of the demolition guard, which was under Brig. Kishen Siñgh of the J&K state forces, were travelling from the Hâji Pîr pass in the direction of Pooñch. They saw some soldiers advancing towards them from the other side of the river. They incorrectly assumed that it was the Pâkistânî Army. So, they deliberately destroyed the bridge.

Thousands of the survivors migrated to Pooñch town. (The river was later renamed Neelum in the occupied parts.)

But almost twice as many Muslims felt compelled to leave the present Jammû and Kathuâ districts. They were the victims of similar massacres in Jammû town, Réâsî, Udhampur, Râmnagar and parts of Kathuâ district.[xxxvi] A few Muslims died in Rajourî proper. Pooñch town was so swamped by emotionally charged Hiñdu-Sikh refugees that the Muslims were overwhelmed and left the town—even though many of them returned later.

Many Jammû Muslims sought refuge in Muslim-majority areas within the state, especially the Valley of Kashmîr, instead of crossing over into 'AJK' or Pâkistân. Given the sudden increase in the proportion of Muslims in Dodâ district—which always had a Muslim majority—and a small increase in Udhampur, it would seem that several thousand rural Muslims, especially from the adjacent villages of Kathuâ, migrated instead to Dodâ (and a handful to the Muslim-majority belt of Udhampur). (The tables in the chapter 'The population of Jammû province' throw some light on what might have happened.)

Beyond dry statistics: While serving in the state, I have come into very close contact with families that personify the tragedy of 1947.

One is a Muslim family from Udhampur, many members of which—including young women—were slaughtered during those killings.

The other is a Brâhmin clan from Rachhwâ (Rajourî), which had for centuries thought of itself as 'half-Muslim' without formally converting to Islâm. Armed marauders decided to complete that formality. They forced this family to convert—which bought its members a few extra months of life. Then, another Pâkistânî group came and dismissed their conversion as a ploy. So, the second group abducted two young women to 'AJK' and killed all the men and old women. The young women were sent back a few years later.

To their credit, neither family let the next generation know what the rest of their clan had gone through in 1947—lest their young grow up with prejudices against 'the other community.' I learnt about the havoc wreaked on these two families not from their own members but from liberals from the other community who were ashamed at what their co-religionists had done.

My former driver, K.K. Sharmâ, is the third shining example of maturity. His parents and other elders, who lived in the parts now called 'AJK,' were slaughtered by some members of 'the other community.' He was a little child then. And yet Sharmâ has no hatred for the Muslims as a whole because a kindly Muslim family of 'AJK' brought him up—

and never tried to impose its religious values on him. When he was twelve they managed to contact one of his uncles, who had survived and fled to Jammû, and sent the boy across to the winter capital.

A conspiracy of silence: There is a huge conspiracy of silence about this era. Most Indian histories don't mention it at all. One or two Indian articles talk only about the brutal ethnic cleansing of Mîrpur, Muzaffarâbâd, Rajourî town and the occupied parts of Pooñch.[18] Pâkistânî accounts—and these are countless—all seem to quote each other (and thus repeat the same exaggerated figures and make the same mistakes, such as referring to places like Saniya, Malatank and Saubha, none of which seems to exist).[19] Besides, the Pâkistânî histories are totally one-sided.

This book, like all my works so far, is an attempt at reconciliation and brotherhood. But all of us who love the people of Jammû—whether they live to the east of the LoC or to its west, or indeed in Siâlkot—owe it to ourselves to reconstruct the truth about what happened in 1947, 1948 and 1949, even if the facts are unpleasant—and they are.

In my mission I have relied on oral histories, old records (Indian, Pâkistânî, British and multilateral) and Alexander Evans, then a British student (and now a civil servant). Alexander's quest is identical to mine—and like me he is sceptical of wild accusations, which can be debunked simply by comparing old census records (1931 and 1941) with the 1961 census. (In 1951 the population was not enumerated by religion.) Alexander will be publishing his findings separately. I would only like to summarise what the records collected by Evans—and census documents and oral histories obtained by me—indicate. I have cited only those oral accounts

---

18 In Pâkistân they officially throttle all voices that dare suggest that the Pâkistânîs' ancestors had slaughtered any Hiñdu-Sikhs. President (Gen.) Musharraf's government, for instance, banned *Khâmosh Pâni* (2003), which is the only Pâkistânî film ever to win the first prize at an international festival (Locarno, at that). The film's sin is that it shows how the Pâkistânis created circumstances in which Sikh women had to either commit suicide or convert.

Gen Musharraf's son had to come to India to watch what is internationally considered the greatest Pâkistânî film ever.

19 Could these now be in Pâkistân Occupied Kashmîr? Maybe, but that is unlikely, because the so-called 'AJK' does not include any part of the old Jammû and Kathuâ districts (except Chhamb, which Pâkistân conquered in 1965 and 1971). Apart from my own very extensive knowledge of the twelve-hundred plus villages of Jammû (each village of which I have toured at least twice, if not three times), even later administrators of these two districts to not seem to have heard of these places. Nor have the Muslim survivors whom I interviewed for this chapter. And if they are in 'AJK' then these three villages would have had Muslim majorities even in 1947.

in which the narrator has spoken of the faults of his own community and of injustices done to the 'other' community.

Mine is a work in progress and if new evidence comes up I am willing to revise, even reverse, all my conclusions. For instance, I have used anecdotal evidence based on oral histories about the killing and migration of Hiñdus and Sikhs and the 'abduction' of Muslim women. I will augment this information whenever official statistics about these two tragedies become available.

The number of people allegedly massacred

Almost all Pâkistânî accounts allege that 2,00,000 Muslims were killed in Jammû province in November (and October) 1947.[xxxvii] The break up of this figure includes 8,000 Muslims allegedly slaughtered at Malatank on October 20; 14,000 Muslims said to have been massacred at Saniya on October 22; 15,000 migrating Muslims apparently killed near the bridge at Akhnoor on October 20,[20] riots in Kathuâ district and in the Jatkatiâñ Mohallâ of Jammû town and 36 Pâkistân-bound trucks, each with around sixty Muslims, attacked on the 5th November (according to other accounts, on the 6th November).[xxxviii]

Mr. Justice Yusuf Saraf, a fairly jaundiced 'AJK' writer, admits that Brigadier Usmân of the Indian Army (whom the Pâkistânîs otherwise consider an Uncle Tom and the Indians a national hero) and his (mostly Hiñdu) soldiers, intervened to halt one of the 6th November attacks on Muslims fleeing Jammû-Kathuâ.[xxxix]

Even if the actual number of Muslims killed is only a fraction of what is alleged, even if the numbers alleged don't square with census figures, even if the October 20 date for the alleged massacre near the Akhnoor Bridge is off the mark by a few (possibly sixteen) days, even if Pâkistânî sources contradict each other about the date of the 5th/6th November carnage and even if the names Saniya, Malatank and Saubha are distortions of the original (or the product of an imperfect collective memory), the fact is that some terrible killings did take place.

This conclusion is based on oral histories collected from the Muslims who stayed behind, as well as liberal Hiñdus. They speak of the massacre of the migrating convoy at Chatthâ-R.S. Purâ and some violence in Sâmbâ tehsîl, rather than at Saniya, Malatank, Saubha or Akhnoor. A Kashmîrî Muslim lady who was in Jammû during those wretched weeks said that she could not recall any violence against Muslims in Jammû town. However, even she recalled the mass murder of some migrating Muslims in the R.S. Purâ area.

---

20 But the mass migration of Muslims had not started till the 5th November.

Memories, of course, can be very imperfect. Hiñdus who were in their mid-teens in 1947 seem to recall their parents locking them up at home because murderous Pâkistânî terrorists were reported to have infiltrated Indian territory all the way up to R.S. Purâ. These reports, as was later seen, were not true.

I have been to several hundred villages in Jammû-Kathuâ which had substantial Muslim populations before 1947 but where not one Muslim lives anymore. I have also been to some villages in Rajourî where not a single Hiñdu is left. The so-called AJK is littered with hundreds of villages every Hiñdu-Sikh of which had felt obliged to flee.

And the Hiñdus, as we have seen, are as liberal with the number of digits in their allegations. Mr Maini, a sober historian, writes that on the 12th November, 1947, the Muslim raiders killed at least 4,000 people in Rajourî. But Rasal, quoting Maurice Cohen, 'an independent [British] observer to the carnage,' claims that 'over 30,000 men, women and children were killed brutally' in that series of incidents in Rajourî. Not only is Dr. Rasal's figure seven times that given by Mr Maini, it is several times the population of Rajourî town—then or even now.

Regarding Mîrpur, Gupta writes that the raiders killed 'more than 18,000 [people, and around] 3,500 wounded and half-dead persons were made prisoners.'

So, with just two places where the Hiñdus had been in a minority, we have allegations about 48,000 Hiñdus killed. Add to that the number of Hiñdu-Sikhs said to have been massacred at places like Muzaffarâbâd, Sudh Nutti, Kotlî and Bâgh and we have another eight thousand or so Hiñdu-Sikhs allegedly killed in the same set of retaliatory massacres.

The origin of these allegations

The figure of two lakh Muslims killed in Jammû, in fairness, is not the product of Pâkistân's extremely hard-working propaganda machinery. Pâkistâni histories claim that it originated in a report in *The Times*, London, (10 October, 1948), which mentioned the killing of 237,000 Muslims. A 1963 book, *Pâkistân*, written by Ian Stephens, a former editor of *The Statesman* (Calcutta), carried a similar figure. Stephens included in the figure people who had died from epidemics and exposure. He claimed that 200,000 Muslims had disappeared.

Pâkistânî histories also quote one Mr G.K. Reddy, 'a Hindu editor of *Kashmîr Times*' as writing on the 28th October, 1947, about "the mad orgy of Dogrâ violence against unarmed Muslims... From the hotel room where I was detained in Jammû, I counted as many as twenty-six villages burning one night."[21]

But are there, or were there ever, twenty six villages encircling Jammû town, leave alone Muslim-dominated ones? Where was this hotel from which one can see more than five or six villages? And in those riots, like all others, while the minority community bore the brunt, a small number of people from the majority community also got killed and lost their houses to arson. We have definite evidence about this both in Jammû, where a few Hiñdus suffered, as well as about Rajourî, where some Muslims were harmed, even though they were in the majority in their respective areas. So, if Mr. Reddy saw houses burn, most of them would, indeed, have belonged to Muslims but the Hiñdus would have owned at least some.

In Jammû, as Hâshmî reminds us, Siddîq 'Chor' ('the thief') poured petrol on 'the multi-storey house of Girdhâri Lâl Sarâf' in Mohallâ Jatkatiâñ and set it on fire after its timber roof was taken over by armed fanatics of Sarâf's community.

However, there can be no doubt that a 'mad orgy of violence against unarmed Muslims' did take place. Hiñdus, who were children at the time, too, recall standing on rooftops and watching entire villages in the hills above the city burn. They were told that Pâkistânî raiders had reached as close to the city as what is now called the Bypass. This, obviously, was not true. Aggressor communities—be they Muslims, in places where they are in the majority, or Hiñdus, in their areas—always try to shield their children from unpleasant facts about themselves.

In Jammû, 'AJK' and Kashmîr they have created the brutal majoritarian fiction that the minorities fled their land not because some members of the majority had terrified the minority witless but because the minority *wanted to* leave, because the minority's loyalties were always with the land that they later migrated to (and not with their original homeland), because some leader persuaded them to migrate...

---

21 Was there a paper called *Kashmîr Times* at the time? How did it come to be edited by a Reddy?

Yes, there was a *Kashmîr Times* but it had nothing to do with the later-day, Jammû-based newspaper of the same name. It was owned by one Mr. Mithâ, a Congressite Muslim. M/s Mithâ and Reddy found themselves in POK in the months that followed Pâkistân's occupation of some parts of the state. During his longish stay in POK, Reddy wrote a number of articles depicting India and the non-Muslims in a bad light. He was obviously doing this to buy insurance—or at least to curry favour—because when he finally returned to India he wrote an even longer series of articles castigating Pâkistân and the Muslims. Mr Reddy later joined *Blitz*, a Bombay-based weekly tabloid.

The migrant minorities, of course, have a totally different take. Though they, too, exaggerate, their accounts are far closer to the truth.

Ershad Mahmud[xl] quotes the 'well-known English writer' Lord Birword as saying that "five lac Muslims had to displace; over a million Kashmîrîs reached Pâkistân by end-October 1947...Hindus erased Muslims from their three districts of Jammû, Udhampur and Kathuâ..." The problems with this quote are: i) Would an Englishman have used the unit 'lac' (especially that spelling)? ii) If five lakh (0.5 million) were displaced then how did a million reach Pâkistân? In any case there were nowhere near that many Muslims in Jammû-Kathuâ-Udhampur. The three districts together had 3,44,330 Muslims in 1941 or around 3.8 lakh in 1947, of whom almost half stayed on in their old districts. iii) That the percentage of Muslims in Udhampur actually rose between 1941 and 1961 has been recorded elsewhere in this chapter. iv) End-October? But 'AJK' and Pâkistân maintain—and rightly so—that the organised evacuation of the Muslims began in early November.

What is important about such evidence is that if the Pâkistânîs can quote Lord Birword ('the well-known English writer'), Ian Stephens, Horace Alexander and Richard Symonds, the latter two being Quaker relief workers based in Pooñch in August 1947—their counterparts in the Indian right have the 'independent observer' Maurice Cohen to cite.

None of these Britons actually went about counting corpses. Each saw some horrible massacres, assumed that only that community had been at the receiving end of violence and then accepted whatever figures members of that surcharged community gave them.

Some of these writers were British civil servants who were either blinded by personal prejudice or by a desire to 'divide [India] and quit' or both. Take Terence Creagh Coen of the Indian Political Service (a British cadre that was somewhat like the ICS, but inferior).

He wrote that even in Jammû province 'the Muslims were in a majority of about 60 per cent to the Hiñdu 40 per cent. (This census-proved fact is often suppressed or denied.) It is true that the Muslims there were massacred wholesale—this was probably the worst of all the 1947 massacres—and the remainder fled to Pâkistân.'

So far Coen is with the facts. The Jammû carnage is, indeed, generally regarded as one of the two worst in the Indian sub-continent in 1947. However, he gives the game away not only by advocating a partition along religious lines but also by adding something that is totally untrue, i.e. 'at present there are practically no Muslims left in Jammû.'[xli]

That kind of total ethnic cleansing took place in the parts now in 'AJK,' and in Pakistan, which Coen has chosen not to mention. In Jammû province to this day the Muslims form more than 30 per cent of the population. And the percentage did not come down from 61.34 per cent in 1941 (which was the Muslim share in undivided Jammû) to a little under 30 per cent after 1950, as biased parties like Coen and Yusuf Saraf would suggest by dishonestly quoting the census figures.

They conveniently ignore that the percentage was brought down not so much by the highly regrettable forced migration of around 1.6 lakh Muslims (and the killing of around seventeen thousand) as by the severing from Jammû of overwhelmingly Muslim areas such as Mîrpur (3.1 lakh Muslims in 1941; around 3.6 lakh in 1947) and parts of Pooñch (at least 1.9 lakh Pooñch Muslims ceased to be citizens of India between 1947 and the 1961 census, mainly because their villages came under Pâkistânî occupation, but some because they migrated to 'AJK').

As far as present Jammû province is concerned, the Muslims would have been around 48.66 per cent of the population in 1941. (My assumptions are: In 1941, there were around 4.8 lakh Muslims in the areas of Mîrpur and Pooñch that were later occupied by Pâkistân. There thus were perhaps 7.3 lakh Muslims in the areas that are still in Jammû, which had a total population of roughly 15 lakh.) Considering that some Pooñch Muslims felt compelled to leave the parts still in Jammû province, one can assume that a little more than 48 per cent of the population of the present Jammû province was Muslim in 1941.

If we subtract the population of Hiñdu-Sikh refugees, it will be seen that, in 1961, the Muslims of the present Jammû province were 38.04 per cent of the original population. (Detailed calculations later in this chapter.)

It is shameful that this percentage declined from 48 per cent in 1941 to around 38 per cent in the 1950s, and that the fall was much steeper in Jammû-Kathua. But that is hardly the same as saying that 'there are practically no Muslims left in Jammû.'

The extent of forced migration

What do we know about the number of people who fled in either direction?

Catherine Rey-Schirr estimates that two million/ twenty lakh people 'fled to the mountains, where many died of hunger and exhaustion as they tried to cross the snow-covered passes.'

An Indian Army Major recalls that when tribal irregulars invaded Rajourî, male Hiñdus fled to the hills. Their women were not allowed to leave. He adds that scores of Muslim villages got burnt in the crossfire, and their residents similarly sought refuge uphill. Some people—from both communities—certainly did seek refuge in the mountains, especially in Pooñch-Mîrpur, but two million? Simply not possible. There weren't that many people in the entire province, as the 1941 census figures show.

Politicians of the 'AJK' Muslim Conference prepared a list of roughly 549,000 people who had allegedly fled Jammû province for 'AJK' between August 1947 and November 1948. A leading politician, Mr. M.A. Gurmani, put the figure at 450,000. In March 1949, Brigadier F.H.Stevens, Director General (Kashmir Refugees) in West Punjâb estimated that in 'AJK' there were circa (approximately) 200,000 refugees, of whom 100,000 were receiving free rations.[xlii]

As we will later see, if the migration figures of the MC, Mr Gurmani or Brig. Stevens are accepted, then no Muslim would have been killed in those riots because there just weren't that many Muslims in Jammû. (And if we accept the figure of 200,000 Muslims killed, then no one migrated to Pakistan or 'AJK.')

The evidence of refugee camps

Rey-Schirr and Evans have separately looked into the records of refugee camps on both sides.

Officers of the 'government' of 'AJK' had the more conservative estimate of around 130,000 Muslim refugees.[xliii]

Of these, 50,000 in Kotlî, 10,000 in Mîrpur and 23,000 in occupied Bhimber received free rations. (The rest would have been well to do.) The refugees in Mîrpur Town had come from those parts of Rajourî, Méndhar and Bhimber where the Indian flag continued to fly.[xliv]

These are the most accurate statistics available, because they jell with the census figures and also because revenue and relief officials, in India as well as Pâkistân, normally have exact names and lists of refugees. Mr. Gurmani and the Muslim Conference obviously had no means to count. They were going by general impressions. As for Brigadier Stevens, he pointed out that his was only an approximate figure.

23,265 Muslims from Méndhar, Pooñch and Rajourî sought refuge in Pâkistânî towns as far away as Wâh in the North-West Frontier Province. The UNCIP (United Nations Commission for India and Pâkistân) team saw 2,619 and 6,664 refugees in the two camps at Siâlkot in March 1949. The better off refugees would by then have moved into houses vacated by fleeing Hiñdus.

So, at the very least, 1,62,000 Muslims from the parts of Jammû which remained under the Indian flag actually reached the parts occupied by Pâkistân. We have established later in this chapter that 1.83 lakh Muslims fled Jammû-Kathuâ. So we have a shortfall of twenty one thousand straightaway. Clearly, many of them had been butchered on their way to 'AJK' and Pâkistân. A few hundred Muslims were killed in the province in the weeks before the tragic exodus of 5 November, 1947. That takes the total to around twenty two thousand.

On the one hand, the '1.62 lakh refugees' figure includes a few thousand Muslims who had fled Pooñch to 'AJK.' Their number should be subtracted because it wrongly lowers the number of missing people from Jammû-Kathuâ. On the other hand, a few thousand 'missing' people from Jammû-Kathuâ had actually gone to Kashmîr (or Udhampur-Dodâ). This incorrectly raises the number of 'missing' Jammû-Kathuâ Muslims.

So, these two sets of figures cancel each other out.

Non-Muslim refugees

Mr Ward Allen, a US Member of the UNCIP, estimated that even as late as in early 1949 there were circa 50,000 non-Muslim refugees housed in temporary camps in 'AJK.' For instance, in Ambore Camp near Muzaffarâbâd, in 1949 there were 760 non-Muslims waiting to move across what is now called the LoC. Some 600 residents of the camp had crossed over and a similar number had gone back to their villages on the India-administered side.

We also learn that Dr Otto Wenger of the ICRC (International Committee of the Red Cross) visited camps in 'AJK' in 1947. At the time there were 2,500 Hiñdu-Sikhs in a camp in Muzaffarâbâd, 1,600 in 'appalling conditions' in Alîbég, 125 in Gobindpar and 700-800 in the Bâgh camp.[xlv]

In turn, the Pâkistân Red Cross told Wenger that the Indian Air Force had bombed its hospitals in Kotlî and Bâgh (both in 'AJK'). Some patients had been killed and hospital facilities had been damaged. The Indian government replied that that the attacks were not deliberate and that the hospitals had not been adequately marked with the Red Cross emblem.

It was the same story on both sides. Thousands of people were, for almost two years, housed in refugee camps in the land of their forefathers. Their sin was that they belonged to communities that were in a minority in that area. They waited for permission to travel to a strange new land across the LoC—which was to be their new home merely because their community was in the majority there.

About 80,000 Hindus and Sikhs fled Western Kashmir (including Gilgit and Skardu) towards places where the Indian tricolour flew.

The change in the Hiñdu-Muslim ratio, between 1941 and 1961

Actually, numbers, especially those followed by four or five (or more) zeroes, convey nothing. Each community plays up its own suffering and denies that of the other. (An excellent example is Khalid Hasan's quote at the beginning of this section.) This is equally true of the figures of Kashmîrî Pañdits who fled Kashmîr in 1990 and Muslims who stayed behind but were killed later. Percentages make infinitely greater sense: whether we talk about 1947-49 or 1990-91. And in both cases these percentages are alarming.

The entire Hiñdu-Sikh community (and many Christians) of the areas now in 'AJK' fled towards the Indian tricolour between 1947 and 1950. In the case of the Muslims of Jammû-Kathuâ the figures (see the chapter 'The population of Jammû province') suggest that the exodus to 'AJK' and Siâlkot (Pâkistân) was tragic but nowhere near as total.

The Muslims' share in the population of Jammû district came down from 37.36 per cent in 1941 to 10.03 per cent in 1961. This would imply that only 73.08 per cent felt pressurised enough to move to 'AJK' and Pâkistân. Or that as many as 26.92 per cent of the Muslims of Jammû district stayed on.

However, the enormity of the exodus from Jammû district was considerably greater than what these figures reveal. That's because the current Muslim population of Jammû city consists mainly of Muslims from Pooñch, Rajourî, Dodâ, Udhampur, rural Jammû and even Kashmîr and Kargil, who prospered after 1947 and moved into the houses evacuated by the original Muslim residents of the city. By the 1950s, Jammû city's Muslim citizens included a few Balti Shias, an entire Gujjar neighbourhood and a small group known as Ahmadi or Qâdiyâni. The only original Muslim residents of the town who still live there are either those who were too poor to bother to migrate or those who fled to or were otherwise in Kashmîr and returned after things had cooled down, or those who lived in Ustad Mohallâ.

The pre-1947 Muslims of Jammû City say that the number of such 'original resident' families would be a few thousand, not more.

Col. Peer Muhammad's young son was one of those who spent a few weeks—three, in his case—in Pâkistân before deciding that they were better off in Jammû. He, and perhaps a thousand or so others, went back to Jammû after the violence was over.

Many Muslims, like Miâñ Abdul Rashîd, who was a superintendent of police, did it the other way around. Rashîd stayed on in Jammû during those turbulent years, only to migrate in 1961—after his retirement from the police.

The cleansing of rural Jammû was even more thorough. It was effected through the brutalisation of the Muslims in Chhamb, Dévâ Batâlâ, Mannawar and parts of Akhnoor. The Muslims accounted for 42.16% of the rural population of the district in 1931. This proportion had plummeted to 8.62% by 1961. The Muslims who stayed on lived mainly in the hills of the district. There were almost none left in the plains.

The above percentages for Jammû district, as well as those for Kathua (below), are based on simple arithmetic. They do not take into account the 1.06 lakh Hiñdu-Sikh refugees who fled from the occupied parts of the province to Jammû-Kathua. By counting this refugee population, we exaggerate the Hiñdu-Sikh percentage after 1948, wrongly deflate the proportion of Muslims who stayed behind and equally incorrectly inflate the percentage of the Muslims who left. It is very difficult to correctly calculate the percentage of Muslims who stayed behind in individual districts after that frenzy. However, it is possible to do so at the provincial level, which we will later in this chapter.

25.45 per cent of the people of Kathuâ district were Muslim in 1941. By 1961 the Muslims' share had dropped to 13.02 per cent. This means that 51.15 per cent of Kathuâ's Muslims felt more secure under the Indian tricolour. (As with the plains of Jammû, the entire Muslim population of the plains of Kathuâ migrated, In both districts the plains border Pâkistân. Also, in both districts, the Muslims of the hills, especially the mountains furthest from the Indo-Pâkistân border, stayed on. My theory is that inflamed Hiñdu-Sikh refugees from West Punjãb and occupied Kashmîr did not reach the hills. However, Muslims were killed in the Billâwar area.)

In the case of Udhampur, the Muslims' share actually rose from 33.17 per cent in 1941 to 33.87 per cent in 1961. And yet (i) I know for a fact that anti-Muslim violence in the Chenaini, Réâsî, Râmnagar and Udhampur towns led to some deaths—and some migration to the Valley of Kashmîr (and some to Pâkistân/ 'AJK'). Perhaps these numbers were not very large. Or (ii) maybe some Muslims migrated to rural Udhampur from the neighbouring villages of Jammû-Kathuâ or from the aforementioned towns of Udhampur.

Both points are supported by this comment in the 1961 census: '[The] proportions [of the Muslims in Udhampur district as a whole] have steadily increased though the increment during the two decades 1941-61 has been comparatively small... [In] the urban population...there has been a phenomenal fall during the two decades 1941-61.'[xlvi]

It is seen from census figures[xlvii] that in 1941 the Muslims' share in the urban population of Udhampur district was 22.52 per cent. This share fell to 4.95 per cent by 1961.

But since the Muslim population in Udhampur district as a whole rose during the same period, it means that in actual numbers the influx of Muslims into rural Udhampur was slightly bigger than their forced migration from the towns (Chenaini, Réâsî, Râmnagar and Udhampur proper).

The Muslims' share in the population of rural Udhampur rose from 33.75 per cent to 35.87 per cent in the same period. This increase does not look as dramatic as the decrease of Muslims in urban Udhampur.

This indicates that in the 1940s very few people lived in the towns of Udhampur compared to the villages. Therefore, while 78.02 per cent of the Muslims of Urban Udhampur felt compelled to leave (or were killed), the actual number involved was very small. It was the equivalent of less than 2.12 percentage points (or 5.92 per cent) of the rural Muslim population.

In Dodâ the increase in the Muslim population was much bigger: from 57.35 per cent in 1941 to 65.01 per cent in 1961. This is an increase of 11.8 per cent. Some of this was because the Hiñdu elite of Bhaderwâh (and some from Kishtwâr) shifted to Srînagar and Jammû towns. Perhaps some Muslims migrated from neighbouring Kathuâ to Dodâ district around 1947.

Comparisons are difficult in the case of Pooñch-Rajourî partly because of the influx of Hiñdu-Sikh refugees from 'AJK' to Pooñch town in particular, and partly because a substantial portion of this area is now under Pâkistânî occupation. (However, the task is not impossible. Village-wise figures are available and should be analysed by some scholar working for a PhD.)

The situation in the areas that later formed the Dodâ district: The present Dodâ district was part of Udhampur till 1948. The 1941 Muslim: Hiñdu ratio in the areas that later joined Dodâ was 57:42. This means that the Muslims were in the majority in some areas while the Hiñdus predominated in others. When communal violence began in one particular town and some villages—for the first time in their history and, except for that town, the only time so far—they followed the 20th century South Asian trend. The majority community bullied the hapless minority. However, most of Dodâ district stayed calm.

The Muslims of neighbouring Chambâ (HP), Dudû-Basañtgarh (Udhampur) and Lowâñg (Banni, Kathuâ) fled to Dodâ in November 1947 following disturbances in those areas. They returned to their villages in May 1948 when things cooled down.

The Hiñdus were at the receiving end of the violence in Bhalés and Khar Punéjâ—and many of them were killed.

In the Bhaderwâh-Râmban-Batote belt, which runs along River Chenâb, it was the other way around. Several Muslims died in Kelârh, Chakrabattî, Khâlû-Mânwâ and Marmat.

There was no migration from the district to Pâkistân or 'AJK'—except for stray individuals. However, there was considerable movement within and between tehsîls: with minorities temporarily shifting to places where their community dominated. The Muslims shifted from Râmban, the Hiñdus from Bânihâl.

Most of Dodâ district—except for the areas mentioned—was untouched by the poison that was injected during that era. The Muslim-majority Dodâ City-Sirâj belt was one such zone of peace. Much of the credit goes to the resolute leadership of the legendary Lassâ Wânî, a Muslim. This illiterate visionary ensured that relations between the two communities remained cordial and that there was no tension, leave alone riots. (He was later elected to the legislative assembly of the state.)

Kishtwâr town and almost all of Kishtwâr tehsîl were peaceful, with Hiñdu-Muslim amity continuing to be as warm as ever. However, six Muslims were killed in Pâdar and a few Hiñdus in Buñjwâñ.

Twelve people died in Bhaderwâh: almost evenly from the two communities. The town has several neighbourhoods. All twelve Bhaderwâhis were killed in areas where their community was outnumbered.

Mr Justice Muhammad Yûsuf Sarâf, who was the Chief Justice of the 'AJK' High Court, informs us that 'the Muslims of Bhaderwâh… could, with a few topîdâr [front loaded] rifles, home-made axes, spears and sticks, not only successfully defend themselves but also drive away a few thousand Hiñdus from the district and push them into Chambâ.'

Regarding the mystery of how the proportion of Muslims in Udhampur district increased in the 1961 census, despite the migration of many Udhampur Muslims to Kashmîr, Pâkistân and 'AJK,' Sheikh Abdul Rehmân, the eminent nationalist parliamentarian and socialist, says, 'There is a scarcity of land in Marmat and Râmban-Bânihâl [all in Dodâ]. It is said that in the 1950s some Muslims from these areas migrated to the Udhampur villages of Chenaini, Lâtî and Sudh Mahâdév.'

Muslim Migration: Summary and Conclusions

In Jammû district there were 1,70,789 Muslims in 1941 but only 51,847 in 1961. The latter number includes around 5,000 Muslims from other districts who migrated to the state's winter capital after 1947. Taking into account the historical annual growth in the Muslim population of Jammû, it can be assumed that in 1947 there would have been around 1,87,000 Muslims of whom at best 36,000 stayed behind in Jammû district. Or that Jammû district alone lost around 1,51,000 of its Muslim population.

45,214 Muslims lived in Kathuâ district in 1941. This number would have swelled to around 50,000 by 1947. In 1961 only 27,005 were left. So, one can assume that around 18,000 Muslims did not migrate. Or that around 32,000 Muslims left the district in 1947.

There is another way to calculate the depletion of the Muslim population. The Muslims were 37.36 per cent of Jammû district's population in 1941 and 10.03 per cent in 1961. Thus, the district lost 73.08 per cent of its Muslims in 1947. So, we can assume that around 51,000 Muslims did not migrate. According to this calculation around 1,36,000 Muslims fled or died in 1947.

Similarly, the Muslims were 25.45 per cent of Kathua district's population in 1941 and 13.02 per cent in 1961. Thus, the district lost 48.85 per cent of its Muslims in 1947. So, 24,425 Kathua's Muslims fled or died in 1947.

By this logic, Jammû and Kathua lost 1,60,425 of their Muslims to migration or death in 1947. However, if the number of Muslims who stayed behind in 1947 by this calculation is projected to 1961, according to the then prevailing rate of population growth, the figures do not match. Therefore, we have to assume the higher figure.

So, around 1,83,000 Muslims left Jammû-Kathuâ, mainly for Pâkistâni Punjãb, some for 'AJK,' a few thousand for Kashmîr and several thousand died (some of them due to epidemics).

Several Muslims migrated from Udhampur-Râmnagar-Réâsî, too, but their number seems to have been too small to show up in statistics. Besides, most of them went to Kashmîr. I would put their number at around 2,000 but won't add them to the 1.83 lakh figure because, as we have seen, the Muslim ratio in the new Udhampur district actually increased. The Muslims who fled because of the riots might well have relocated in villages within the district.

Hiñdu-Sikh Migration: Summary and Conclusions

The migration of Hiñdu-Sikhs from Pooñch-Mîrpur (i.e. from within the state) began quite early. According to Lamb, 60,000 Hindu-Sikhs had fled towards Jammû by 13 September.[xlviii]

In 1941 there were 63,576 Hindus and 12,111 Sikhs in Mîrpur district. By 1947 there would have been around 70,000 and 13,500 of them, respectively. All but 790 of them migrated in 1947, and the rest in the early 1950s.

7.55 per cent of Kotlî tehsîl was Hiñdu in 1941. 1.28 per cent of the population was Sikh. All of them fled.

In Muzaffarâbâd there were 5,846 Hiñdus and 12,922 Sikhs in 1941. There would have been around 21,000 of the twin communities put together in 1947. All of them left.

So, at least 1,06,000 Hiñdus and Sikhs migrated from the territories now in 'AJK.'

The calculations: A note of caution

As we have seen, at least 1,06,000 Hiñdu-Sikhs migrated from the territories now in 'AJK.' They settled mainly in Jammû and Kathuâ, which, in 1941, had a combined Hiñdu population of 3,80,096 (or 62.4%), and 9582 Sikhs. The two added up to 3,89,678. By 1947, the Hiñdus and Sikhs of these districts would have numbered more than 4.3 lakh.

With the arrival of 1.06 lakh Hiñdu-Sikh refugees from the occupied parts of the state (but not including those who came from Pâkistân), the Hiñdu-Sikh population jumped up by a quarter. (The Sikhs' share in the population of Jammû district almost tripled, from 2.45 per cent in 1941 to 6.34 per cent in 1961. In Kathua it increased more than fivefold from 0.24 per cent to 1.23 per cent during the same period.)

The inclusion of these refugees in the 1961 population of Hiñdus and Sikhs, thus, gives the impression that the share of the Muslims in the original population fell more drastically after 1947 than it actually did. Or that the Hiñdu-Sikh share rose higher than what really happened.

By 1961, the refugees would, through natural growth, have increased to around 1.4 lakh.

Therefore, we should deduct this figure from the 1961 population of the present Jammû province. In that case, the population of the districts of Jammû that remain under the Indian tricolour would have been 14.32 lakh in 1961. The proportion of Muslims who remained in the province as a whole is correctly 38.04%.

It is very difficult to subtract the Hiñdu-Sikh refugee population from the 1961 population of individual districts such as Jammû and Kathua, but it can safely be said that the extent of fall in the Muslims' share is much less than what simple arithmetic suggests.

Conclusions regarding the killings

What we can say for certain is that around 22,000 (perhaps minus 5,000) Muslims had definitely died in Jammû province in October-November, 1947, due to killing or epidemics.

The number could be five thousand lower than twenty two thousand because i) I have assumed that two thousand Muslims died in the pre-migration riots. This figure is certainly on the higher side. Besides, it could well have been counted twice in the above calculations. ii) At least two to five thousand Muslims from the Kâhnâ Chak-Sambâ belt crossed the border on the 14th August, 1947. I am certain that they were not among those whom the UNCIP saw in the two Siâlkot refugee camps in 1949.

On the other hand the number could be somewhat higher because i) my very rough estimate of the population in 1947 could be slightly wrong; ii) the 1961 Muslim population of Jammû included some non-Jammûites (Kashmîrîs as well as Muslims from Central India).

Two people whom I greatly respect—a Muslim whose patriotism and liberalism is legendary and an Englishman who has made every attempt to get to the truth—feel that the actual number was close to twenty thousand Muslims killed. Neither source is given to exaggerating the Muslims' woes: but in both cases theirs is a gut feeling and not a precise figure. In fairness to Yusuf Saraf, he only alleges that around twenty or thirty thousand Muslim civilians were killed in 1947 in Jammû province.[xlix] Though the tone of his writings reeks of prejudice and onesidedness, his lower figure is not very far from the truth.

After researching this issue for almost a year, I am of the opinion that given the wide margin of error in all such exercises, the number of Muslims killed in the riots and epidemics of 1947 was somewhere around seventeen thousand, but certainly under twenty-two thousand. The reason why I am prepared to accept such a wide margin is that no one has scanned village-level records and compared them with refugee records in the other country.

The number of Hiñdus and Sikhs killed was less than half that of the Muslims—i.e. it was between four and nine thousand. That's because the number of Hiñdu-Sikh refugees was in a 1:1.7 ratio with that of Muslim refugees, because Hiñdu-Sikh allegations of death at the hands of 'the other community' are roughly in a 1:2 ratio with similar Muslim exaggerations and also because that's what such evidence as we have—including neutral eyewitness accounts—suggests. (The Muslims were mainly killed near Jammû, a capital city, where relatively impartial observers such as journalists from outside the state were more likely to be present. The Hiñdus, on the other hand, were killed in remote places like Mîrpur and Sudh Nutti.)

The rule of thumb about the killings in Jammû-Kathuâ, observed by a very senior Indian Army officer who served there in 1947-49, is that the river bed that runs from Jammû to Akhnoor is the dividing line. This mostly dry river bed is better known in military circles as the 'chicken's neck.' The Hiñdus massacred Muslims to the east of this line, and the Muslims butchered a large number of Hiñdus to its west.

'Abducted' women

'Abducted' women from 'the other community' had to wait, some till 1949, before they could join their family and co-religionists across the cease-fire line (as the LoC was then called). Between 1948 and 1950, the dormitories of Jammû's Néhâ Ghar were filled with such women—whom their captors from 'AJK' and Pakistan had pushed back across the LoC, but whose families were hesitant to take them back, because they had been 'defiled.'

There must, doubtless, have been similar dormitories in Pâkistân and 'AJK,' where they would have lodged the 256 Muslim women and children (as well as 167 male Muslim refugees) who came over from Jammû city's Ustâd Mohallâ camp on 21 January 1949. The same day 140 non-Muslim women and children from Pâkistân's Dathyâl camp crossed over into India at the Siâlkot border post.

This thing about women abducted (and I am using the legally correct euphemism) by the 'other community' goes far beyond anecdotal evidence.[22] An Indian Army Major, whose unit pushed the tribal invaders back from the villages near Rajourî town, recounts that when his men and he reached the raiders' newly abandoned camp they found that the tribals had set up a harem with 160 abducted women.

In Chhamb village, the other community set up a harem of nineteen women in the house of Mehr Dîn Lohâr. The poor Lohâr had no option but to acquiesce. He was assured that his womenfolk would not be touched if he let the abductors use his house. (He did and they weren't.) At least one member of this harem recalls that she was under pressure to convert to the religion of the abductors. (From Y. Sarâf's article in Rad's book.)

Chaudhary Hamidullâh Khân's daughter was one abducted girl who was never heard of again. The two teenaged daughters of Atâ Muhammad of Mastgarh forced their father to kill them when bullets started flying past their house.

Other abducted women, too, committed suicide or were killed. Some were allowed to run back to their own menfolk shortly after the 'abduction.' Some, as the classic *Khâmosh Pânî* [2003] and the blockbuster *Veer Zaara* [2004] show, stayed on in the abductors' country. But, in 1949 alone, a few thousand such women crossed over into the country that the rest of their families had migrated to. An Army officer recalls a field near Rajourî town which was littered with female hair and the bodies of women and children. (Their menfolk had fled to the hills.)

As late as in April-May 1949, delegates from the ICRC found 151 Muslim women and children in a camp in Amritsar, 60 non-Muslim women and children in a similar camp in Lahore and 180 Muslim women

---

22 This author, for instance, has met two such women. I could not get myself to ask them about their experiences. So, liberal people from the abductors' community filled me in with the broad details about what some of their co-religionists had done to those women.

and children in Jammû. All of them were waiting to cross over into the other country. If there were that many 'abducted' women in January and May 1949, the number in 1947 must have been at least ten times greater.

Some abducted women realised that they were better off marrying the more decent of their abductors than returning to a life of disgrace in their own community.

Three years after her abduction, an affluent Pathân landlord from Udhampur heard that his wife was in Bombay. He waited outside the house where he had been told his wife now lived. He saw her in a car with a man and two little children. The gatekeeper of that house later informed the Pathân that the woman was the wife of the man who had been driving the car and those were their children. The Pathân decided to close that chapter of his life. This was around 1950 and he was still quite young. He got married again and started a new family.

In the mid 1970s, a woman from a prominent Syed family of Dalpatiâñ Mohallâ turned up at her ancestral home—after almost three decades. With her were her Sikh children, who had flowing beards by then.

Both incidents indicate that the abductors were not people from Jammû province but outsiders—almost certainly refugees from West Pâkistân.

The number of 'abducted' women was so large that an all-India effort went into their rehabilitation—and an elaborate administrative structure had to be created. Mridulâ Sârâbhâi, the daughter of an eminent technocrat-industrialist from Gujarât, a Kashmîr-lover and a close friend of the Sheikh Abdullâh family, oversaw much of this effort. Officers from the state were sent to Mahâtmâ Gâñdhî's hermitages at Sévâgrâm and Wârdhâ to receive training in rehabilitation.

Sheikh Abdullâh then appointed Mrs. Wâgéshwari Dhar as the 'Abducted Women Recovery Officer.' Her job was mainly to help women who had been abducted from India, taken to Pâkistân or 'AJK' and then pushed back into India. However, this courageous (and unprejudiced) lady raided the house of a Deputy Inspector General of Police (the second highest rank in the state police), who was a Kashmîrî Muslim. Mrs. Dhar recovered two Muslim girls, some members of whose families had been killed in those riots, from the DIG's house. The DIG had initially offered shelter to the girls but later refused to let them go.

The government set up a home for 'recovered women' and widows at Chenaini, a home for orphaned boys at Nishât (Srînagar) and a similar home for orphaned girls at Râj Bâgh (also Srînagar), a vocatiobnal training centre for boys in Kathuâ and sub-centres all along the border/ LoC, especially in Rajourî, Pooñch and Delînâ (Bârâmullâ). At Jammû's Néhâ Ghar, 'recovered women' were trained to become nurses and teachers. The government made efforts to get some of these young women married.

Begum Sheikh Abdullâh, who had only just given up the custom of staying behind the veil, led this effort. 'Mahârâni Târâ Devi attended some of these marriages personally and awarded a part of the dowry in each case from her own pocket,' Mr Justice Sarâf recalls.

The rehabilitation effort went on till at least 1963. Pâkistân would, doubtless, have launched a similar effort. However, after Sheikh Abdullâh was removed from office in 1953 (see the volume on 'Kashmîr'), Mridulâ Sârâbhâi fell out with his successor.

Jammû and Kashmîr was not the only state affected, leave alone being the main one. Things were much worse in undivided Punjãb, the NWFP, Sind and, to a lesser extent, Bengal. At the national level, the Government of India created the institution of the 'High Powered Officer for Recovery of Abducted Women and Children, India.'

This officer published a massive tome called *List of Non-Muslim Abducted Women and Children in Pâkistân and Pâkistân Side of the Ceasefire Line in Jammû and Kashmîr State*, New Delhi (1954). The book runs to more than 1,400 pages and lists almost 22,000 people—mostly women but also some children. About a third of the book relates to Jammû and Kashmîr. It gives the names of 2,614 women (and children) abducted from Mîrpur district, 1,655 from Muzaffarâbâd, 3,309 from Pooñch and 25 women (mostly Sikh) from Bârâmullâ.[l]

The issue is much like what the Chinese and Koreans call Japan's sex slaves, except that here there were offenders on both sides.

Roots pulled out

The people who fled left behind some very fine architecture—now being used by people who just don't fit in those elegant houses and caravan-sarais. (Religious shrines are another matter. If anyone in 'AJK' or Siâlkot happens to read these words, I would like to reassure them that in the plains of Jammû-Kathuâ, every Thursday evening Hiñdus and Sikhs light lamps at the graves of Muslim saints, and periodically place new, embroidered, green silk sheets on them. This is as true of grand shrines as of little-known, roofless graves.)

Secondly, the Government of Jammû and Kashmîr has temporarily allotted the 'evacuated' houses to others, and not given them away forever. The idea is that the evacuees' descendants might come back some day and claim their ancestral houses and forefathers' lands.

A reaction to events in the Punjãb?

Evans writes, 'The waves of violence, reprisal and counter-reprisal that emanated from the Punjâb spread north into the state of Kashmir. In November 1947, a series of pogroms took place against Jammû's Muslim population.'[li]

Catherine Rey-Schirr, has an identical take on that unfortunate era, 'With news of the killings in Punjâb, however, the strife spread to Jammû, a region in southern Kashmir with a preponderantly Hindu population,[23] where Muslims were massacred.'[lii]

Every Jammûite whom I have interviewed, Hiñdu as well as Muslim, agrees with Evans and Rey-Schirr.

The Hiñdus, however, maintain—and Evans finds these accounts plausible—that the butchery was carried out not by Jammû's Hiñdus and Sikhs but by those who fled West Punjãb (the part now in Pâkistân) because of the riots there, where they had been at the receiving end.

Some Pâkistâni websites, too, suggest this. One of them quotes Douglas Brown as having written in the *Daily Telegraph*, London (12 January, 1948), "Yet another element in the situation is provided by Sikh refugees from the West Punjâb who have seized Muslim lands in Jammû.... They originated the massacres there last October, to clear for themselves new Sikh territory to compensate for their losses in Pâkistân.'

There seems to be some truth to this because violence started in the Punjãb as early as in March 1947, but in Jammû mainly in November—after a tense, and somewhat brutal, October. Even Khalid Hasan concedes that 'After the June 3 [partition] Plan was announced, Hiñdu and Sikh refugees had started pouring into Jammû from areas that were going to become Pâkistân.'[liii]

The late Ashfâq Ahmed, a Muslim Federation leader from Jammû, always spoke of the *nazar kâ lihâz* (lit. 'regard for eye-contact') that has traditionally characterised Hiñdu-Muslim relations in Jammû—till the 1930s as well as today. This means that people want to be able to look friends from 'the other community' in the eye. Even if they hate 'the other community' as a whole they will never harm (or cheat) any individual with whom they have had a relationship of 'eye-contact.' Ashfâq would insist that it were anonymous Hiñdus and Sikhs from very distant places who killed or drove out the Muslims of Jammû-Kathuâ, and not people whom these Muslims knew personally.

And as we have seen, the ones who massacred Hiñdus and Sikhs in places like Mîrpur, Chiñgas and Rajourî were all unknown outsiders, and not local Muslims. The Hiñdu-Sikh gangs that looted foodgrains from the already impoverished rural Muslims of Pooñch were all refugees from Pakistan and what is now called 'AJK'—and not local Hiñdus and Sikhs.

---

23 Not correct. The Jammû region was overwhelmingly Muslim. (See the chapter 'The population of Jammû.') The Hiñdus predominated only in the Dogrâ belt of Jammû-Kathuâ-Udhampur.

In the case of women who were abducted and later set free, not one of them had been kidnapped by a local Hiñdu, Muslim or Sikh.

Mîr Pooñchi, too, seems to recall that the people who fled 'AJK' were responsible for some of the [retaliatory] killings in parts of Jammû province.

Hordes of Hiñdu and Sikh refugees from the Punjãb

Since most clues point to revenge-seeking Hiñdus and Sikhs from West Punjãb, how serious was that problem? Some records[liv] indicate that between March and September 1947, 8,00,000 to 10,00,000 Hiñdus and Sikhs and 3,00,000 to 4,00,000 *Muslims* from the Punjãb sought refuge in Jammû province. Yes, Punjãb's ethnic cleansing had started before the August 1947 partition of India. And the Punjãbî Muslim's faith in the people of Jammû was intact till as late as mid-1947.

The Mahârâjâ's administration sent the Muslims to West Punjâb and the Hiñdus and Sikhs to East Punjâb.

By early September it was no longer just Hiñdus and Sikhs from the Punjãb. Alistair Lamb records that 60,000 Hindus and Sikhs had fled Pooñch-Mîrpur (which were within the state) towards Jammû by the 13th September.

These people, who had fled the Punjãb (and, later, Pooñch-Mîrpur) because of 'the other community,' obviously poisoned the minds of their co-religionists in Jammû—and destroyed the innocence of that paradise. The first lot of Punjãbî refugees does not seem to have killed anyone in Jammû. The killings began in October. Either a fresh wave of refugees had entered Jammû or the old lot's arguments found a newly receptive local audience because of the Pâkistânî invasion and devastation of the state. It would seem that the Hiñdus and Sikhs of Jammû were more incensed by the September migrants from Pooñch-Mîrpur and neighbouring Siâlkot than by the earlier refugees from the Punjãb.

Even though the Hiñdus were in a majority in Jammû-Kathuâ-Udhampur, in October-November 1947 they, too, lived in fear—of being killed by people from what is now Pâkistân. They heaved a sigh of relief when the Mahârâjâ of Patiâlâ sent his mainly Sikh-Hiñdu forces to Jammû to help the Government of Jammû and Kashmîr—ostensibly to maintain the order. The Muslims of Jammû did not see the soldiers from Patiâlâ in quite the same way. These soldiers are 'alleged to have contributed to some of these communal incidents--or at least have stood back without intervening.'[lv]

Under pressure from India's Prime Minister Nehru, the Mahârâjâ of the state appointed Sheikh Muhammad Abdullâh the Head of the Emergency Administration of Jammu and Kashmir. This happened on the 30th October,

1947. According to a legend,[lvi] the Sheikh insisted that he would accept that post only after the forces of the princely states of Nabha and Patiala[24] were replaced by Indian Army units from Madras [Tamil Nadu]. The latter units were believed to be above sectarian considerations. (The legend is slightly off the mark because this replacement started taking place five or six days after the Sheikh assumed office.)

The first thing that the Government of India did—after the 5/6 November massacre of fleeing Muslims—was to send Dalîp Siñgh, a senior officer, to prepare a list with the name of every Muslim who boarded a bus for Pâkistân. These lists would be given to the Pâkistânî authorities at the border, who would certify whether every passenger on that list had reached Pâkistân safely. Thus was the killing of Pâkistân-bound refugees brought to an end.

'Ajmal' recalls, 'Two days later [i.e. from the 9th Nov. onwards], caravans from [the Jammû] Police Lines started reaching Siâlkot without being attacked. My grandparents and some other relatives reached Pâkistân on the 9th November 1947.'

*

In the year 2005 the Prime Minister of India, Dr Manmohan Siñgh, and the President of Pâkistân, Gen. Pervez Musharraf, took the first step towards undoing some of the damage. They agreed to let people travel once again on the Râwlâkote ('AJK')-Pooñch road—for the first time after the 1940s. In November 2005, people from Poonch and Rawlakote travelled across the LoC for the first time in several decades.

References

i Report on an IPS fellow's visit to Jammû: The Hard Realities of Jammû by Ershad Mahmud and published in *The News* (Pâkistân), July 25, 2001.

ii Sinha, Lt. Gen. SK, 'Jammû & Kashmîr: Past, Present and Future' (28 April 2005) Maj Gen. Samir Sinha Memorial Lecture, United Service Institution of India, New Delhi. Page 6.

iii Sinha, op. cit., p. 6.

---

24 'Ajmal' refers to them as the 'Indian army from Nabha and Patiala.' This explains the mystery why in countless Pâkistâni/ 'AJK' histories we are told that the 'Indian army' attacked the convoys travelling from Jammû to Pâkistân. There was no Indian Army on that route on the dates given (Oct.20 etc). The first Indian Army units reached the state on the 27th October—and they flew straight to Srînagar. They reached Jammû several days later, by when many of the alleged massacres were over.

iv Maini, K.D., 'A decision that changed the fate of Poonch,' *Daily Excelsior*.

v In the volume about 'Kashmîr' I had incorrectly given the date as 24 October.

vi Sinha, op. cit., p. 7.

vii From 'My Life In Kashmir' a series of articles posted on the Internet by a right-wing Jammû Muslim who later migrated to Pâkistân.

viii Rashid, Prof. A., Solving the Dispute, *Greater Kashmîr*, 10 and 11 September 2001.

ix Private conversation, the 18th March, 2005.

x Amin, Maj (Retd) Âghâ Humâyun. 'The war of lost opportunities.' From the internet.

xi Amin, Maj (Retd) Âghâ Humâyun. 'The war of lost opportunities.'

xii Amin, op. cit.,

xiii The time of that call, as well as the 27th October date, are both from an e-mail sent by Andrew Whitehead.

xiv From Amîn, op. cit.

xv Andrew Whitehead very kindly shared this insight with me by e-mail.

xvi Kishtwâri, Wali Mohd. Aseer, *Focus on Jammû and Kashmîr* (2003) Crescent House Publications, Jammû. Page 257.

xvii Amîn, op. cit.

xviii Rasal, Dr. Ravindra 'J & K's Accession to India: Betrayal by the Muslim Sub-Units of the J&K State Army' (2002-2003) Shivajinagar Nanded-431602 India. Email: ravi273@yahoo.com

xix Rasal, Dr. Ravindra 'J & K's Accession to India'

xx Khân, Major Sardar Shaukat Hayat, *The Nation that Lost Its Soul*, Jang Publishers-Lahore-1995. Cited by Maj. Amîn, op. cit.

xxi Rasal, Dr. Ravindra 'J & K's Accession to India'

xxii Amîn, op. cit.

xxiii From 'My Life In Kashmir' a series of articles posted on the Internet by a right-wing Jammû Muslim who later migrated to Pâkistân. His name is not clear but someone called Zack or ZA (Zakaria?) annotated them and posted them on the net. The author claims that his family was always pro-Pâkistân and used to finance the Muslim League. His father—probably called Ajmal—could have invented this retrospective Pâkistâni patriotism to curry favour with the country of his adoption, because there were very few (if any) such families in Jammû. Despite the anti-Hiñdu and anti-India bias of the articles, they contain useful material about the plight of the Muslims of Jammû during the tragedy of 1947.

xxiv Hasan, Khalid, 'Jammû 1947: gone but not forgotten,' *Friday Times*, Pâkistân. Reproduced in *The Kashmîr Times*, 29 May 2005.

xxv Kishtwâri, Wali Mohd. Aseer, *Focus on Jammû and Kashmîr* (2003) Crescent House Publications, Jammû. Page 256.

xxvi Maini, K.D., 'Rajourî Reclaimed,' *Daily Excelsior*, 15 April, 2001.

xxvii Rasal, Dr. Ravindra 'J & K's Accession to India.'

xxviii Gupta, CP, 'Mîrpur Carnage,' *Daily Excelsior*, 21 November, 2004.

xxix Kishtwâri, Wali Mohd. Aseer, op. cit., p. 256.

xxx Maini, K.D., 'Rajourî Reclaimed,' *Daily Excelsior*, 15 April, 2001, page 3, col.2.

xxxi Rasal, Dr. Ravindra 'J & K's Accession to India'

xxxii Maini, K.D., 'Rajourî Reclaimed,' Daily Excelsior, 15 April, 2001.

xxxiii Pathik, p.325.

xxxiv Rasal, Dr. Ravindra 'J & Ks Accession to India'

xxxv Reproduced in *The Kashmîr Times*, 29 May 2005.

xxxvi These two paragraphs are based on revenue records, which leave no one in doubt about the thorough ethnic cleansing that took place—in both directions.

xxxvii Evans, op. cit., quoting Tahir Amin, *Mass Resistance in Kashmir* (Islamabad: Institute of Policy Studies, 1995) p27

xxxviii These figures can be found on any of several websites on the Internet. In print, Evans, *Communal Violence in Jammû Division: 1947*, quoting Meraj-ud-Din, 'India too should shun rigidity' *Pâkistân Observer* (5 November 2004)

xxxix Evans, op. cit., quoting Yusuf Saraf, in Rehmatullah Rad and Khalid Hasan (eds.), *Memory Lane to Jammû* (Lahore: Sang-e-Meel Publications 2004) Ibid, p181

xl Mahmud, Ershad, 'Census in Kashmir - An Analysis,' *The Nation*, Pâkistân, Oct. 11, 2000

xli Terence Creagh Coen, *The Indian Political Service: a study in indirect rule*, London, 1971, pp. 138-9: the relevant excerpt was sent to me by Andrew Whitehead.

xlii UNCIP, Report of the Sub-Committee on Western Kashmir 31 March 1949. Ref: S/AC.12/WK/1. Annex 17: Memorandum by Brigadier Stevens on Refugee Problem p118-119. From the personal archives of Alexander Evans.

xliii Evans, op. cit., quoting the UNCIP, Report of the Sub-Committee on Western Kashmir 31 March 1949. Ref: S/AC.12/WK/1. p82

xliv Evans, op. cit., quoting the UNCIP, Report of the Sub-Committee on Western Kashmir 31 March 1949. Annex 20. Ref: S/AC.12/WK/1. p. 128-129.

xlv Rey-Schirr, Catherine, 'The ICRC's activities on the Indian subcontinent following partition (1947-1949)' *International Review of the Red Cross* (No 323) 30 June 1998.

xlvi Census of India, 1961, Vol. VI Jammû & Kashmîr, Part 1-A (iii), General Report; MH Kamili, Superintendent of Census Operations, page 240.

xlvii Census of India, 1961, Vol. VI, op. cit., p. 236.

xlviii Lamb, Alastair *Incomplete Partition*, Roxford 1997, p.123, extract posted on a Pâkistâni website.

xlix Evans citing Yusuf Saraf, *Kashmîrîs fight for freedom* (Vol II, 1947-1978) (Lahore: Ferozono Ltd, 1979) p. 841.

l Andrew Whitehead, Director, India, of the BBC World Service Trust, very kindly summarised that massive book and sent me this information.

li Yogendra Sikand, *Sacred Spaces: Exploring Traditions of Shared Faith in India* (Delhi: Penguin India 2003) p219, quoted by Evans.

lii '*Partition and the strife in Punjâb*,' by Catherine Rey-Schirr, a historical research officer at the ICRC, who assisted in the preparation of a history of the ICRC for the period 1945-1955.

liii Hasan, op. cit.

liv UNCIP, Letter from the Prime Minister, Jammû and Kashmir to the Chairman of the Economic and Political Mission, 14 September 1948. Ref: S/AC.12/66 p27, cited by Evans, 'Communal Violence In Jammû Division: 1947.'

lv Evans, op. cit.

lvi Recorded on 'AJK'/ Pâkistâni websites.

* * *

The So Called "Azad" Jammu and Kashmir (Pok)

15

A History of 'Azâd' Jammu and Kashmir[1]

After Pâkistân occupied Mîrpur, Muzaffarâbâd-'Neelum' valley and parts of Pooñch-Rajourî, it officially established the Government of 'Âzâd' ('free') Jammû and Kashmîr ('AJK') on the 4th October, 1947.

In theory, 'AJK' was a free land and not a part of Pâkistân. Quâid é Âzam Muhammad Ali Jinnâh, the founder of Pâkistân and an upright man, did not want Pâkistân to forcibly annex Jammû and Kashmîr. He wanted to leave the matter to the Kashmîrîs to decide. 'The [Indian government, led by the Congress] wanted the people of the [princely] states [of undivided India] to have the right of deciding their right while the Muslim League leadership [which ruled Pâkistân] wanted the rulers to have this right,' Mr. Amânullâh Khân of the Jammû and Kashmîr Liberation Front (JKLF) points out.[i]

Indeed, 'AJK' based Kashmîri nationalists like Habîb Kaifee, held this against Mr. Jinnâh. In 1984, Kaifee told a predominantly non-Kashmîri

1. The total area of Jammû and Kashmîr is 2,22,236 sq. km. Of this the Indian tricolour flies over 45.62 per cent. Pâkistân is in the illegal occupation of 35.15 per cent of the state. China has illegally occupied 37,555 sq. km. (16.9 per cent). Pâkistân has gifted 5,180 sq. km. (2.33 per cent of J&K) of the territory occupied by it in Shaksgam (Ladakh) to China.

   Pâkistân has divided POK (Pâkistân Occupied Kashmîr) into three broad entities: i)the so-called 'AJK' (which is mainly occupied Jammû plus the Muzaffarâbâd area/ Kishen Gañgâ valley of occupied Kashmîr); ii)the so-called Northern Areas (which initially consisted of 28,000 square *miles* in occupied Ladâkh-Gilgit: India later liberated some of this land), and iii)Shaksgam. People wrongly assume that 'AJK' and POK are synonyms. 'AJK' is only one part—and a very small part, at that (5134 square miles/ 13,297 square kilometers)—of POK. The quotation marks around the word Azâd and around the acronym AJK draw attention to the fact that 'AJK' is not an independent political entity but an occupied territory.

audience (i) that the Quâid was wrong when he decreed that the Mahârâjâ should decide the fate of the kingdom, and (ii) that non-Kashmîri Pâkistânis were wrong when they abused the hugely popular Sheikh Abdullah (because the Sheikh, like the Congress, wanted the people of Kashmîr to choose their own destiny). Kaifee asked the Pâkistâni establishment to 'take back' (i.e. renounce) both positions. (Mr Kaifee was the General Secretary of the Muslim Conference. He made this famous speech at the Writers' Guild.)

In practice, as we shall see later, 'AJK' is an occupied land, with none of the economic benefits enjoyed by the four states of Pakistan.

Mr. Anwar became the first 'President' of this region. His provisional presidency lasted twenty-one days (4 October 1947-24 October 1947).

Sardâr Ibrâhim the right man in the wrong camp

The Pâkistân Government then installed Sardâr Mohammad Ibrâhim Khân (b. 1915; d. 2003) of the Muslim Conference as the President of 'AJK.' Ibrâhim was rewarded for blocking his own party's move to pass a resolution asking for independence from Pâkistân. This divided the party.

In the mid-1940s Sardâr Ibrâhim had emerged as, what Ershad Mahmud calls, 'a consensus leader from Pooñch.' He studied law at London University and received his Bar-at-law from the Lincoln Inn.

The Sardâr was Anglicised and 'not a religious man. He spent his whole life in the Western way. Although, he enjoyed friendship and trust of the local clergy but their interpretation of religion-politics relationship remained an enigma for him. During his stay in England, the British lifestyle fascinated him exceedingly.'[ii] (As I plan to show in another book, mature, traditional, religious types like Mahatma Gandhi, Khân Abdul Ghaffâr Khân, Sheikh Abdullâh and the Déobañdi Muslims stood for a united, multi-religious India, while young, urban, educated and irreligious Hiñdu, Muslim and Sikh leaders have normally emphasised the separateness of their communities.)

In 1946, while still in his early thirties, the Sardâr became a member of the Mahârâjâ's J&K Assembly. The Muslim Conference made him its parliamentary leader shortly thereafter. When the emergence of a Muslim Pâkistân became a certainty, the Sardâr felt that the predominantly Muslim region should opt for Pâkistân.

Even though the Sardâr, like many other Westernised people, joined the 'two-nation theory' camp, his heart was in the right place. Mahmud writes, 'Contrary to other leaders of AJK, he was a true believer in cultural plurality of Jammû and Kashmîr State and quite often publicly regretted over the forced exodus of Hindus and Sikhs from the territory [Muzaffarâbâd, Mirpur and occupied Rajourî-Pooñch] in.,. 1947.'

Sardâr Ibrâhim Khân became the founder president of the 'Âzâd' Jammû and Kashmîr government 'when many veterans like Mirwaiz Yusuf Shâh had blatantly refused to head the interim set up.'[iii] He spoke for Pâkistân at the United Nations in 1948 when discussions on Kashmîr came up.

Within the leadership of the Muslim Conference (MC), the Sardâr had been fairly junior. Therefore, not everyone in his own party welcomed his elevation. The influential Mirwâiz Muhammad Yûsuf Shâh, for one, rejected this move. The Sardâr had the support of many powerful top-rung Pâkistânî civil servants. The Mirwâiz retracted a while later and agreed to serve under the Sardâr as a member of his cabinet. However, the top leader of the MC, Chaudhary Ghulâm Abbâs, then in a jail in Srînagar, remained unreconciled. This would lead to trouble later.

Chaudhary Ghulâm Abbâs reaches 'AJK': but is not amused

In February 1948, Sheikh Abdullâh, who was the Prime Minister of the Indian state of Jammû and Kashmîr, released Chaudhary Ghulâm Abbâs from jail, and allowed him to cross over into 'AJK.'

The Sheikh asked the Chaudhary to try to get the Pâkistân government to agree to tripartite talks between the leaders of India, Pâkistân and Kashmîr. Mr Jinnâh rejected the idea—perhaps because, like his Indian counterparts, he considered Kashmîr a bipartite issue with India alone. (Both countries follow this line partly because the Indian Independence Act, 1947, does not accept any third nation, province or state as a successor state to British India.)

Instead, an agreement was arrived at between the Pâkistân Government and the MC on April 28, 1949. M.A. Gurmani, Minister without Portfolio, signed on behalf of the Government of Pâkistân. Sardâr Mohammad Ibrâhim, 'President', signed for 'Âzâd' Jammû and Kashmîr and Chaudhary Ghulam Abbas for the All-J&K MC, of which he was the President. Under this accord the MC is required to look after Pâkistân's interests not only in the Pâkistân-occupied territory but also in the part actually administered by India.

This came to be known as the Karachi Agreement. It gave Pâkistân temporary administrative control over the occupied territories.

Worse, it hived Gilgit-Baltistân (which Pâkistân calls the 'Northern Areas') off from 'Âzâd' Jammû and Kashmîr and gave Pâkistân direct control over this huge region. This cynical decimation of its territory is the biggest trauma that 'AJK' has suffered in its entire existence.

Neither of the 'Kashmîrî' signatories was from Gilgit-Baltistân (or even from the Valley of Kashmîr). Two Jammûites, thus, bartered away the destinies of the people of Gilgit-Baltistân, whose representatives were not consulted. However, in fairness, Sardâr Ibrâhim and Chaudhary Abbas had specified that what they were ceding to Pâkistân was only for a while.

Now that the Chaudhary had crossed over to 'AJK,' he was, naturally, offended to find his junior, Sardâr Ibrâhim Khân, presuming to be the President of the occupied region. He started persuading Mr Liaquat Alî Khân the leader of Pâkistân (who was later assassinated in 1951), to remove Sardâr Ibrâhim from the highest office in 'AJK.'

At the time 'AJK' was governed by Rules of Business—a substitute of sorts for a constitution. These laid down that the President of 'AJK' could hold his office only during the pleasure of the General Council of the Muslim Conference. Ch. Ghulam Abbas was the President of the MC. Mr. Abbas used the power that the Rules gave him to remove Sardâr Ibrâhim from his post. (The Sardâr's first stint lasted from 24 October 1947 to 30 May 1950.)

Ibrâhim retaliated 'by threatening to form a parallel Government.'[iv] His supporters took to the streets and, as we shall see, a very bloody confrontation with Pâkistân followed. It is generally believed in 'AJK' that the Government of Pâkistân got these two stalwarts to fight each other, so that Pâkistân had an excuse to intervene in the dispute and annex 'AJK' in the process. Even if this conspiracy theory is wrong, the fact is that the Pâkistâni establishment preferred Ibrâhim at that point of time.

The Sûdhans' revolt, martial law and direct control by Pâkistân

The Sûdhans—and, at one remove, all Pooñchîs—have a long martial tradition.[2] They revolted against the Lahore-based empire twice—in the 1830s and in 1847. More than 20,000 Pooñchîs served in the Indian Army in World War I. The number tripled during World War II. These British army veterans were as pro-Pâkistân in the early years (1947-1950) as some of their descendants have been angry with that nation ever since.[3]

2. I don't believe that there is any 'race' that is genetically martial. However, communities with long histories of taking part in warfare—the Gurkhâs, for instance—become martial. The Kashmîrîs, on the other hand, were de-martialised by the Mughals between 1586 and 1589. Four hundred years of non-participation in wars—and not some genetic defect—made them a 'non-martial' people.

3. What a see-saw sub-continental loyalties have been since 1947. The Muhâjirs—Muslim immigrants from Central India—were the ones who, since the late 1930s, had been asking for a Muslim Pâkistân to be carved out of British India. Punjâb, Siñdh and Balochistân were indifferent to the idea, while the NWFP (Frontier Province) opposed it vehemently. By 1990, it was the other way around. The Muhâjirs wanted independence from Pâkistân. The Punjâbis were left to defend the idea—and integrity—of Pâkistân.

Things went wrong in 1950 when Sardâr Ibrâhim who was a Pooñchî, was dismissed. The Sûdhans rose in armed revolt. Pâkistâni forces opened fire on the Sûdhan-led agitators. Some Sûdhans died. This incensed the community further. Pâkistân imposed martial law on 'AJK' in order to control the situation. (According to Evans, 'In 1954 there was, unrest following the removal of a Sudhan politician from power.'[v])

In March 1950, the Pâkistân Army rushed its 160 Brigade 'to deal with Sardâr Ibrâhim, who had a large following among the local Sûdhan tribes.' Pâkistân's 25 Brigade replaced it in July. In turn, the 100 Brigade took over in September. (The quote and the dates are from 'Pâkistân Army—War 1965' a semi-official but fairly honest Pâkistâni military history. It will thus be seen that the Army was sent in a good two months before—and obviously in preparation of—Sardâr Ibrâhim's dismissal.)

The Army decided that the best way to crush this brave martial community was to humiliate it. Soldiers went from house to house—entering bedrooms and ladies' chambers—to flush the Sûdhan warriors out.

Things were so sordid that it is said that most Sûdhans born during that fateful year deny having been born during that period when soldiers were stomping through their parents' homes. They claim instead to have been born a year before or after, lest others cast aspersions on their paternity.

After defeating the Sûdhan warriors militarily, the Army singled out all the main fighters, tied them to trees, and made them bark like dogs and salute shoes. (Sardâr Qaiyûm hints at this in his book *Muqaddamâ é Kashmîr* [The Kashmîr Trial].)

Then the media started demonising the Sûdhans.

Since the 20th century one of the worst insults for a Muslim is to be called a Jew. However, it was not always so. There have, since olden times, been vague suggestions that the Muslim Sûdhans might be of Jewish origin. (The most plausible theory is that the Sûdhans have descended from the Sadozai tribe of Durrânî Afghâns and that they migrated to Jammû province in the 1700s and early 1800s.)

Ziñdagi, a leading publication, carried an article entitled '*Âzâd Kashmîr meiñ Israel âbâd.*' ('The Israel within Âzâd Kashmîr.') It implied that the Sûdhans' loyalties were with Israel—the perceived enemy no.1 of all Muslims—and not with Pâkistân or fellow Muslims.

This outraged the Sûdhans. Some people beat up the editor of Ziñdagi.

All this resulted in the secession of the Sûdhans from 'AJK.' They set up a parallel government, which was crushed through police action in 1954.

Because of the Sûdhans' numbers, as well as their tradition of having been rulers and leaders, the Râjpûts and they have held most of the important political positions in 'AJK.' However, few Sûdhans have forgotten the shame that their ancestors had to suffer.

The Pâkistân Army, which calls the shots in 'AJK,' as in Pâkistân itself, generally prefers Muslim Conference leaders who advocate Kashmîr's accession to Pâkistân over those who want 'AJK' (or J&K as a whole) to be an independent country.

In any case, it was then that Pâkistân brought 'AJK' under its direct control. With the two top leaders of the MC squabbling, Sardâr Abdul Qaiyûm took over the leadership of the party. Since then the MC has broken up 'a number of times but the main faction always remained identified with Qaiyûm.'[vi]

Rapid turnover of 'Presidents'

Being an old-world type of South Asian leader, Chaudhary Abbâs thought it beneath himself to move into an office that his junior had held. So, he got a protégé from Mîrpur, Sayyed Alî Ahmed Shâh, an army veteran, installed as President (30th May 1950 to the 2nd December 1951). Abbâs gave himself a designation that was higher still: Supreme Head. (Chaudhary Abbâs was the 'Supreme Head' of 'AJK' from the 8th January 1951 till almost the end of the year.)

This irked Mirwâiz Muhammad Yûsuf Shâh. He parted ways with both the government and the Muslim Conference. Other members of the MC (by now renamed the AJKMC) were equally unhappy with the Chaudhary. They persuaded the Government of Pâkistân to sack him, abolish the post of Supreme Head and make the Mirwâiz the head of 'AJK.'

The Mirwâiz lasted less than half a year (2 December 1951-18 May 1952). He rubbed a powerful Pâkistânî civil servant the wrong way. This cost him his job. (His designation had been 'acting Administrator' rather than 'President.') The fact that the Mirwâiz was from the Valley of Kashmîr—and was not a native of the areas occupied by Pâkistân—went against him. He knew no English. Officers of the federal government, by then based in Râwalpiñdî, made him sign some papers, which he thought were the budget of 'AJK.' They were, instead, his resignation.

Râjâ Mohammad Haidar Khân (18 May 1952-21 June 1952) was the 'President' for a month or so. Col. Shér Muhammad (or Ahmad) Khân, another army veteran, was the next President (21 June 1952-30 May 1956). However, he wasn't Chaudhary Ghulâm Abbâs' man. Abbâs persuaded the then Prime Minister of Pâkistân, Chaudhary Muhammad Alî (1955-Sept 1956), to sack the colonel and replace him with Sardâr Qaiyûm instead.

However, the Mirwâiz had another stint as the 'acting Administrator' for a few months (30 May 1956-8 September 1956) before Sardâr Abdul Qaiyûm Khân (born circa 1924) of the AJK Muslim Conference could become the President (8 September 1956-13 April 1957) for a brief while.

The next Prime Minister of Pâkistân, Hussain Shaheed Suharwardy, was not happy with his predecessor's choice. He changed the 'AJK' leadership. Sardâr Mohammad Ibrâhim Khân had his second innings as President from the 13th April 1957 to the 27th April 1959.

Every subsequent change of regime in Pâkistân has seen the 'President' (and, later, Prime Minister) of 'AJK' being replaced. The top official in 'AJK' has, thus, often been an appointee of the Government of Pâkistân, rather than an elected representative of the people of 'AJK.'

Meanwhile, Field Marshal Ayûb Khân took over the Government of Pâkistân, first as its Chief Martial Law Administrator (1958) and twenty-one days later as the self-appointed President of Pâkistân. Naturally, he wanted his own men to head 'AJK.' (In all, Ayûb ruled from 1958 to March 1969.)

Mr Khurshîd Hassan Khurshîd (b. 1916) became the next President of 'AJK' (1 May 1959-7 August 1964).

Abdul Hamîd Khân was the President of 'AJK' from the 7th August 1964 to the 7th October 1969. Abdul Rahmân Khân followed, as an interim President (7 October 1969-30 October 1970).

By now 'AJK' had run out of potential leaders. So, a game of musical chairs began. The military leader of Pâkistân[4] brought Sardâr Qaiyûm of the AJKMC back (30 October 1970-16 April 1975)

Shaykh Mansûr Mas'ûd was the interim President of 'AJK' for a few months (16 April 1975-5 June 1975).

Then, Pâkistân's Prime Minister, Zulfiqâr Alî Bhutto (1971-77, including a stint as President), brought Sardâr Muhammad Ibrâhim back as the President of 'AJK.' (5 June 1975 -30 October 1978), this being the Sardâr's third tenure.

Elected governments—at last (and for brief spells at that)

In June 1975, almost twenty-eight years after its occupation by Pâkistân, 'AJK' had its first elections. Abdul Hamîd Khân (June 1975-August 1977) became its first Prime Minister. Abdul Rahmân Khân (August 1977-Oct 1978) followed, as an acting PM.

While Mr Zulfiqâr Ali Bhutto was Prime Minister of Pâkistân, his People's Party of Pâkistân (PPP) became quite popular in 'AJK' (as well

4. Gen. Yâhyâ Khân, one would assume. However, at least one history of 'AJK' insists that it was Ayûb. The problem with that version is that Ayûb had left by then—with his power and popularity both at their lowest.

as in the so-called Northern Areas). Ever since, the polity of 'AJK' has revolved around a two-party system: during those short spells when Pâkistân is not under a military government. The contest, in other words, has generally been between Sardâr Sikañder (b. 1932?) on the one hand and his estranged colleague Sardâr Abdul Qaiyûm Khân and Qaiyûm's son Sardâr Atîq Khân, on the other.

However, this experiment with democracy was not to last.

Gen. Ziâ ul Haq (1977-88) sacked Mr. Bhutto in a military coup and appointed Brig. Muhammad Hayât Khân (30 October 1978-1 February 1983) the President of 'AJK.' In October 1978, Ziâ also abolished the newborn institution of Prime Minister—which remained in abeyance till May 1985.

The 'AJK' Presidency saw a change on the 1st February 1983, when Abdul Rahmân Khân was brought back for the second time. He held that office till 1985.

In 1985 Sardâr Abdul Qaiyûm Khân of the AJKMC was back as President for the third time. He stayed on that post till the 11th July 1991. However, he now had a Prime Minister as well: Sardâr Sikañder Hayât Khân, also of the AJKMC (May 1985-July 1990).

Sardâr Abdul Qaiyûm is a Dhoñd Abbâsi from Pooñch. At the time he believed that 'AJK' should join Pâkistân. His views were so unpopular in places like Dadiâl that the audience at his 1985 election rally started hooting him with venom. A huge contingent of the army had to be called in to protect him and whisk him away from the rally. (His politics, as we shall see, have changed somewhat since.)

'AJK' and the question of nationhood

The High Court of 'Âzâd' Jammû and Kashmîr has delivered a landmark verdict in which it has asked Pâkistân to transfer the control and administration of the 'Northern Areas' to the Government of 'AJK.'

At other times the honourable court has questioned the right of governments and rulers in Pâkistân to legislate on behalf of 'AJK.' For instance, in the mid-1990s it held that the Extradition (Fugitive Offenders) Act was null and void. The said Act had been promulgated by Gen. Ziâ ul Haq, who was the military dictator of Pâkistân in the 1980s.

The 'AJK' High Court held that only the legislature of 'AJK' had the power to enact such legislation. Therefore, no matter what the Act said, no citizen of 'AJK' could be handed over to the Pâkistânî police.[vii]

In theory, Sardâr Sikañder stands for the 'liberation' of the state. However, the thrust of his politics suggests that he does not plan to change the status quo. Sardâr Atîque's[5] position is similarly ambivalent.

5. The name is spelt Atîque as well as Atîq by the Pâkistânî press, often in the same news report. The latter seems the preferred spelling.

That of the pro-independence JKLF, led by Mr Amanullah Khân, is not. It refuses to accept the Pâkistân Constitution or affirm on oath that 'Kashmîr will become [a part of] Pâkistân' (*Kashmîr baneygâ Pâkistân*). As a result, JKLF is prevented from contesting elections. Therefore, writes Khaled Ahmed, 'the JKLF has not been able to show its strength in the Âzâd Kashmîr Assembly. In 1992, it attempted a mass crossing of the Line of Control in protest against India, which demonstrated its popularity in the region.'[viii]

The *Daily Excelsior,* Jammu, comments, 'This resistance [on the part of the JKLF] is daring considering that the chances of their oppression are high in a society that has been made inaccessible for the international media.'[ix]

Because the JKLF does not contest elections, it can afford to be so bold. Ruling party politicians can not. Section 56 of the 1974 provisional constitution of 'AJK' 'authorises Islâmâbâd to sack any government in Muzaffarâbâd if it is a threat to Pâkistân's stand on Kashmîr. Islâmâbâd uses this constitutional provision as a sword of Damocles over the head of rulers of ['AJK'] to keep them under control,'[x]

Prime Minister Mumtâz Rathore of the PPP was one victim of this provision, in 1991. But, three years later, when his party was in power in Islâmâbâd but not in 'AJK,' his followers (and those of the then 'AJK' President Sardâr Sikañder) started pressurising Islâmâbâd to use the same power to dismiss the MC government headed by Qaiyûm. Unfortunately, Rathore justified the need to dismiss Qaiyûm thus: 'Sardâr Qaiyûm [is] taking steps which [a]re detrimental to Pâkistân's foreign policy relating to Kashmîr.'[xi]

AJK's elected representatives live under the constant threat of being sacked by Islâmâbâd. That Qaiyûm's party, the MC, held 40 of the 48 seats in the Legislative Assembly of 1991 was of no help once the government in Islâmâbâd changed and the PPP came to power there.

Every PPP leader of 'AJK' (notably Rathore, Sardâr Akhtar Rabânî and Sardâr Sikañder, as well as the federal minister Sher Afghan) kept Qaiyûm on tenterhooks by threatening to use the dreaded Section 56 against him. Therefore, people like Qaiyûm have raised private militias (called Al Mujâhid in his case), ostensibly to wrest Kashmîr from India but actually to protect themselves against Islâmâbâd.

Party bosses in Islâmâbâd treat with the same disdain whoever heads the 'AJK' unit of their party. Mrs Bénazîr Bhutto certainly did. After Barrister Sultân Mahmood merged his Liberation League with the PPP, she started trying to oust Rathore from the helm of her party in 'AJK.' Fortunately for him (but unfortunately for democracy and the dignity of political leadership) Pâkistân's dreaded Inter-Service Intelligence (ISI) was allergic to the barrister.

It is the same ISI that had held Sardâr Qaiyûm aloft for almost fifty years. He later drew close to Mr Nawâz Sharîf of the Pâkistân Muslim League, but survived in the 1990s mainly because of ISI's support. No wonder he needed an Al Mujâhid to ensure some degree of independence vis a vis the government and party bosses in Islâmâbâd.

When he found that neither a majority in the legislature nor friends in the ISI nor even a private army of *mujâhids* ('holy warriors') were helping in the war of nerves that the PPP—then in power in Islâmâbâd—was playing with him, Qaiyûm threatened to 'set on fire' all of 'AJK' in case his government was removed through the dreaded Section 56.[xii]

It worked. He was allowed to complete his five-year term in office.

Other irritants with Pâkistân

The people and politicians of 'AJK' have from time to time demanded that Pâkistân give 'AJK' a share in the income generated by the Mañglâ Dam. For instance, in 1994, Sardâr Abdul Qaiyûm Khân of the AJKMC, who was the Prime Minister of 'AJK' at the time, did this. Pâkistân ignored his plea.

Pâkistân has also always glossed over AJK's repeated insistence that, as a successor to the Dogrâ government, 'AJK' is the inheritor of all properties owned by the erstwhile princely state in what is now Pâkistân. (In India, Jammû and Kashmîr inherited all state properties in Delhi and Bombay—including the Mahârâjâ's palace in which I lived when I wrote much of this book).

The Dogrâ government owned properties worth 'billions of rupees in Lahore, Râwalpiñdî, Karâchî, Quetta, Péshâwar and Sheikhupurâ. [In Lahore its assets included] Governor's House, Chamber House, Pooñch House, Landa Bazâr and Harbañspur.'[xiii] These properties, Sardâr Atîque Ahmad reminded his people, should yield an annual income of crores of rupees. None of those revenues have ever reached 'AJK.'

The Kâlâbâgh and Bhasha Dams are issues about which 'AJK' is as concerned as are the Pâkistânî states of Sindh, Balochistân and NWFP. The status of those parts of occupied Kashmîr which Pâkistân calls 'the Northern Areas' bothers the people of 'AJK' as much as their own place under Pâkistânî occupation. As pointed out elsewhere in this book, the people of Mîrpur have emotionally seceded from Pâkistân. The Sûdhans, too, have had to be controlled, at times, through the imposition of martial law.

The Mañglâ Dam and the exodus of the bitter Mîrpurîs

The Mañglâ Dam was inaugurated in 1967, near Mîrpur. About 250 villages were submerged in the reservoir created by the Dam. This provoked the Mîrpurîs, who already had one foot in Britain, and the people of Kotlî to migrate en masse. Around half a million (five lakh) people from 'AJK'—mostly from Mîrpur and Kotlî—now live in Yorkshire, Luton, Bradford and Birmingham in the UK. Some of them return to their native land for extended periods. Evans estimates that more than ten thousand British passport holders can be found in the Mîrpur area on any given day.[xiv]

The British authorities clubbed the new immigrants with the general Pâkistâni-Punjâbi population. For a people who had been driven out of Pâkistân because of the Punjâb-centric Mañglâ Dam, this was extremely offensive. It was also unprofitable. Some British government resources and jobs (e.g. as translators) could be earmarked specifically for the Mîrpurîs if they were classified as a non-Pâkistâni community. Besides, this would give them separate representation on the boards of hospitals.

The Mîrpurîs were also fed up of being 'racially stereotyped [by the Pâkistânis] as uneducated hill-people with little culture.'[xv] If they continued to be classified as Pâkistânîs, they would keep languishing as a subaltern group within the overall Pâkistâni community in Britain. By getting a separate identity they could meet the Pâkistânis as equals in the community of British South Asians.

Because Mîrpur was a part of Jammû and Kashmîr—a state that is sometimes called 'Kashmîr' for short—the Mîrpurîs have taken to calling themselves 'Kashmîrîs.' As Evans points out, 'being Kashmîrî has more status than being Mîrpurî.'[xvi]

Shabîr Choudhry of the Jammû and Kashmîr Liberation Front explains it thus, '[W]e would like to be called Kashmîrîs rather than Mîrpurîs, a term used rather cynically [pejoratively] by Pâkistânîs to insult the people of Mîrpur.'[xvii]

The Mîrpurîs of Britain have kept up their links with their relatives back home. So, their insistence that they are not Pâkistânis is increasingly getting echoed in Mîrpur itself.

In 1999, 41 British MPs (Members of Parliament) supported a motion in the Commons, urging 'the Office for National Statistics to revise the ethnicity category for the 2001 census and include Kashmîrî as a distinct ethnic group.'

There are around three hundred families from the Valley of Kashmîr in Britain. Strictly speaking, only they qualify to be called Kashmîrî. Evans reports that these 'Valley Kashmîrîs' treat 'Mîrpurîs with much the same condescension as their Punjâbi counterparts.' They insist that "they are Kashmîrîs—and Mîrpurîs are 'nouveau Kashmîrîs.'"[xviii]

The marginalisation of migrants from Kashmîr

There was no mass migration from the Valley of Kashmîr to 'AJK' or Pâkistân in 1947. Indeed, the only Muslims who fled India in large groups that year were from East Punjab-Jammû and some parts of Bihâr. However, in October 1947 several thousand Valley Kashmîris found themselves stranded in the areas now called 'AJK,' when Pâkistân occupied that region. They stayed on.

Migration from Uttar Pradésh, the Central Provinces (Madhya Pradésh), much of Bihâr and the Valley of Kashmîr occurred in the form of individual families between 1950 and 1969. These later migrants were better educated than the ones who had fled en masse in 1947. Muslim migrants from Central India to Pâkistân (but not from J&K or East or South India) are called Muhâjirs.

In the 1950s and '60s, the Muhâjirs came to have a disproportionate presence in the civil services and professions of Pâkistân. Migrants from Kashmîr enjoyed a similar position in 'AJK.'

The first few Chief Justices of 'AJK' were all migrants from Kashmîr: Khwâjâ Muhammad Yûsuf Sarâf of Bârâmullâ, Khwâjâ Mañzoor Gîlânî, Khwâjâ Saeed (who went on to become the Chief Justice of Pâkistân) and, later, Khwâjâ Sharief (a Pahârhî).

Indeed, Valley Kashmîris—from Mîrwâiz Muhammad Yûsuf Shâh to Hamîd Mumtâz—made a huge contribution to the educational system, and distinguished officers like Ghulâm Ahmed Pañdit to the civil services of 'AJK' during its first two decades.

An anti-Valley Kashmîri backlash began in 'AJK' between 1969 and 1972. (It was the same period when anti-Muhâjir feelings started brewing in Pâkistân.)

This became evident when Sardâr Qaiyûm published a work, the title of which means 'The seven lakh spies [in 'AJK' and Pâkistân].' He estimated the number of migrants from the J&K areas still under the Indian flag at seven lakh [seven hundred thousand]: a figure that was a wild exaggeration. He suggested that all migrants from Kashmîr were disloyal to 'AJK' and Pâkistân and that India need not send any spies over because it already had a huge fifth column there.

The persecution of Valley Kashmîris had begun much before, as early as in 1952, when Mîrwâiz Muhammad Yûsuf Shâh was tricked into resigning.

At any given moment there can be only one Mîrwâiz of Srînagar. Yûsuf Shâh and, after him, his son Mîrwâiz Ahmed, claimed this position: which has the hereditary loyalty of lakhs of followers—and their considerable tithes.

When followers from Srînagar visited Mîrwâiz Yûsuf Shâh in 'AJK' they were horrified to see the straitened circumstances that their spiritual leader was living in. They asked him to return to Srînagar rather than live in ignominy.

Yûsuf Shâh's brother, Mîrwâiz Noor ud Dîn, wrote to the Indian Prime Minister, Pt. Nehru, asking him to allow his brother and him to return to India. It is said that this request set off alarm bells in certain circles in Srînagar, which feared a loss of their position in case Yûsuf Shâh and Noor ud Dîn were to come back to Srînagar.

These circles were extremely close to the rulers in New Delhi—never mind their public posture. They prevailed upon the government not to let Yûsuf Shâh and Noor ud Dîn come back. (Mîrwâiz Ahmed later shifted to Asgharmâl, near Râwalpiñdî in Pâkistân.)

Khwâjâ Sanâullâh Bhat—one of the most incorruptible, insightful and intellectually honest journalists India has produced—was the other Valley Kashmîri hounded out in the 1950s. This fearless young man was the editor of the weekly 'Kashîr.' His articles did not find favour with Sardâr Abdul Qaiyûm. So, Sanâullâh was deported from 'AJK' and pushed into the Valley of Kashmîr, even though under the laws of 'AJK' this could not have been done. (Logically, this incident would have occurred in 1956 when Mîrwâiz Yûsuf Shâh was removed from power for the second time and Sardâr Abdul Qaiyûm took over from him. However, according to my source it happened in 1952.)

Khwâjâ Sanâullâh went on to found the 'Daily Âftâb,' which became Srînagar's biggest selling newspaper. He stuck to his principles—and the truth—even during the violent 1990s when militants attacked his office more than once and threatened his life.

Mr. K.H. Khurshîd, an ethnic Kashmîri from Jammû, was an extremely close aide and associate of the Quâid é Âzam. Such is the respect for Mr. Jinnâh in Pâkistân that even his barber is treated with deference. But this regard was denied to Mr. Khurshîd, because of the community that he belonged to.

Mr. Justice Khwâjâ Muhammad Yûsuf Sarâf distinguished himself as a historian by writing *Kashmîrîs fight for freedom*, a two-volume history of the Kashmîris' struggle for freedom from monarchy. It is a meticulously detailed book, though—obviously because of the horrors that Mr Sarâf witnessed and experienced in 1947—very one-sided. Mr Sarâf was a votary of Kashmîriyat (Kashmîriness). He would trace out members of the (Valley) Kashmîri diaspora, no matter which part of the world they had migrated to. His book records the contributions of and sacrifices—regardless of their size—made by every individual Kashmîri to the movement. And he has written very kind things about the hero of that struggle, Sheikh Muhammad Abdullâh.

This did not go down well with communities other than Valley Kashmîris. The rulers of Pâkistân and 'AJK' loathe Sheikh Abdullâh. They consider him an Uncle Tom for his Indianness. Sardâr Abdul Qaiyûm got the book removed from all libraries. Apparently, it was made sure that Mr. Sarâf did not receive his royalties either.

Worse was to come. A Sûdhan judge found Mr. Sarâf—who had by then retired and was practising as a lawyer—guilty of contempt of court, and sentenced him to a prison term. The judge curtly asked Mr. Sarâf, 'Do you think you are still the Chief Justice (of this court)?' Mr. Sarâf's sin was that he did not approve of AJK's annexation by Pâkistân and favoured independence.

(Under Article 257 of the Constitution of Pâkistân, if the people of Jammû and Kashmîr ever decide to formally accede to Pâkistân, they will determine the terms of that accession. Till then their relationship with Pâkistân is conditional.)

There is also an unwritten rule that Valley Kashmîris are not to be recruited to the AK ('Âzâd' Kashmîr) forces. As a result, Bhats from the Valley have started calling themselves Bhatti—a 'martial' community native to the region—in order to join the armed forces.

In 1975, Mr. Mumtâz Rathore moved a resolution in the legislative assembly, because of which all senior Valley Kashmîris in the civil services were forcibly 'retired' from government service. 'Sons of the soil' replaced these refugees from the Valley.

The Pâkistân Prime Minister, Mr. Nawâz Sharîf, himself of Kashmîri ancestry, tried to set things right. He appointed Khwâjâ Sharief as the Advocate General and, later, as a judge of the High Court. However, the 'sons of the soil' started a campaign against Mr. Nawâz Sharîf, accusing him of being Kashmîri-*parast* ('a worshipper of the Kashmîris.') It did not help Mr. Nawâz Sharîf that his *peer* (spiritual guide) also happened to be a Valley Kashmîri.

Not that migrants from Jammû City were treated much better. (Now we are talking of Pâkistân rather than 'AJK.') On the one hand, some of them rose to high positions in Pâkistân—a few Âfrîdîs from Jammû even took active part in Pâkistân's frequent military coups. This made them objects of envy—and suspicion.

The family of Air Marshal Asghar Khân—the de facto head of the Jammû Âfrîdî clan in Pâkistân—is the best example of both phenomena: high positions and persecution.

The Air Marshal won a formidable reputation for his uprightness. During his tenure as the air chief, the Pâkistân Air Force purchased a large number of aeroplanes from the USA. The manufacturer of the aeroplanes gave the Air Marshal kickbacks at the usual rate. Asghar Khân bought an aeroplane with that money and added it to the Pâkistâni fleet.

Some people felt threatened by the popularity that Asghar Khân had begun to enjoy with the common man.

Prime Minister Mr Z.A. Bhutto feared that the Jammû Âfrîdîs' very ability to help him take over power from Gen. Yâhyâ Khân might some day be used to get rid of him. So he hounded them out first.

Asghar Khân's only son, Omar Asghar, was a vocal member of the Pâkistân Muslim League. He became a minister in the federal cabinet. However, he was strangulated to death in 2003.

The 1990s: political changes

In the 1990s, Sardâr Mohammad Ibrâhim published a new edition of his book, *Kashmîr Saga*, in which he suggested that Kashmîr should be made a buffer state between Pâkistân and India. This idea was anathema to the Pâkistânî leadership, which shouted him down with ferocity. His son, Khâlid Ibrâhim, too, persuaded him not to take an anti-Pâkistân stand. So, the Sardâr quickly backtracked and reverted to what Pâkistân calls its *usoolî mauqif* ('principled stand') i.e. that Kashmîr should accede to Pâkistân.

Sardâr Ibrâhim had helped set up a unit of the People's Party of Pâkistân in 'AJK.' When General Ziâ ul Haq ousted Pâkistân's Prime Minister ZA Bhutto in a military coup in 1977, Sardâr Ibrâhim happened to be the President of 'AJK.' Out of loyalty to Mr. Bhutto, he refused to work with the military junta. This cost him his job.

However, Mr. Bhutto's daughter, Bénazîr, was not impressed by this sacrifice. When she became the prime minister of Pâkistân she made Râjâ Mumtâz Hussain Rathore, a junior PPP/ AZKP leader, the Prime Minister of 'AJK.' Sardâr Ibrâhim felt humiliated by this decision. He resigned from the PPP and started his own political group. Rathore was the Prime Minister from July 1990 to July 1991.

In June 1991, Prime Minister Râjâ Mumtâz Hussain Rathore (PPP) refused to accept the results of what he called 'massively rigged elections.'[6] For daring to speak out against the Pâkistân establishment, he was bodily removed from the office of Prime Minister and shunted to a Rawalpindi jail. This was done under the aforesaid Section 56 of the 1974 Provisional Constitution of 'AJK,' which allows the Government of Pâkistân to sack any government in 'AJK' that dares to dévîate from the

6. Were those elections really rigged? The Election Tribunal investigated the allegation and concluded that elections to seats like Muzaffarâbâd-Khawara had certainly been rigged. AJK's superior courts agreed with the Tribunal's decision.

official Pâkistânî line. It is for reasons like these that it is a cruel joke to call the occupied territory 'âzâd' (free).

Sardâr Muhammad Ashraf (5-11 July 1991) was the acting PM for a week. Sardâr Râjâ Abdul Qaiyûm Khân of the AJKMC (July 1991-31 July 1996) formally took over as PM from him. Simultaneously, there was a change in the Presidency as well: Sardâr Sikañder Hayât of the AJKMC (July 1991-25 August 1996) assumed that office.

Sardâr Ibrâhim, Sardâr Abdul Qaiyûm Khân and KH Khurshîd were never very happy about the political humiliation of the people of 'AJK' by Pâkistân [through 'the most ostracised {by the people of 'AJK'} ministry of Kashmîr Affairs'[xix]], because Pâkistân rarely, if ever, allowed the people to choose their own representatives and leaders. Ershad Mahmud writes that these three 'struggled hard to get a proper democratic election system for the people of Âzâd Kashmîr.'

Sardâr Ibrâhim and Chaudhary Ghulâm Abbâs remained at daggers drawn till they died. The Sardâr felt that the Chaudhary, who was what Ershad Mahmud calls the 'most trusted person of Rawalpindi,' had sabotaged his political career.

After the June 1991 elections, as we have seen, Sardâr Sikañder Hayât Khân became the President of 'AJK' and Sardâr Abdul Qaiyûm the Prime Minister. Hayât began to lash out at Qaiyûm's son, Atîq, whom he accused of being corrupt and of acting as an 'extra-constitutional centre of authority.' (In the finest of South Asian traditions, some sons and, at times, wives and daughters, of top ranking politicians in power issue orders—mostly illegal ones—to civil servants, purportedly on behalf of their parents. Such people, who issue orders without a legal right to do so, are called 'extra-constitutional centres of authority.')

Hayât had wanted to spite Qaiyûm politically. However, he wound up damaging the MC as a whole. The MC lost to the PPP in the 1996 elections. However, Hayât and Qaiyûm-Atîq continued their spat.

He who lays traps for others...

For AJK, 'watching Pâkistân's interests' has, unfortunately, meant allowing Pâkistân to run camps that lodge and train so-called *jihâdîs* (lit. 'holy warriors'), from where these terrorists are pushed across the LoC to the Indian side. This happened in 1965 and it has been happening since 1989.

While these *jihâdîs* have created mayhem on the Indian side, they have been dangerous for the society, polity and economy of 'AJK' and Pâkistân, too. For instance, in the mid-1990s, when some *jihâdîs* were assembling a bomb at the Kashmîr 'refugee' camp near Nagosh Colony, ten kilometres from Kotlî (in AJK), the bomb went off by accident and killed ten of the people standing near it.[xx]

With such a large concentration of *jihâdîs* brought in from outside (very few, if any, are from 'AJK' itself), turf battles had to break out. By 1994 rival groups of militants being trained for the *jéhâd* in Kashmîr were at loggerheads with each other in Kotlî, Abbotâbâd, Garhî Dupatta, Naikal and Khuiratta (all in 'AJK.').

The main war was between the pro-Pâkistân Hizb ul Mujâhidîn and the JKLF. A news agency, IPA, reported that thirteen persons were killed in the last week of September 1994. It added, 'The victims were said to be supporters of the pro-independence JKLF group, which has started a campaign against ISI control of subversive camps in POK and parts of Pâkistân.'[xxi]

The *jihâdîs* were also employed to settle political scores within 'AJK.' As we have seen above, around 1994 Mrs. Bhutto's PPP started a campaign to remove the MC's Sardâr Abdul Qaiyûm from power. Qaiyûm survived partly because the ISI did not want to see him replaced by someone it did not like. IPA reported at the time that 'besides the ISI, [the] Hizb [ul Mujâhidîn] has the direct support of the [AJK] government headed by Sardâr Abdul Qayoom Khân, who fears that he may be toppled by the [Pakistan] government... led by Ms. Bénazîr Bhutto.'

The Sardâr was obviously buying multiple insurance for himself.

A Mîrpuri—at last

Sardâr Mohammad Ibrâhim Khân became the President for a fourth time (25 August 1996-25 August 2001). Sultân Mahmood Chaudhry of AZKP/PPP was the PM (31 July 1996 -25 July 2001). Mahmood was the first Mîrpuri make it to a high position, after five decades of Sûdhan-Râjpût domination.

The Muslim Conference won 30 of the 48 seats in the State Assembly in July 2001. The party swept the polls because of Sardâr Abdul Qaiyûm and his son Sardâr Atîq. The latter was the president of the party. Twenty-two of the party's legislators were with the father and son duo.

Denying the people representatives of their choosing

The Army felt uneasy at having to deal with leaders with a genuine following. Besides, the political stance of Qaiyûm and Atîq had rattled the military junta that was then ruling Pâkistân.

Qaiyûm had, in public statements in London and Muzaffarâbâd, spoken well of Indian Prime Minister Vajpayee's sincerity to resolve the problem in Kashmîr. He had said that Mr Vajpayee's visit to the Mînâr-é-Pâkistân in Lahore in February 1999 was proof that he genuinely wanted peace with Pâkistân. Qaiyûm condemned the pro-Army Jamaat-e-Islami for using violent jehadis in Kashmîr. He also came out against Pâkistân's insistence that the Hurriyat Conference should be included in negotiations between India and Pâkistân about Kashmîr. This display of political independence panicked the junta. (It will be recalled that Qaiyûm had, in 1994-95, thumbed his nose at Pâkistân's Prime Minister Mrs Bhutto and had threatened to set 'AJK' on fire.)

So, the Pâkistân Army appointed Sardâr Sikañder Hayât Khân as the Prime Minister of 'AJK' even though (or, perhaps, because) at the time Mr. Khân's position within his own party was shaky.

With the office of 'Prime Minister' gone, Atîq decided to contest for 'President.' The Army pre-empted this by installing an Army man to this post. Maj Gen Mohammed Anwar Khân of Rawalakot was made to resign his commission in the Army. He was rushed to Muzaffarâbâd where 'Muslim Conference legislators had been ordered to elect him as the President. The legislators were taken aback but could not defy the order.'[xxii]

Relations between India and Pâkistân began to improve. 'Sardâr Atîq took advantage of the changed scenario to once again stake his claim to [the] Prime Ministership of POK,' Baid writes. 'His support in the Muslim Conference legislat[ure] party remained intact. The Army [did] not have much choice between Prime Minister Sardâr Sikañder Hayât and Qaiyûm and his son Atîq. It [tried] to be neutral between them. It fear[ed] that a further flare-up in the Muslim Conference intra-party crisis [would] demoralise Pâkistân's supporters in Kashmîr' and give them the impression that if Kashmîr were a part of Pâkistân it would suffer the same fate as the people and leaders of 'AJK.'

On 25 July 2001, Maj. Gen. Sardâr Sikañder Hayât Khân of the AJKMC was sworn in as PM for the second time. Sardâr Muhammad Anwar Khân (b. 1945), also of the AJKMC, became the President a month later, on 25 August 2001.

As this book went to the press, there were reports that the Pâkistân Army was trying to get the two factions to sort things out. The Pâkistânî media reported that the Corps Commander of Rawalpindi Lt Gen Ashfaq Kiyani had asked Atîq 'to tolerate the Prime Minister (Hayât) for another four to six months.' It seems that the Pâkistân Army has given up on Sardar Sikandar Hayât Khân, though he has been allowed to last five years as P.M.

The Pâkistânî establishment is extremely unhappy with Sardâr Abdul Qaiyûm Khân, too. The PPP on its part has given up on its own leader and former 'Prime Minister' Barrister Sultan Mehmood. In January 2006 it 'suspended' him, as well as three other PPP legislators, following serious differences with PPP secretary general Jahangir Badar. This led to a split in the party. Nine members of the 'AJK' Legislative Assembly and one freshly elected member of the 'AJK' Council belonging to the People's Party of 'Azad' Kashmir resigned from the party.

The year 2005 witnessed major developments. Buses started plying between Muzaffarâbâd and Srînagar once again after almost six decades. The Governments of India and Pâkistân began negotiations about the movement of goods across the LoC. They also agreed to a similar bus service between Pooñch (India) and Râwlâkote ('AJK').

People—divided families as well as civil society leaders and media people—began to travel to the other half of the state, again for the first time in ages.

The by now legendary Sardâr Abdul Qaiyûm Khân was the highest ranking 'AJK' visitor to India. During his longish stay in Delhi he did and said all the right things—from the point of view of bringing peace back to Kashmîr and giving realistic advice to the militants. Among other things he said that Kashmîr could not become an independent nation in another hundred years.

This greatly disappointed Pâkistânî hardliners. Their leading spokeswoman in Pâkistân's English language press wondered in her column what it was about India's soil that the moment leaders from Pâkistân and 'AJK' set foot on it they began to sing a tune different from what they would within Pâkistân.

As 2005 drew to a close, nature brought the two halves of Jammû and Kashmîr together through its ultimate weapon: grief. The worst earthquake to hit the region since 1885 tore through the state on the 8th October. While the destruction in Urî, Tañgdhâr and Pooñch on the Indian side was terrible (around 1,300 people, including forty-two Indian soldiers, died), 'AJK' was devastated. In a few minutes, more than seventy-three thousand people were killed in 'AJK' and the adjoining areas of Pakistan's Frontier Province. Thus 'AJK' lost more than 2 per cent of its population in that earthquake. Maj. Gen. Shaukat Sultan of the.Pâkistân Army said, 'Râwalâkot has been destroyed. Muzaffarâbâd is 70 per cent destroyed. There is not a single family that has not suffered.' Bâlâkot and once prosperous Bâgh, too were affected very badly. Almost twentyone lakh (2.1 million) people lost their homes in 'AJK' and the NWFP.

Pâkistân had helped India with high quality relief materials when Gujarat had been similarly ravaged a few years before. Now it was India's turn to reciprocate, which it speedily did. The Indian Prime Minister agreed to let Pâkistânî officials pass through Indian territory along the LoC in order to reach AJK's frontier villages affected by the earthquake.

After the 'quake the Indian soldiers posted on the LoC noticed a sudden lull in the activities of the Pâkistân Army. Apart from the loss of three to four hundred soldiers, Pâkistâni units on the LoC seemed to have lost contact with their headquarters.

One of the Pâkistâni sentry posts overlooking the Indian Army had collapsed. During that shared tragedy the sentry saw his Indian counterparts not as people who might kill him but as the only comrades he had at that moment. He asked them if they could help him rebuild his watchtower—and they did. They, too, saw the Pâkistâni sentry as a fellow victim of a terrible calamity and not someone whose tower was meant to keep an eye on their movements.

Quake hit Pâkistâni soldiers at the Kamân Post (ahead of Uri) told the Indians that they needed shovels and pickaxes. Once again, the Indians helped. They crossed the Peace Bridge to 'AJK' twice, without weapons, something they would not even have considered a year or two before. They helped the Pâkistânis recover their own weapons, which had to be dug out from under the debris.

Pakistani militants rose superbly to the occasion, rescued people and distributed relief materials. And yet, in the July 2006 legislative assembly elections, all 33 candidates of the Muttahida Majlis-e-Amal, an alliance endorsed by the militants, lost. Less surprisingly, the people voted out 13 of the 33 legislators of the ruling AJKMC, including eleven Cabinet ministers. The Peoples Party, which won seven seats, mainly in earthquake-affected Muzaffarabad and Neelum Valley, accused President Musharraf of "manipulating" the election results. In Narowal it was proved right. The AJKMC, under Sardar Atique Khan, emerged as the biggest party in the 49-member Kashmir legislature. (Eight seats are reserved, five of them for women.)

While the international community did its bit to help the devastated people of 'AJK' and the NWFP, it was felt that it was easier to deliver relief materials from the Indian side.

This change of mood was formalised at Islamabad on the 29th October, 2005, when India and Pakistan decided to 'open' the Line of Control at five points. These were Chakan da Bagh and Tatta Pani in the Poonch district (Jammu) and Kaman, Haji Pir and Tithwal in the Baramulla and Kupwara districts of Kashmir.

When the first of these points was opened on the 7th November, 2005, thousands of residents of the devastated Rawlakot area of 'AJK' turned up at the LoC. Their excitement was palpable. The Pakistan Army had to fire tear gas shells to keep them from crossing over to the Indian side.

A few days before, Pakistan's President Gen. Pervez Musharraf had declared that through the 29th October, 2005, agreement 'I have made the LoC irrelevant.' While the word 'irrelevant' can be debated, there can be no doubt that the LoC has become softer than at any time since 1965.

References

i 'Amanullah: Jinnah had agreed to Kashmir's independence,' *Khabrain*, Pâkistân, 7 Januray 199?.

ii Mahmud, Ershad 'Sardar Ibrahim remembered' *The News*, Pakistan August 7, 2003.

iii Ibid.

iv Baid, Samuel, op. cit. 'Political Crisis In POK The *Daily Excelsior,* 1 April 2004

v Evans, Alexander, 'Kashmîr: A tale of two valleys,' *Asian Affairs* (Vol. 36, I), March 2005, p. 35-47.

vi Baid, 'Political Crisis In POK The *Daily Excelsior,* 1 April 2004.

vii "AJK High Court holds void act imposed by CMLA Ziâ ul Haq.' The *Jañg*, Pâkistân, 16 Dec 199?.

viii Ahmed, Khaled, 'Demands of a diaspora' Reprinted in *The Indian Express*, Monday, August 9, 1999, from *The Friday Times'* (Lahore).

ix 'Any Doubt? -It's 'Âzâd' Kashmîr!' The *Daily Excelsior* 28 August 2004.

x 'Qayum revolts against Pâkistân,' *Daily Excelsior,* 18 July 1994.

xi 'Pâkistân Prime Minister can dismiss AJK PM, says Rathore,' *Khabrain*, Pakistan, 27 January 1995.

xii 'Gang warfare in POK intensifies,' the *National Herald,* India, 5 October 1994.

xiii 'AJK Government seeks custody of its properties in Pâkistân,' *News*, Pâkistân, 21 January, 199?.

xiv Evans, op. cit., p. 2.

xv Evans, Alexander, 'Kashmîr: A tale of two valleys,' the manuscript of an article based on a lecture that Mr. Evans delivered at the Royal Society for Asian Affairs in December 2004. Page 10.

xvi Evans, op. cit., p. 10.

xvii 'Pak envoy has it quite wrong,' *The Asian Age*, 24 July 1994.

xviii Evans, op. cit., p. 10.

xix Mahmud, Ershad 'Sardar Ibrahim remembered' *The News*, Aug. 7, 2003.

xx '10 killed as bomb goes off in Kotlî refugee camp,' The *Dawn*, Pakistan, 16 September 199?

xxi 'Gang warfare in POK intensifies,' the *National Herald,* India, 5 October 1994.

xxii Baid, Samuel, 'Political Crisis In POK *The Daily Excelsior,* 1 April 2004.

* * *

16

Jammû Province

(1950 and after)

1952-53: The Prajâ Parishad agitation

Pâkistân managed to illegally occupy several Muslim-majority areas of the state in 1947. The Muslims continued to be in an overwhelming majority (64.19 per cent in 2001) even in the parts of the state physically administered by India. The composition of the Jammû and Kashmir Constituent Assembly reflected this. It had 75 members, of which 50 were Muslims.[1,i]

This irked a Jammû-based, right-wing Hiñdu political party called the Prajâ Parishad. Mahârâjâ Hari Siñgh, as we have seen, had been strictly neutral between the various religious communities of his state and also between the various geographical regions. This had annoyed the more conservative of his co-religionists. But when he was removed from the position of Mahârâjâ, his dismissal became a major issue for the Hiñdu right.

Yuvrâj (crown prince) Karan Siñgh agreed to become the first Regent of the State, with the designation of Sadr-é-Riyâsat ('head of state'). He would be a kind of a constitutional monarch (without being called one), while real power would vest in the elected Prime Minister of the state. The Hiñdu right saw Dr. Siñgh's installation on November 15, 1952, as a sell-out. They called it a `traitorous act' and alleged that it was "tantamount to selling the Dogrâs out to the Kashmîrîs".[ii]

Within days the Prajâ Parishad took the matter to the streets. Its mass movement had the blessings of the Bharatiya Jan Sangh, the Hindu Mahasabha, the Punjâb Arya Samaj and the Râm Rajya Parishad (all being Hiñdu nationalist parties), as well as some Akali (Sikh) leaders. The government arrested Prem Nâth Dogrâ, who was the leader of the Parishad, as well as his colleague, Shâm Lâl.

1. Another 25 seats were earmarked for the areas occupied by Pâkistân.

The Parishad had launched its movement in February 1952 with a slogan that anti-autonomy politicians use to this day, *'Ek desh mein do vidhân, do nishân, do pradhân, nahîñ chalégâ, nahîñ chalégâ'* (Two constitutions, two flags and two chiefs [Prime Ministers] cannot be allowed to exist within the same country,).

This agitation gained momentum when the so-called Delhi Agreement was signed between the Government of India and the Government of Jammû and Kashmîr. Finalised on the 24th July 1952, the Agreement spelt out in some detail which aspects of governance would be looked after by the national government, which by the state government and which by the two concurrently.

The Prajâ Parishad wanted Article 370 of the Constitution of India to be deleted so that the State could be 'fully integrated' into the Indian Union and so that the Constitution of India could be enforced directly in Jammû and Kashmîr, as in other Indian states, instead of through Article 370. It wanted to get rid of the distinction between 'state-subjects of Jammû and Kashmîr' (who alone could purchase immoveable property or seek employment under the state government) and other Indian citizens (who can do neither in the state).

In a word, the Parishad wanted the complete integration of the State with the rest of India and the abolition of the autonomy that Article 370 had granted to the state. The Hiñdu nationalist leader Dr. Syama Prasad Mookerjee summed up the position of the Parishad thus, "There cannot be a republic within a republic... Consciously or unconsciously, [the pro-autonomy National Conference is] creating a new sovereignty for Jammû & Kashmir... India has been torn into two by the two-nation theory. You are now developing a three-nation theory, the third being the Kashmîrî nation. These are dangerous symptoms."

The Parishad started demanding the secession of Jammû province from the state of Jammû and Kashmîr. It felt that Jammu could either be made a full-fledged state of the Indian Union, or it could be merged with neighbouring (East) Punjãb.[2]

Behera writes, 'Prime Minister Jawaharlal Nehru appreciated the legitimate grievances of the Jammû people but castigated the narrow communal approach of the Praja Parishad movement.'

The Parishad intensified its agitation in early 1953. 'The state authorities replied with considerable violence,' writes Kishtwâri.[iii] This upset the

2 In 1949, Chhéwâñg Rigzin, the President of the Buddhist Association of Ladâkh, had petitioned Pt. Nehru to remove Ladâkh from the state and integrate it with Jammû instead. A similar anti-Kashmîr sentiment resurfaced in Ladâkh in 1952. This further alarmed Delhi. (Kishtwâri, Wali Mohd. Aseer, op. cit., p. 333.)

national leadership of the Jan Sañgh. Dr. Syama Prasad Mookerjee left for Jammû in May 1953. At the time there were no railways in the state. One had to travel to Pathânkot (Punjãb) by train and then take a bus to travel to Jammû and Kashmîr. Lakhanpur was, and remains, the first town that one enters in the state from that direction. On the 11th May, the state police arrested Dr. Mookerjee at Lakhanpur, as he was trying to enter the state. He was sent to Srînagar where he was detained in a Dak Bungalow near the Mughal gardens.

While in custody, Dr. Mookerjee died in a government hospital on the 23rd June, 1953. Kishtwâri writes that even before his arrest Dr. Mookerjee reportedly had a heart condition. He adds, "It was generally suspected that [Dr. Mookerjee] had been murdered...[This] gave rise to a wave of national anger against Sheikh Muhammad Abdullâh although he repeatedly [announced] that the Jan Sañgh President had died of a heart attack.'

And yet, the Parishad's agitation failed because it excluded the majority of the population: Hiñdu peasants as well as all Muslims. It only represented the urban middle-class and the rural elite. As Behera points out, 'The Parishad also failed to mobilise the support of the small but influential Hindu minority of Kashmîrî Pañdits in the Valley and the Ladakhi Buddhists who shared its antipathy for Sheikh Abdullâh.'

1963: Attempts to destabilise Jammû province

An event took place on the 27th December 1963 that rocked the Valley of Kashmir to its very roots. (See the volume on 'Kashmîr.') This is generally known as the Hazratbal Incident in which a hair from the beard of the Holy Prophet of Islâm (peace be upon him) was stolen. This resulted in what was easily the most serious law and order situation in the state between 1947 and December 1989.

The more this author looks at the records of that month the more it becomes clear that a malign power was trying to stir up trouble in the state. Identical incidents took place in Jammû city, Dodâ 'city' and Kishtwâr around the same time. In each case the result was the same—the public got extremely angry and vented its anger on the government.

Mysterious fires broke out in both Kishtwâr and Dodâ. The most venerable shrine of Kishtwâr, that of Syed Shâh Asrâr ud Dîn Walî Sâheb, was burnt completely. Someone similarly set on fire the shrine of the Syed's even more respected father, Syed Farid ud din Sâheb of Baghdad, at Dodâ.

Just four days after the theft of the Holy Relic at Srînagar, on the 31st December, word went around the state's winter capital, Jammû, that two idols had been stolen from a Hiñdu temple. If in Srînagar, Dodâ and Kishtwâr it were the Muslims who were livid, in Jammû it was the Hiñdus. In all four cases the idea clearly was to provoke the majority community of that area.

The agitation in Jammû continued into 1964—till February, when someone pointed out that the said temple had ceased to be used for prayers several decades before and the idols had been eroded by time.

1965: The Pâkistânî aggression

'In mid-1965,' an American record points out, 'Pâkistân sent guerrilla forces into the Indian part of Kashmir in the hope of stirring up a rebellion that would either oust the Indians or at least force the issue back onto the international agenda. Pakistani forces did not find as much support among the Kashmîrî population as they had hoped.'[iv] In fact, they did not find any support at all.

(See the volume on 'Kashmîr' for more details, especially for the overall picture and also for the subsequent Indo-Pâk peace talks in Tashkent.)

In all, Pâkistân trained a force of thirty thousand infiltrators during the course of that year. These included 'irregulars' as well as soldiers in Kashmîrî plainclothes. Wali Mohd. Aseer Kishtwârî points out that the men had been trained by Pâkistân's Gen. Malik and 'some of [them] had been identified as Pâkistânî regular army officers.'[v]

Field Marshal Ayûb Khân consulted only Gen. Mûsâ Khân while deciding to push infiltrators into India, Air Marshal Nûr Khân would later recall. Ayûb did not take the chiefs of Pâkistân's air force and navy into confidence.[vi] However, some members of Ayûb's council of ministers knew. (Ayûb Khân was the President and military dictator of Pâkistân, Mûsâ Khân the chief of the Pâkistân Army and Nûr Khân the chief of the Pâkistân Air Force at the time.) According to Air Marshal Nûr Khân, 'The infiltration started on August 6. However, the Indians came to know about it in mid-August.' (The good air chief has got the first date wrong by a few hours.)

The main infiltration took place on the night of the 5th August. India and Pâkistân share a very long international boundary (IB) in Jammû and Kashmîr, and an even longer, 750 kilometre 'line of control' (LoC), which was then called the cease-fire line (CFL). It is impossible for the armed forces to guard every inch, especially mountain peaks and ridges.

The infiltrators were well supplied with arms, food, Indian money and communication equipment. They formed little groups of two or three and slipped across the CFL wherever they found a gap in the Indian patrol. A few hours later they assembled in bigger groups at designated places.

'They were organised into eight 'Forces' composed of six companies of 110 men,' Pathik writes. 'In most case, the companies were commanded by Pâkistân Army officers of the rank of Major, while the platoon commanders were either junior commissioned officers [i.e. corporal and below, or] senior non- commissioned officers [i.e. sergeant and above].'[vii]

The Indian Army decided to cross over to the Pâkistânî side of the CFL so that it could capture and seal off the more frequented gaps and passes through which the infiltrators were pouring in.

The Hâjî Pîr Pass was the most important of these. It links Poonch and Rajourî (both in Jammû) with Urî (Kashmîr). Whichever country occupies this pass can call the shots in an area of roughly 3,500 square kilometres. At the time the Pâkistân Army administered this vital pass. Before 1947 a wide, metalled highway between Kashmîr and Jammû ran through the Hâjî Pîr.

Pâkistân began to shell Indian positions in Tithwâl, Urî and Poonch on the 19th August. Clearly, the Hâjî Pîr had to be brought back under Indian control to put an end to the constant torture inflicted by Pâkistân. Brig. Z.C. Bakshî was the commander of India's 68 Infantry Brigade. Acting on his orders, 1 Para captured Sar, on the right flank, on the 25th August. However, it could not take the critical Sankh.

On the 26th August, Major (later Lt. Gen.) Ranjît Singh Dayâl, an exceptionally imaginative and daring Indian officer, led a band of a hundred 'paratroopers' into the territory controlled by Pâkistân. The mountainous terrain was so difficult that it could be negotiated only in daylight. So, an unconventional decision was taken: to start at two in the afternoon of the 27th. Pâkistânî soldiers saw them and fired on them. To make things worse, there was a heavy fog and a drizzle at night. All the same, Dayâl encouraged his tired men to reach the base of the pass.

Brig. (later Lt. Gen.) Z.C. Bakshî is one of the greatest military geniuses of free India—and one of its most highly 'decorated' soldiers. As soon as he learnt of the fog, he detached a company and sent it to the pass to make an alternate attempt to capture it. His strategy assumed that Pâkistân had very substantial forces at the pass. The idea was also to secure Poonch.

When the fog lifted, Dayâl saw that his men and he were overlooking the Haji Pir Pass and Pâkistânî soldiers were brewing tea at the pass.

By the morning of the 28th August Dayâl and his men were close to their goal, the pass itself. Dayâl took his men up by a route used rarely because it is longer. The idea was to take the Pâkistânîs by surprise. At 4.30am they reached the old, disused Urî-Pooñch road. That was when Dayâl allowed his men a short nap. They resumed their advance half an hour or so later and by six they were just below the pass. The Pâkistânîs began to fire on them.

Maj. Dayâl divided his men into two groups. One group took the Pâkistânîs on by firing on them. Dayâl led the other group. They climbed up the mountain that towered above the pass. They rolled down from that height to the pass, where they took the Pâkistânî soldiers unawares. Caught between gunfore from two sides, the Pâkistânîs panicked and deserted the pass.

By 10.30 that morning, the Indian tricolour was flying on the Hâjî Pîr Pass. This was one of the most significant battles won by the Indian Army after 1947. In less than forty-eight hours India had captured critical Pâkistân-controlled border 'posts' such as Bedori (13,000'), Burfi Pathrî, Kuthanar ki gallî and Sañkh (Point 9591). (The Hâjî Pîr pass was returned to Pâkistân as part of a bilateral pact between the two countries.)[viii]

The Pooñch-Urî link: After 1947, as we have seen, the Indian district of Pooñch did not have a good road link with Urî (in Kashmîr). In the first week of September 1965, the Indian Army started working to change that. It captured around thirty Pâkistânî 'posts' and, on the 10th September, 1965, linked these two frontier towns with each other. This was another major Indian victory.

The failure of Pâkistân's guerrilla strategy: So far India and Pâkistân had been fighting an undeclared war, with the Indian forces sorting out infiltrators rather than a formal army. The Pâkistânîs had hoped that the local Muslims would support the infiltrators, feed them and house them. They were sorely disappointed.

Ch. Muhammad[ix] Din, a Gujjar from Tañgmarg (Kashmîr), who was later awarded the Padma Shri, was the first to alert the Indian government about the infiltration. Several other Muslims—of Jammû as well as Kashmîr—gave vital clues to the Indian Army. (Later, Pâkistânî terrorists killed Ch. Dîn because of his loyalty to India.)

Pâkistân, writes Pathik, had only two options now, 'either to…admit the failure of the [guerrilla] operation or commit their country to an all-out war with India.'[x] It chose the latter on the 1st September.

The Battle for Siâlkot: Briefly, Indian tanks entered Pâkistân proper (as opposed to Pâkistân occupied Kashmîr), in the direction of Phillaurâh. Pâkistân's 6th Armoured Division responded by moving its tanks from Badiâñ and Pasrûr to where the Indians were. Thus began what Pathik describes as 'the biggest [tank battle] since World War II. [The battle continued] without break for fifteen days. [66 Pâkistânî] tanks were destroyed [during the Battle of Phillaurâh on September 11, while India lost] only six.'[xi]

The details: On September 3, a Pâkistâni patrol crossed over into India and abducted an Indian despatch rider. The Indian courier was apparently carrying the complete details of an invasion of Siâlkot planned by India's 1 Armoured Division.[xii] No one in the Pâkistâni Army took that intelligence coup seriously. All of them assumed that the blueprint had been deliberately planted on them by India.

Around 3:30am on September 6, a small Indian force began to shell the Pâkistâni bridge on River Râvi at Jasser, and then attacked it. The Pâkistâni company commander ordered the demolition of the bridge. He also vastly overstated the size of the Indian force in his report to his seniors. This led the Pâkistânis to believe that Jasser was where the Indians were planning to attack. So, by noon they sent a brigade with an additional armoured regiment to Jasser.

The Indians attacked Pasrûr-Chawinda-Phillaurâh instead. The Pâkistâni commander asked the freshly despatched brigade to rush from Jasser to where the attack was. This confused the Pâkistâni troops thoroughly. Worse was to come, because Brigadier Ismail, the inept[3] commander of the Siâlkot division, would continue to issue contradictory orders.

Early the next morning the Indian infantry formed a bridgehead and a 'defended area' for its men—on Pâkistâni soil. At 10:30am on September 7, India's 1 Armoured Division started marching into Pâkistân. Even though they found no opposition from the paralysed Pâkistânis, the cautious Indians did not capitalise on Pâkistân's internal disarray. They thought they were being led into an ambush.

This conviction got reinforced when the Indians advanced from Pasrûr to Phillaurâh (both in Pâkistân) before dawn on September 8. Major Muhammed Ahmed, a squadron commander of the Pâkistâni armoured regiment, and his men hid in a grove of trees when they saw the conquering Indian tanks roll past them. They opened fire and hit many tanks of the leading Indian unit, as well as some that followed.

3. That he was inept is the Pâkistâni assessment, not mine.

Meanwhile, another unit of the Indian armoured division reached Chawinda (Pâkistân). When its officers heard of the ambush at Phillaurâh, they decided to halt at Chawinda for a while. Men from that Pâkistâni armoured unit moved to Chawinda and fired on the Indians, killing many and hitting more Indian tanks. The Pâkistânis call this 'the greatest tank battle since the Second World War.' (But no, that was at Asal Uttar, where India destroyed a few hundred Pâkistâni Patton Tanks.)

The next day (September 9) the Pâkistâni GHQ (general headquarters) ordered Pâkistân's second armoured division to proceed to the Siâlkot sector. After that a series of battles followed, some going in favour of one country while the rest gave the other country the upper hand.

Because of its huge overall success in this sector, the Indian Army conquered 268 sq. km. of Pâkistânî territory in Siâlkot, including major trophies such as the Alhar Railway Station. While India did not conquer Siâlkot town, its Army was only five or six kilometeres short. Besides, India had captured most of the territory leading to Siâlkot.

Chhamb-Jauriâñ: Pâkistân attacked Jammû's Chhamb-Jauriâñ sector with ninety armoured tanks—mainly of the Patton variety—and an infantry brigade before dawn on September 1, 1965. Pâkistân has the strategic advantage in this area.

Actually, in 1965 Pâkistân enjoyed more than just good topography. It had, around 1958, got hold of India's military plans (for the entire border and not just Chhamb-Jauriâñ) in all their details, thanks to an Indian Brigadier whose wife had an expensive hobby. What the Brigadier allegedly sold were India's entire offensive and defensive operational plans. This crucial revelation was made by Gohar Ayûb Khân[xiii], whose father Field Marshal Ayûb Khân was then the military dictator of Pâkistân. Gohar was 28 at the time. (There's a moral in it for all Indians who would sell their nation to Pâkistân: The Pâkistânî whom you hand the secret documents to will merrily spill the beans on you in his memoirs, which will be a bestseller on both sides of the border for that reason.)

The Indian Brigadier, who had once been India's Director of Military Operations[xiv], was paid Rs.20,000 ($4,000 at the then exchange rate) in London. As a result 'President Ayub ordered [the] deployment of Pâkistânî forces where [the] Indians planned to attack.' But God was clearly not on Pâkistân's side. The Lahore Military Commander, Maj. Gen. Sartâj, 'moved his forces late, to the disappointment and annoyance of top [Pâkistânî] military commanders,' Gohar Khân adds. Besides, a careless Pâkistânî tank driver accidentally hit and knocked off an Indian bridge that the Pâkistân Army needed to cross in order to annex Indian territory.

In any case, after Pâkistân had moved all its defensive forces, 'the Pâkistân Army launched its attack at [Chhamb-Jauriâñ] that was left unguarded by Indians as indicated by their secret war plan. No Indian soldier was found to defend the border and the Pâkistân Army started its advance secretly.'

In the event, Indian troops withdrew to River Munnawar Tawi. Had Pâkistân been able to advance a little further, into Akhnoor, it would have severed the main road link that Rajourî and Pooñch had with the rest of India and thus, possibly, would have conquered that region.

And had Pâkistân been as successful from the Siâlkot side as it had been in Chhamb, it could have captured Jammû city and the national highway as well. In that case India would have lost its road link with Kashmîr and Ladâkh as well.

That was what the Pâkistân Army had set out to achieve—and what the Indian Army had to prevent.

On the 3rd September Pâkistâni tanks rolled further into Indian territory, in the direction of Jauriâñ. The Indian Army withdrew again. The next day Pâkistânî tanks advanced across the almost dry Munnawar Tawi river and captured more territory.

India, which had not been expecting the attack, hit back with enormous ferocity four days after the Pâkistânî invasion. On the 5th September it regained some territory by pushing the Pâkistân Army back across the Munnawar Tawi.

The same day India took the offensive by attacking not only Pâkistân's Siâlkot area, which borders Jammû, but also the distant Lahore sector. This halted the Pâkistân Army's conquering spree in this sector. Now that they had to defend their own territory, the Pâkistânîs reduced their pressure on Chhamb and Akhnoor.

Asal Uttar: Indian soldiers withdrew from Kasur to a place near Khémkaran-Asal Uttar. There they hid themselves in fields of sugarcane. When the Pâkistânîs marched in to the area, thinking that they had conquered the stretch without any resistance, the Indian troops trapped them between themselves and a stream.

The Indian Army killed a Pâkistânî General Officer Commanding as well as the Artillery Commander. They also captured 97 Pâkistânî tanks, fourteen officers—including two Lieutenant Colonels and six Majors—and several men.

The cease-fire: The Security Council of the United Nations recommended a cease-fire in the hostilities between the two neighbours. This took place on the 23rd September, 1965. At the time India held around a thousand square kilometres of Pâkistânî territory: including

Pâkistânî land in the Lahore region as well as some Pâkistânî areas bordering Râjasthân. 'The credit for this victory,' Pathik writes, 'goes to the able leadership and strategy of [Gen.] J.N. Chaudhari.'[xv]

1965-a summary: The war achieved nothing for Pâkistân. Instead it lost twenty aircraft, two hundred tanks, and 3,800 troops, according to a US estimate[xvi] that adds, 'Pâkistân's army had been able to withstand Indian pressure, but a continuation of the fighting would only have led to further losses and ultimate defeat for Pâkistân.' In his book, *My Version*, the then Chief of the Pâkistan Army, Gen. Muhammad Mûsâ shared the view that Pâkistan gained nothing from the 1965 war and that, on the contrary, Pâkistan failed to achieve its objectives.

Why Pâkistân did not succeed: Apart from military reverses, Pâkistân failed because, as Gohar Ayûb Khân points out[xvii], it based its entire strategy on the assumption that the people of Jammû and Kashmîr were on its side. Khân recalls that the top Kashmîrî leaders whom Pâkistân relied on had assured Pâkistân that the Kashmîrîs would rise in revolt against India after a few thousand Pâkistânî commandoes had infiltrated into the state.

According to Khân, the then foreign minister of Pâkistân, Mr Zulfiqâr Ali Bhutto, received this assurance from pro-Pâkistân leaders in Kashmîr and conveyed it to Field Marshal Ayûb Khân. It was only after that Ayûb launched Operation Gibraltar.

Khân told *The News* (Pâkistân) that this wrong assumption 'led to a big disaster and resulted in [the] killing and captur[e] of Pâkistânî commando[e]s after Indians closed their entry and exit points at Kargil and other areas.'

The Pâkistânî commando[e]s who managed to reach the Valley of Kashmîr 'sent horrifying reports back home [because] the earlier assurances and information of Kashmîrî leaders turned out to be "doctored" and the commando[e]s were trapped [in Kashmîr].'

Lt. Gen. Kamal Matinuddin,[xviii] who was Pâkistân's brigade major in Khém Karan at the time, supports Gohar Ayub's version that 'the reports on the so-called uprising in IHK [Indian Held Kashmîr] were doctored. The Sadâ-é-Kashmîr radio station, located in Murree [in Pâkistâni Punjãb], was broadcasting fictitious achievements in IHK: "Revolutionary Council takes over all authority in Kashmîr. Patriots cut Jammû-Srînagar road. Panic grips Srînagar. Enemy [i.e. Indian] battalion wiped out." Such propaganda based on total falsehood never achieves the desired results.'[4]

---

4. True. But that did not deter Pâkistân from planting even more incredible stories in its media after 1989.

Initially, Pâkistân told its own citizens that India had forced that war on Pâkistân. (As I had said in the previous chapter, aggressor communities do not want to shatter their citizens' illusions about the innocence of their nation/ ethnic group.) However, every retired Pâkistânî general has since admitted that Pâkistân was the aggressor.

Matinuddin writes, 'Ayub's confidence...had increased because [Pâkistân] had received state-of-the-art weapons after joining US-sponsored, anti-Soviet military pacts... With the death of Nehru...India's destiny was [guided by] Lal Bahadur Shastri [who] was, in the eyes of the Pâkistânî military leadership, a weak leader.' Besides, Pâkistân thought that the world powers, especially the immediate neighbourhood, were with Pâkistân.

'It was the security environment, which was in Pâkistân's favour at that point of time,' Lt. Gen. Matinuddin adds, 'which led Ayub Khân to give the go ahead signal to try and resolve the issue of Kashmîr militarily...

'The war was not conceived in its totality. It began with [Pâkistânî] raids [on Indian territory]. When that did not produce the desired results and our vital areas in Azad Kashmîr were threatened, a full-fledged attack on Akhnur was launched. When that stalled, reserves were pulled out from the Lahore sector. When the Indians attacked Lahore, the armoured division was launched in a hurry, without adequate infantry support...When that ended in a disaster [for Pâkistân], emphasis was shifted to the Sialkot sector where a purely defensive battle was fought.'

Each Pâkistânî invasion of India has assumed that the Indians are a bunch of idiots and wimps, that the vegetarian Indian Army is no match for Pâkistân's rugged, meat-eating, 'martial' soldiers (each of who can bash up twenty Indian soldiers), that the people of Kashmîr are all closet Pâkistânîs and, therefore, the Pâkistân Army simply has to march into Kashmîr (indeed, all of India) and occupy it 'with a smile'—i.e. without any resistance from the Indian side. ('Hañs ké léiñgé Hiñdustân.')

Lt. Gen. Matinuddin writes that the Pâkistânî military believed that India, under Prime Minister Shastri, 'was not expected to resort to an all-out war against Pâkistân even if Kashmîr was attacked.'

As a result of such delusions, all that Pâkistân has achieved though its various invasions has been the needless death of thousands of Kashmîrî civilians, as well as Indian and Pâkistânî soldiers. And each time thousands of Kashmîrîs have kept Indian soldiers informed about the whereabouts of the Pâkistânî infiltrators—often sacrificing their own lives in the process.

1965: The important battles: The main battles fought in Jammû & Kashmir and the neighbouring areas of the Puñjâb were at Hâji pîr (August 26-31), Raja Picquet-Chand Tékri (September 5-6), Jauriâñ-Kalit (September 2-5), Kâli dhâr (September 1-Oct. 5), Sanjoi-Mirpur

(September 3-12), Point 9013 (September 20-21), Op Hill (NL 1053) (November 2-3). Hostilities on the state's boundaries with Pâkistân/ occupied Kashmîr began on August 5 and continued till November 3.

Echoes of the Parméshwari case in Jammû

In 1967 a Kashmîrî Pañdit woman, Parmeshwari, got married to a Muslim, Ghulâm Rasool Kañth. This enraged the Kashmîrî Pañdits. They launched the most intense agitation the Valley had seen since 1963. (See the volume on 'Kashmîr' for more details.)

The Hiñdus of Jammû, too, rose in protest. Things got ugly and the politicians of Jammû brought up the issue of what Aseer Kishtwâri refers to as 'regional discrimination' (i.e. alleged discrimination by the government against Jammû province in the matter of employment and the allotment of developmental funds). This gave the agitation a fresh lease of life and prolonged it.

Things in Jammû were brought under control only when the Government of India constituted the Gajendragadkar Commission of Inquiry to look into the allegations and complaints of the people of Jammû. Mr (Justice) Gajendragadkar had retired as the Chief Justice of India.

The 1971 war with Pâkistân

The genesis of this war between India and Pâkistân, and incidents connected with Kashmîr have been mentioned in some detail in the volume about 'Kashmîr.'

Briefly, in 1971, Pâkistân ruled over Bâñglâdésh, which was then called East Pâkistân. At the time a military junta governed Pâkistân. Elections, internationally accepted as fair, were held in Pâkistân to transfer power to a civilian government. The East Pâkistân-based Awâmî League won the majority of seats in the national parliament. Politicians and generals from West Pâkistân were alarmed at the prospect of Pâkistân being ruled by 'the Bingos.' So, they refused to let the elected government assume charge. A civil war broke out in East Pâkistân.

Pâkistân was sore that India was providing refuge to the East Pâkistânis, some ten million of whom had crossed over into India, fleeing the reign of terror of the Pâkistân Army. So, to quote an American history, "on December 3, [1971] Pakistani forces began hostilities in the west with attacks on Indian airfields. [A major Pâkistâni land attack on Chhamb, where Pâkistân had done well in 1965 and where it has the strategic advantage, followed. On the whole] they [Pâkistân] had little success, and within twenty-four hours India had seized air superiority, launched attacks against West Pâkistân, and blockaded the coast."[xix]

The Indian Army's objectives in the west (i.e. Jammû and Kashmîr, the Puñjâb, Râjasthân and Gujarât) were limited. The idea was to conquer as much Pâkistâni land as possible and concede the least possible Indian territory. The Pâkistân Army's aims were a mirror image. Both knew that there would be negotiations after the war. Whichever side seized more land would be in a better bargaining position.

Perhaps for that reason, Pâkistân concentrated its forces in the West.[5] (And suffered an innings defeat in the East.) In 1965, Pâkistân's Army and Air Force had some of the world's best tanks, aircraft and other supplies, while thitherto pacifist India was still limbering on with its World War II craft and weapons. By 1971 the gap with Pâkistân's technical superiority had narrowed somewhat. The Pâkistân Air Force had Starfighters, the latest Chinese F-6s and state of the art F-86 Sabres. Its Army had new Chinese T-59 tanks as well as the once-dreaded American Patton tanks. (India's new, USSR-made weapons are mentioned in 'The Battle of Chhamb' later in this chapter.)

India's western border with Pâkistân, as military analysts point out, is longer than the distance between Paris and Moscow. For either side to capture the other's territory can only be by losing a large number of men—not to mention the expensive loss of armament. That is why the Army divisions of both countries are mostly defensive ('holding') formations, rather than offensive ('strike') ones.

The Indian Army had drawn up three missions in which India would attack Pâkistân and capture its territory: i) 26 Division would try to enter the Siâlkot area. ii) 1 Corps would try to capture the 30 kilometre 'Shakargarh bulge.' iii) A division of India's Southern Command would attempt to snap the rail link between Pâkistân's Puñjâb and Sindh provinces.

Siâlkot: Indian Army Headquarters abandoned the Siâlkot mission. Major General Z.C. Bakshi, who commanded India's 26 Division, later wrote. "After the Pakistani thrust at Chhamb, [Army] Headquarters was in a flap and they took away one of my brigades and told me not to attack [Siâlkot]. All those brilliant plans prepared before the war went to waste all because people could not keep their cool in the heat of battle and let one temporary reverse cloud their judgement.'[XX] (If it is any consolation, exactly the same happened in Pâkistân, too, several times during that war.)

---

5. This interesting insight comes from the military history website, ttp://www.subcontinent.com/1971war/west.html.

   As a civilian I notice countless references to Pâkistân's smugness in the East. They never thought that India could breach their defences in the East. So, obviously Pâkistân was very well armed in the East. By 'concentrating forces in the West' what is perhaps meant is 'a disproportionate retention of forces in the West,' considering that the war was really about the East.

The Puñjâb-Sindh area is not relevant to this book, because it does not border Jammû or Kashmîr.

The Shakargarh bulge: It was here that one of the bloodiest battles was fought. Lt. General K.K. Siñgh was the commander of India's only 'strike' corps, the 1 Corps, the headquarters of which were at Pathânkot. On the other side of the border was Pâkistân's 1 Corps, a 'strike force' with a good reputation.

The Shakargarh 'bulge' protrudes into the region between Pathânkot in north Puñjâb and Sâmbâ in south Jammû. Indian hills are to its east and the Pâkistân border on its west. The 'bulge' is vulnerable to Indian forces from three sides. India decided to attack from all three.

The badly depleted 39 Division, under Major General B.R. Prabhu, attacked from the western tip. Its initial thrust into Pâkistânî territory was perhaps its only success. Inside Pâkistân it got trapped in minefields. The 39 Division was supposed to cover the flanks of the other two attacking Divisions—54 Div from Sâmbâ and 36 Div from the south—but was unable to, thus impeding their efforts.

54 Div, under Major General W.A.G. Pinto, did quite well, considering that two-thirds of his Division had been sent to protect Chhamb, where the Pâkistânis were on top. Brigadier A.S.Vaidya, who led an armoured brigade, and his brave men captured the main positions above Pâkistân's Shakargarh-Zafarwal road.

India was now ready for the next big task: to build a bridge across River Basañtar, and a road to the bridge. Pâkistân had sensed the Indian intention. So, its army mined that area to a 'depth' of 1.4km. To thwart the Indian attack it had also deployed four armoured brigades, which it later augmented with two infantry brigades and one armoured brigade. This was infinitely more manpower and armour than the invading Indian forces had.

Indian engineers continued their work even as the Pâkistân Air Force fired from the air and the Pâkistân Army from the land. The commanding officer of an Indian battalion and a very large number of men were killed in the process.

The road and the bridge were completed on the 15th December. Pâkistân sent its 8 Independent Armoured Brigade to destroy the bridge. India lost the better part of two tank regiments while defending the bridge. The situation on the Indian side, as can be imagined, was quite grim. India had seized Pâkistâni land but holding on to it, leave alone further advances into Pâkistân, was proving very difficult.

At last, 17 Horse, an Indian armoured regiment, aided by three infantry battalions, managed to contain Pâkistân's valiant counter attack. Both sides were at the end of their tether and fought as best they could.

Pâkistân lost forty-six tanks that day. 17 Horse lost all but three tanks, and now faced Pâkistân's entire 13 Cavalry armoured squadron, commanded by Major Nisâr. India's Captain V. Malhotra led the three tanks that paralysed 13 Cavalry by hitting most of its tanks.

Second Lieutenant Arun Khétarpâl, fresh out of military school, scored most of the Indian hits, till Major Nisar's tank smashed Khetarpal's. Though mortally wounded, Khétarpâl managed to cause equal damage to Nisar's tank before succumbing to his wounds. Major Nisar jumped out of his tank. He found that of the Indian squadron commanders only Captain Malhotra was alive. Had Khétarpâl abandoned his tank, as his seniors had ordered him to, he might have survived. But he was more intent on destroying Major Nisar's tank—which he achieved at the cost of his own life.[6]

Jarpal: Major Hoshiâr Siñgh and his men of 3 Grenadiers captured Jarpal village from Pâkistân. The Pakistanis brought in a battalion, in an effort to regain the village. Maj. Hoshiâr Siñgh received serious injuries in that battle. Later that evening, when the 'cease-fire' came into effect, Siñgh's men found the bodies of eighty-five Pakistani soldiers.

The Indian Army captured the territory leading to—and only seven kilometres short of—Zafarwal.

The Battle of Pooñch and the Thân Pîr operations

'Within the range of the Pâkistânî artillery' Other than Chhamb-Akhnoor, what Pâkistân had concentrated all its energies on was the conquest of Pooñch. Its 12 Infantry Division was given this task. Two Indian picquets, 405 and 406, built on a hill northeast of Pooñch—and overlooking it—defended the town. They were manned by detachments of India's 93 Infantry Brigade—especially 6 Sikh.

Pâkistân chose to attack Chhamb-Akhnoor and Pooñch because these were the two places where it had the strategic advantage—and the greatest chance of success. Maj. Gen. (then Lt Col.) R.N. Chibber points out that the entire belt near Pooñch town—which included Thân Pîr, the Chañdak Spur and the Kalai Bridge—was within the range of the Pâkistânî artillery.[xxi]

Around the middle of November 1971, the Indian Army had started noticing a 'conspicuous increase in Pâkistânî movements and activities opposite Pooñch town.'[xxii] Pâkistân had begun to shift its 7 Infantry Division from the NWFP and Sindh to its border and LoC with Indian Punjãb and Jammû.

6. This account is based on Major Nisar's extremely gracious telling of the story.

The Indian Army Commander reacted immediately. He ordered the 'move' of the 33 Infantry Brigade from Sâmbâ to Pooñch, which was done on the 23rd and 24th November. 8 Jât, which was part of this brigade, was detached and placed under the 93 Infantry Brigade (Pooñch Brigade). It was directed to defend the Durangali Nullâh (stream) all by itself, station itself on the Bâñdî Chéchiyâñ spur and reinforce the defence of picquets 405 and 406. India's 11 JAK Militia was responsible for the area in which Thân Pîr and the Chañdak Spur are located.

This was a very difficult task because the mountainous terrain was forbidding and it was cold. More important, the Pâkistân Army could see every Indian movement in this area. So, as Maj. Gen. Chibber recalls, 'The work had to be carried out at night—and against time.'

There were villages nearby. This meant that the Indian Army could not lay mines everywhere to make the imminent Pâkistânî invasion difficult because some of the mines would have hurt the village people as well. The village people—all of them Muslim and many of them Gujjar—appreciated the gesture and reciprocated as they always have since 1947. They helped the army carry ammunition, rations and other stores wherever needed.

Miâñ Bashîr, the legendary Gujjar leader to whom (and whose family) the Gujjars of the Himâlayas (J&K, HP, Uttarâñchal, north Punjâb and even 'AJK') owe allegiance, and who was a minister in the J&K Cabinet at the time, came all the way from the state capital, camped on the spot and personally ensured that the Indian Army received all the help that it wanted.[xxiii]

A Pâkistânî victory: In the first of the three phases of its surprise attack, around 7.45 on the night of the 3rd December, Pâkistân infiltrated a battalion with a company of Pâkistân's elite SSG (Special Service Group) through the Durangali Nullâh. By then the Indians had had around ten days to prepare their defences, 'which were ready though not fully but substantially.'[xxiv] By the morning of the 4th December Pâkistân had captured the Chañdak Spur as well as the Thân Pîr ridge.

This critical ridge is just above the all-important Kalai Bridge, which was the only link that Pooñch town had with much of India. Pooñch town and 93 Infantry Brigade were thus cut off from Rajourî and Mañdî valley. Pakistan's 9 AK Brigade now dominated Pooñch town as well the road to Mañdî valley. From the Indian point of view, things were desperate.

The main attack of Pâkistân's 2 AK Brigade, also on the night of 3/4 December, was on the outlying posts, 405 and 406 (6 Sikh) and the Bâñdî Chéchiyâñ spur (8 Jat). The Pâkistânis 'shelled' the Indian defences massively. 6 Sikh and 8 Jat replied with equally intense 'artillery, infantry mortars and MMG [medium machine gun] fire. The [Pâkistânî] attack was brutally broken up by this fire' by the morning of the 4th December.[xxv]

The Indian reply: Early on the morning of the 4th December, the headquarters of 25 Infantry Division asked Brig. M.S. Panwar (Para), who was the commander of 33 Infantry Brigade to clear Thân Pîr, Chañdak Spur and areas above the Kalai Bridge.

Panwar immediately drove to the Kalai Bridge. With him were the Artillery Regimental Commander, Lt. Col. Rânâdé, and the Brigade Major, Maj. H.S. Chaudhary. The Pâkistânîs, who now dominated the Bridge, started shelling this top-level reconnaissance party rather heavily. That was the Pâkistânîs' undoing, for it gave Panwar and his officers a precise idea about how the Pâkistânîs had spread themselves out in the area. (Pâkistân's Liâquat Company (SSG) had been given the task of killing Panwar, whom his colleagues describe as a 'go-getter.')

Brig. Panwar instructed his Artillery Regimental Commander to engage the Pâkistânîs with artillery fire. Lt. Col. Rânâdé got the direction of his guns changed towards the Pâkistânîs' new position. In less than half an hour the Indians were able to reply to the Pâkistânî infiltrators in kind.

Panwar also asked Col. N.B. Siñgh, the CO (Commanding Officer) of 13 Mahâr to move his battalion to the Kalai Bridge. 13 Mahâr acted at once. Maj. Chaudhary organised the shifting of the battalion to its new 'firm base.' Maj. Gen. Chibber writes, 'Though the area was new to 13 Mahâr, it must go their great credit that without loss of time they got after the [Pâkistânîs].'

Shortly after 2 p.m. on the 4th December, the peerless 13 Mahâr had wrested the Chañdak Green Ridge—which is close to the bridge—back from the Pâkistânîs. Indian traffic began to ply on the Kalai Bridge once again.

Why Pâkistân failed: Pâkistân failed because its back up force could not link up with its daring infiltrating unit. When the Indians fired back—'brutally' as Maj. Gen. Chibber puts it—Pâkistân's infiltrating soldiers began to rush back to their side of the LoC. Some soldiers of Pâkistân's Liâquat Company were unable to go back in time. They were 'rounded up by the local [Muslim] civilians who handed them over to the nearest Indian Army unit.'[xxvi]

Some Pâkistânî soldiers, who were from East Pâkistân (now Bangla Desh), surrendered to the Indian troops. (There were a number of defections in the Hîrânagar and Sâmbâ sectors as well. The most famous of these was of a Lieutenant Colonel from East Pâkistân who drove into India in his official jeep, bag and baggage, flying a white flag. This officer went on to play a very important role in the army as well as politics of Bangla Desh.)

The recapture of Thân Pîr: The Pâkistânîs sitting on Thân Pîr started shelling 13 Mahâr heavily.

Just before dawn on the 5th December, the brave soldiers of 13 Mahâr started climbing the narrow, sharp-edged, steep and dangerous ridge that led from Chañdak Green to Thân Pîr. They attacked the Pâkistânî force at six that evening. R. Saksena writes that a 'fierce battle took place at close quarters. The attack was a complete success and the [Pâkistânîs] ran helter-skelter, abandoning [a] huge quantity of arms, including a Chinese 76mm. Recoilless Gun, as well as their dead soldiers.'[xxvii]

Saksena adds, '13 Mahâr attacked Thân Pîr at the incredible ratio of 1:1...the feature was recaptured without a single casualty.'

Casualties: Elsewhere in that series of battles 8 Jat lost an officer—Capt. Kuldeep Siñgh Râthee—and six Other Ranks (ORs). Maj. Gen. Chibber says that Capt. Râthee, who was one of his best officers, died on the 7th December when a Pâkistânî shell ricocheted and hit him. No officer of 6 Sikh died, but some ORs did. Indian military historians describe these casualties as 'nominal' compared to the Pâkistânîs and considering the situation. An East Pâkistânî officer who defected informed the Indian Army that Pâkistân lost 350 officers and ORs in the Pooñch-Thân Pîr battles. Many of them got caught in Indian minefields. The dead included a large number of PoK villagers, some as young as twelve, whom the Pâkistân Army had employed to carry its equipment.

Among the Pâkistânîs who died were Lt. Col. Ahmed Nâsir Khân, the Commanding Officer of 9 AK Batallion, Maj. Jâvéd, Battery Commander, and twenty soldiers. The Indian soldiers who found their bodies buried them 'with full religious [Islâmic] and military honour,' Maj. Gen. Chibber writes, adding, 'However, Pâkistânî troops have a very despicable record of inflicting brutality on prisoners of war [POWs], as also mutilating their dead bodies by gouging their eyes, cutting off their genitalia and slitting their throats. They had done this to some 11 J&K Militia personnel taken prisoner by them, whose bodies were recovered by 13 Mahâr after the capture of Thân Pîr. The same was inflicted by Pâkistânî troops on POWs in the Kargil operations of 1999.'

A failed back-up: In fairness to the Pâkistânîs they lost after a famous initial victory, achieved by Lt. Col. Khân and his brave men, because something had gone terribly wrong. They were supposed to invade India with two brigades and a battalion. In actual fact they came with a much smaller force. Except for the bold and successful thrust by

Lt. Col. Khân and his men, the Pâkistânî attack was intriguingly feeble. There was no back up at all.

The Indians won hands down in Pooñch-Thân Pîr but paid a price elsewhere. 25 Division, military experts feel, could have handled the Pâkistânî invasion of Pooñch all by itself. Some Indian officers overplayed the Pâkistânî threat (which, as mentioned above, did not materialise wholly). 33 Infantry Brigade was abruptly moved from 39 Infantry Division, causing some damage to the Division. Worse still, it was not used fully and was given only a limited role.

The Battle of Chhamb

Major General Gurcharan Siñgh Sandhu feels that this was 'the most serious reverse suffered [by India] in the 1971 war[xxviii] *From the Pâkistânî point of view 'it was this battle that sustained the morale of the army in West Pâkistân and provided much needed credibility to sustain and preserve the [Pâkistân] army's image in the wake of the traumatic events of December 1971 [i.e. defeat in Bangladesh].*[xxix]

In 1965, Pâkistân's Maj. General Akhtar Hussain Malik had swiftly moved his men and machines into Chhamb. Pâkistân's Operation Grand Slam then continued its march towards Akhnoor, though without similar success there.

At the time, India had not given Chhamb its due importance and had stationed only a single Infantry Brigade there, with a squadron of outdated French AMX-13 tanks. Pâkistân vastly outgunned India. It had two armoured regiments: and modern American Patton tanks.

Things were very different in 1971. Chhamb now had all of an Infantry Division (with two Border Security Force battalions also under it), heavy fortifications and Russian T-54/55 tanks to protect it.

There are two ridges, parallel to each other, north of Chhamb. They are called Mandiâlâ North and South. They shielded the town from the Pâkistân Army. River Tawi was another obstacle for the Pâkistânis, though it is quite shallow in winter.

The battle line-up was: India's 10 Infantry Division was defending Chhamb with a hundred and four tanks (ninety of them made in the USSR). Pâkistân's 23 Division with 129 tanks (of which only seventy-four were T-59s; the rest were Sherman 11/M-36/B2) had been asked to wrest the area from India.

The Pâkistân artillery had one hundred and thirty guns in all. India was only four short of that number. Pâkistâni as well as Indian military historians feel that India's Russian-made tanks gave it the technology edge this time, because America had stopped giving Pâkistân military aid after 1965.

As in 1965, the Pâkistânis wanted to move from Chhamb to Akhnoor, capture the bridge there and thus cut off all of Rajourî, Pooñch and Akhnoor from the rest of India.[7] Besides, had Pâkistân captured Akhnoor, it could have threatened Jammû town itself, not to mention Réâsî-Udhampur and beyond.

India does not covet Pâkistâni territory. However, Pâkistân's crucial Grand Trunk Road is only fifty or sixty kilometres from Chhamb. The Pâkistânis always felt that so long as Chhamb was with India, the GT Road would be vulnerable to the Indian Army. Besides, there is no river or stream to hinder the Indian Army had it decided to advance into Pâkistân.

The first attack: The Pâkistân Air Force bombarded the area on the evening of the 3rd December, after which, at 8.20pm, Pâkistân's 66 Brigade invaded India. By two in the morning it accomplished its mission of capturing Indian territory to a depth of 3000 yards. Pâkistân's 111 Brigade had been given an identical task: to seize India's Moel village that evening (and Chhamb by the 5th December). However, the Indian Army stopped it in its tracks.

Pâkistân's 11 Cavalry Group needed a three-kilometre strip in order to lodge its men and then 'break out.' The 66 Brigade had done the needful for it.

The Battle Of Mandiâlâ: The Indians had thought that Pâkistân would attack from the south. That probably was why India had not deployed any armour to protect Déwâ Mandiâlâ, from which a passage led into Indian territory.

The 11 Cavalry Group captured Gurhâ the next morning. The tanks of India's Deccan Horse struck back at Mandiâlâ. India held the heights. Therefore, historians of both countries agree, within a few minutes Deccan Horse destroyed seven T-59 tanks and two recoilless guns. Meanwhile, 11 Cavalry's tanks arrived from behind Mandiâlâ North and captured that ridge by three in the afternoon—though only after losing many of its tanks and men. (By the end of December 4, eleven Pâkistâni tanks had been hit in this area.)

India lost the Commanding Officer and four other officers of 7 Kumaon's O Group. Meanwhile, the heroic 5 Sikh and the tank troops of Deccan Horse continued to hold Mandiâlâ South.

---

7. And that was what happened when, in September 1992, an enormous flood washed the historic Akhnoor bridge away. By then an alternate route to Rajourî-Pooñch had been built through Réâsî, but the Akhnoor Bridge remained India's most convenient link with the two and a quarter districts across the river. Pâkistân would have loved to take advantage of India's extended discomfiture in 1992-93—the bridge took more than a year to rebuild—had the same floods not devastated its own territory—and bridges—even more ruthlessly.

4/5 December: Pâkistân's 13 AK Battalion captured the Mandiâlâ bridge. However, India's 9 Horse thwarted its attempts to get its tanks to cross River Tawi into Indian land.

By the *morning of the 5th December*, the Indians were once again in control. Not only was Pâkistân's 26 Cavalry Squadron unable to advance into India, it lost three tanks. Pâkistân's Maj. General Eftikhar Khân Janjua, a great strategist and a man not easily unsettled by failures, began to modify his plans to capture Chhamb. He decided not to engage Indian troops but to look for gaps in India's defences, instead.

India had begun to think that Pâkistân would continue to invade from the north, as it had on the two previous days. India did not expect Pâkistâni forces to come up from Jaimal Kot. But that was what they did on the night of 5/6 December. By the morning of the 6th, Pâkistân's 23 Balûch captured ill-defended Bakan and Paur.

The Indian Army had left an opening in its minefield between Barsala and Jhanda. Pâkistâni historians feel that India had created this gap to enable Indian soldiers to invade Pâkistân someday. Pâkistân's 2 Armoured Brigade looked for the gap, found it and entered Indian territory through it. By 5.30 that evening (6 December), it annexed Chak Pañdit.

On that same evening, Pâkistân's 4 AK Brigade captured Mandiâlâ South—after a tough two-day battle with 5 Sikh. A few hours later, 2 Armoured had Pallâñwâlâ—Pâkistân's biggest prize in the 1971 War till then.[8] India's 39 Medium Field Artillery and 216 Medium Regiment lost a hundred and seven gunners in the battle of Chhamb.[xxx]

At 7.30 that evening, Major General Jaswant Siñgh, the GOC of India's 10 Division, decided to concede the western bank of the Tawi. He ordered the 191 Brigade to withdraw to the eastern bank of the Tawi. The crucial Mandiâlâ bridge was destroyed at midnight. The Indian withdrawal meant that Pâkistân's 2 Armoured Brigade could now walk into Chhamb, which it did the next day (7 December)—but not without resistance from the Indian Air Force.

Brig. Saeed Ismat, SJ, was the first Pâkistâni to set foot in Chhamb. He recalls[xxxi] that Radio Pâkistân announced that 'Chamb had fallen to our valiant forces' when in fact 2 Armoured Brigade 'was barely at Chak Pañdit.' Ismat and Captain Tariq, GSO-3, flew over Chhamb the next morning, They found Pâkistâni troops 'digging two miles southeast of Chamb.

8. Pâkistân ruled over this entire area for several months, till it returned much of the captured land after the Simlâ Agreement. During the months that it governed this area, which had lost its Muslim population in 1947, Pâkistân built a fairly big mosque in Pallâñwâlâ, which can still be seen.

The small town of Chamb was deserted and 2 Armoured Brigade was nowhere near it…I landed the aircraft in a grassy field in Chamb, switched off the engines and started a long wait for [Pâkistâni] troops to arrive. We entered the Indian brigade command post and when we came back to my aircraft, [four] Indian SU-7s were on us throwing all sorts of munitions. It was a miracle that my little L-19 standing proud in the middle of the ground was intact. I took off to urge 10 Balûch and 2 Armoured Brigade that had stopped in their tracks after the air attack to resume their advance. I landed back at Chamb. It was in the late afternoon that 10 Balûch entered Chamb.'

Pâkistân's 111 Brigade was asked to move further into the Pallâñwâlâ-Jauriañ area. General Eftikhar (Iftekhâr?) had planned the attack in detail. However, his helicopter crashed on the evening of the 9th December. The general later succumbed to his wounds. The loss of his brilliant leadership meant that the Pâkistâni forces did not achieve as much as they were capable of. The 'officiating' (temporary) command of the division was given to Brig Kamal Matin. 28 Cavalry, which had only twenty-eight tanks left after the operation at Chhamb, remained the armoured component of the Pâkistâni attack.

The infantry attack started an hour after the midnight of 9/10 December opposite the Darh and Raipur ferries. By the next afternoon, the Pâkistânis had created a bridgehead that was a kilometre deep and four kilometres wide. The Indian Army reacted swiftly. Maj. Gen Sartâj Siñgh, the Commander of the 15 Corps deployed 7 Kumaon, 5/8 Gurkha, 10 Garhwâl and 3/4 Gurkha and a squadron of the 72 Armoured Regiment. India succeeded in containing the bridgehead.

Now the Pâkistânis made a series of mistakes. 28 Cavalry Regiment had succeeded in crossing River Tawi by 1pm on the 10th December. It asked 111 Brigade for support, which was denied. Major Nazar Hussain, the brigade major (BM) of 111 Brigade, wrongly reported that 28 Cavalry had just four tanks left. At 2pm on the 10th December, the top brass of Pâkistân's 23 Division ordered that 111 Brigade should be withdrawn. At 6pm, 28 Cavalry was asked to withdraw west of River Tawi and concentrate on the Singri area. Col Tauqir ul Islam of Pâkistân comments, 'These were strange orders because till 12 December the entire area upto [Pallâñwâlâ] remained un-occupied by [Indian forces].'[xxxii]

From the Pâkistâni point of view, as Maj. Agha Humayun Amin would later write, 'The Battle of Chamb [sic] was a battle of lost opportunities.'

The Darûchiâñ disaster: After Pâkistân's attack on Pooñch, which was successful initially, the Indian Army became concerned about its defensive position, especially in that sector. It decided to go on the offensive, even if to a limited extent, all along the LoC. On the night of 10/ 11 December it captured Nañgî Tékrî, Jungle Tékrî and Bump.

As a result the Pâkistân Army was no longer able to use the Kotli-Madarpur-Hajirâ road in thitherto occupied Kashmîr.

Darûchiâñ is a conical strip of mountainous land in Pâkistân occupied Kashmîr. It is located on the LoC in the Pooñch sector. Its importance is that it blocks the Balnoi neck of the Kotli-Balnoi road between River Pooñch and the LoC. The Indian Army decided to recover it for India because that would straighten out the LoC and make it easier to defend at that point.

Some geniuses—especially Col. Hattal, the Indian Commanding Officer—decided that the best way to wrest Darûchiâñ from Pâkistân was to assault it from all three sides and deploy every single company of 14 Grenadiers for this. A senior Indian officer who was posted nearby points out that it should have been obvious that when a narrow projection is attacked from three sides some shells fired from the left are bound to fall on fellow soldiers attacking from the right, and vice versa. And a few shells fired from behind will certainly fall on fellow soldiers on the other two sides. And that is what happened.

The Pâkistânîs, on their part, defended Darûchiâñ valiantly.

The Indian soldiers did not have adequate fire support. The Pâkistânîs, on the other hand, could fire on them at will. Col. Hattal was too far removed from the scene of action to influence the battle. His colleagues say that his ideas of warfare were 'weird.'

In the event, fifty-two Indian fighters died in that disastrous offensive operation. This figure includes five young officers, who had been leading from the front, as well as four junior commissioned officers.

'Who was to blame?' an Indian military historian has asked. 'All the commanders from the divisional commanders downward for having approved such an unsound plan.'[xxxiii]

(I obtained these figures from the Internet,[xxxiv] by doing a Google search. There were only four references to this battle with that spelling: and two of them were postings made by some secular Indian non-Muslim who was talking about the Muslim martyrs of the modern Indian Army. The Grenadiers have a very high percentage of Muslims and a large number of the Indian soldiers who died at Darûchiâñ were Muslim.)

1971: The important battles: The main battles fought in Jammû & Kashmir and the neighbouring areas of the Puñjâb were at Chhamb (December. 6-10), Laleali-Picquet 707 (December 3-8), the defence of Pooñch (December 3-7), Thanpîr (December 4-5), Gutrian (December 3-7), Banwat (December 3-4), Nangi Tekri (December 10-11), Turtok, Ladâkh (December 6-14), Shingo River Valley, Ladâkh (December 7-17), Brachil Pass and Wali Malik (December 7-12), Basañtar River (December 5-17) and Sâmbâ (several days in December 1971).[xxxv]

1971—A summary: Pâkistân continues to occupy much of Chhamb to this day. Several thousand Hiñdu-Sikhs fled Chhamb and sought refuge in other parts of Jammû district. India made gains in the areas where it had taken the retaliatory initiative—especially in Ladâkh, where it regained Turtuk (which it had lost in 1947-48). Later, as part of an agreement with Pâkistân, India returned most of what it had conquered—but retained areas like Turtuk.

Wali Mohd. Aseer Kishtwâri writes, "According to the White Paper [published by] Pâkistân [in] 1977, India gained 340.88 square miles and lost 58.38 square miles."[xxxvi]

The Kishtwâr agitations of 1969 and 1974

High school students and other youths of Kishtwâr boycotted school for days on end and took out large processions through the streets of the town. They wanted the government to establish a college for undergraduate studies in Kishtwâr. The government's problem was that if it created a college in Kishtwâr, it would be obliged to do the same in several other similar towns of the state, which it could not afford.

The agitation went on for so long that the government called the student leaders to Srînagar for negotiations. The students agreed to resume their studies when the government promised to set up the college that they wanted. This was in 1969.

The people of Kishtwâr waited five years for the college to be founded. When it did not materialise, the students took to the streets once again. This time their elders joined them. Another long agitation followed. Not just the political leaders of the area, politicians from other parts of the state started visiting Kishtwâr in support of the students' demand.

Somehow the agitation turned violent on the 13th September, 1974. The police fired on the procession. Four youths— Abdul, Gyân, Mohd. Iqbâl and Ravinder—died. Many others were injured. Never in their known history had the civilians of Kishtwâr been so brutalised till then.

This turned the whole town hostile towards the government, then headed by Syed Mîr Qâsim. The people of Kishtwâr town shut down their shops and brought all normal activity to a halt. When this had gone on for a month, the government did exactly what it would in similar circumstances in the Valley of Kashmîr. It requested the most popular leader of the state, Sheikh Muhammad Abdullâh—who did not have an official position at the time—to help pacify the incensed people of Kishtwâr.

The Sheikh persuaded the people to call off their agitation. He took them to Srînagar where they met the Chief Minister. As a compromise it was agreed that a vocational college (as opposed to a college that taught the liberal arts and sciences) would be set up in Kishtwâr.

The degree college failed to materialise this time as well.

1978-79: The Pooñch agitation

In December 1978 began what perhaps was the most momentous agitation in the history of Jammû province. It was so serious that several Jammû leaders tried to use the anger among the people to separate Jammû from Kashmîr and either form a state of its own or join neighbouring Himâchal Pradésh.

It all started in Pooñch town (with an immediate echo in nearby Rajourî town) when unemployed, educated urban youths complained that they were not being given jobs, which were being diverted instead to youths with inferior educational qualifications in the rural areas.

At some stage things got out of hand in Pooñch town and the police killed ten agitating youths. This was infinitely worse than what had happened in Kishtwâr. All the major towns of Jammû province rose in sympathy with the people of Pooñch.

Life in Pooñch and Jammû towns was paralysed for the next four months. Other towns were affected to a lesser extent. Politicians, cutting across party lines, converted the unrest into an agitation against '"regional imbalances", that is to say, the general neglect of Jammû region [and a] preference for Kashmîr valley,' Aseer Kishtwâri records.[xxxvii]

The agitation was called off in March 1979 when the state government, then headed by Sheikh Muhammad Abdullâh, constituted the Sikri Commission of Inquiry to look into the allegation that Jammû was being given short shrift in matters of economic development. Mr (Justice) Siîkrî was an eminent retired judge from outside the state.

1990-2006: Most of Jammû province stays away from militancy...and reaps the peace dividend.

Jammû is a big and posh city with a clear Hindu majority. However, many mosques and other symbols of Muslim heritage can be found all around. It is a peaceful city and life is quite normal here. Apparently, Hindus and Muslims are living peacefully...Not a single organisation hailing from Jammû is member of the 23 party [anti-status quo] alliance, the APHC.

Ershad Mahmud, *The News* (Pâkistân) July 25, 2001[xxxviii]

Throughout its history Jammû had been the second city of the state of Jammû and Kashmîr—in terms of size, population, infrastructure, quality of life and availability of modern facilities. This remained true even during the 101 years when a dynasty of Jammûites ruled the state. Srînagar had the better schools, colleges, hospitals, clubs, libraries, cinema halls, restaurants, bookshops and intellectual life, and better known doctors and dentists—just everything, including a trendier partying set.

Well to do Jammûites would choose to educate their children in Srînagar. They would maintain a summer residence in Kashmîr and also go there to shop, consult doctors—and party.

The phase of Kashmîr's history that began in December 1989 changed all that. Indeed, it inverted the equation.

Jammû has historically been a generous host. With silent lips it has sought out the tired, the poor huddled masses yearning to breathe free. The 'wretched refuse of teeming shores' always knew that they would find solace and a comforting shoulder in Jammû city. In the eighteenth century (and for a while later) it was the Muslims of Delhi and the Punjãb who sought Jammû. After 1947, the refugees of Mîrpur and Chhamb as well as West Punjãb fled to Jammû.

And now, between January and May 1990 another tempest-tos't people, rendered newly homeless, leaving their comfortable—and, often, considerable—homes behind, sought refuge in the city where tigers and goats have traditionally sipped water from the same pool and lived together amicably.

Around 1.5 lakh (150,000)[xxxix] Kashmîrî Pañdits and other (Punjãbî- and Bhaderwâhi-speaking) Hiñdus from Kashmîr migrated en masse from the troubled Valley to Jammû city, Kathuâ town, Udhampur town and, later, Delhi. So did some Kashmîrî Muslims.

The population of Jammû city suddenly increased by around a quarter. The prices of vegetables and groceries immediately shot up, and stabilised only towards the end of the year. The cost of housing plots jumped up, and has been rising ever since.

The Kashmîrî Pañdits are an almost entirely-literate community with educational levels well above those of the Kashmîrî Muslims and Jammûites.

Now a pool of well-educated teachers and office workers became available to Jammû. They were willing to work for around a third less than the then prevailing wage. (The government gives migrants from Kashmîr a monthly allowance in cash and kind over and above what they might earn in the private sector.) On the one hand less qualified and/ or better paid local teachers and clerks got displaced in the private sector. On the other, the services of talented doctors (including some medical superstars), journalists, teachers and other professionals became available to Jammû.

Around the same time—the early 1990s—other unrelated things started happening. Pilgrim traffic to the holy shrine of Srî Mâtâ Vaishno Dévî jî began to increase at the rate of around twenty per cent a year. Pilgrims need hotels to stay in, buses and taxis to travel by (because there are no trains) and souvenirs (mostly Kashmîr's dry fruits, Jammû's basmati rice and *râjmâ* {red beans} from the Jammû hills) to take home..

Within a few years the people who sold almonds, walnuts and dried apricots became exceedingly rich. Though these dry fruits grow in Kashmîr (and Ladâkh), bulk customers now decided that they would purchase them only from peaceful Jammû. Dry-fruit shops were renovated with expensive black granite and marble.

This prosperity virtually wiped out unemployment at least in the lower rungs of the economic ladder.

Around 1992, an economic boom swept all of India as well.

The pharmaceutical trade shifted its state headquarters from Srînagar to Jammû, as did some other categories of private business.

Before 1989 many Kashmîrî Muslims had favourite doctors who happened to be Pañdit. Others would not dream of letting their school-going children seek private tuition from anyone except certain renowned Pañdit teachers. After the mass-migration of Kashmîrî Pañdits, both categories of Kashmîrî Muslims took to shifting to Jammû for several weeks at a time, to be with the doctor or teacher of their choice.

The 1990s were also a time when expensive schools and private as well as more-prestigious government-run colleges started springing up in Jammû. On the other hand, disturbances in Kashmîr meant that schools and colleges in the Valley would often announce unscheduled 'holidays.' Besides, all-India chains of educational institutes (especially those that taught the then newly emerging science of computers) opened shop in Jammû but not in Srînagar during the early 1990s, when militancy was at its peak in Kashmîr. So, middle-class Kashmîrî Muslim parents started sending their children to Jammû to study not only at formal colleges but also at these hole-in-the-wall institutes that offered short courses of study. (Rich Kashmîrî Muslims started sending their wards to Pune, Manipâl and other parts of India, Bangladesh and the former Soviet Union where students with indifferent school-leaving grades can buy their way into professional colleges.)

I once gave half a dozen Kashmîrî Muslim students a lift from the Jammû airport, because there was a strike in town that day and there were no taxis. They asked me to drop them at an 'engineering college' that I wasn't even aware of. It turned out to be a biggish house on the outskirts of Jammû city—rather undersized for a professional college. Several such low-profile, privately owned—and, sometimes, mercenary—engineering, management and law colleges were built in Jammû during that eventful decade.

During the 1990s Jammû also got its first engineering college (run by the government and, therefore, trusted and sought after) as well as its first private medical college (which caters mainly to affluent Kashmîrî students). Jammû has become an educational capital of sorts for the region—which includes the neighbouring districts of the Punjãb and Himâchal Pradésh.

Jammû district cemented its position as the most literate district in the state. The surprise gainer was peaceful Kathuâ, which displaced Srînagar for the number two position. Since 1947 Kathuâ has been the most law-abiding, least troublesome, easiest-to-administer district in the province. Little wonder then that it has made such spectacular developmental gains.

Those who own buses, trucks and taxis (i.e. the 'transporters') mostly belong to Jammû's prosperous rural hinterland. Now that they had even more money than before they started shifting to Jammû city. Posh new housing 'colonies' started springing up all around Jammû city. The better off Hiñdu migrants of Kashmîr needed houses. So did rural Jammûites who benefited from the booming tourist economy. By the late 1990s middle class Kashmîrî Muslims—some of whom had plenty of money to spare despite militancy in the Valley—started setting up winter homes, also in the suburbs of Jammû. Muslims from Kishtwâr and other parts of Jammû province followed suit. Housing 'colonies' often reflected the district (or even tehsil) in Kashmîr in which their Kashmîrî Muslim residents had their summer homes.

To put it another way, Jammû city grew almost three and a half times between 1981 and 2001.

Attempts to ignite Jammû: It is not as if there were no attempts to stir things up in Jammû. In July 1990 someone used RDX (an enormously powerful explosive) to blow up a room in my office complex. I was the head of the district administration and blowing up the First Office of the district had enormous symbolic significance. A terrible fire ensued and many people got burnt very badly. If they pulled through it was because of the protection of God, because medically there was no reason for them to survive.

And if you do not believe in God then I wonder how you will explain these: (i) A couple of youths from one particular community went to the Ranbîr School, Jammû, to blow up the classrooms where schoolchildren of the 'other community' from Anantnag, Kashmir, were taking an examination. The bomb exploded in the hands of the would-be saboteurs. (ii) Terrorists from a third community were assembling a bomb inside an abandoned house of worship of their community. To make the bomb even more lethal they mixed tiny metal pellets, nails and screws into the paste. The bomb went off while it was being made. The pellets sliced the veins of the persons making the bomb. (iii) Two well to do youths of the same community were assembling a bomb in the bathroom of their well-appointed house near Murgi Chowk. They got into a scuffle during which the bomb exploded accidentally. (iv) 'Nationalists' from another community were assembling a bomb inside the state headquarters of their very well-known right-wing party. When the bomb went off by accident they spread a rumour pinning the blame on construction workers from the other community who were whitewashing the walls of their office.

All these incidents took place between 1990 and 1992. In all these cases the bombs went off by mistake, killing the would-be killers instead of their intended victims. Clearly a higher power was protecting the people of Jammû.

The agents of a neighbouring country tried their best to inflame the Sikhs by setting fire to the interior of the Bîbî Châñd Kaurâñ gurudwârâ. That was when another miracle took place—the holy scripture, the Guru Grañth Sâheb, was untouched by the blaze.

Kishtwâr town was not so lucky. The Jâmâ Masjid was set on fire during this wretched phase of history. The reaction was exactly what the saboteur had expected: An outraged public burnt down shops, public property, liquor vends and a private school called Âdarsh Bâl Nikétan, writes Aseer Kishtwâri.[xl]

The easiest way to incense the Hiñdus is to kill a cow. Saboteurs did that, too. We somehow managed to contain passions, which had threatened to take a violent turn.

Enemy agents (who were later caught and identified as Pâkistânî Punjãbîs) then planted a very powerful bomb in the Jâmâ Masjid of Tâlâb Khatîkâñ. Many Muslims died. Things could have taken a very ugly turn and the Muslims might have assumed the worst had Hiñdu youths, led by a party identified with Hiñdu extremism in Mumbai, not landed up at the hospital to donate blood for the wounded Muslims.

The Muslim Federation—again associated with hard postures—played an equally responsible role: especially when the 'nationalists' mentioned above were mauled by their own bomb. The leadership of both radical organisations has substantial property. The last thing that they wanted was sectarian riots. Fortunately, the leaders of both 'extreme' groups were clear headed and mature. They could see a pattern in these attempts to damage the shrines of various communities. More than us in the government, they realised that some people from across the border were trying to instigate riots.

Jammû was destined to reap the peace dividend.

References

i *A signal from Jammû* by Navnita Chadha Behera, Reader, Department of Political Science, Delhi University. (From the internet.)

ii Behera, op. cit.

iii Kishtwâri, Wali Mohd. Aseer, op. cit., p.332.

iv From the website: Library of Congress Country Studies: Pâkistân http://lcweb2.loc.gov/cgi-bin/query/r?frd/cstdy:@field(DOCID+pk0152)

v Kishtwâri, Wali Mohd. Aseer, op. cit., p.363.

vi 'Pak army responsible for '65 war: former Pak Air Chief,' *The Kashmîr Times,* August 3, 2005, quoting *Dawn*, Karachi.

vii Pathik, Jyoteeshwar, *War and Warriors of Jammû and Kashmîr* (1996), Jay Kay Book House, Jammû.

viii Shorey, Col. (retd.) Anil, 'The Saga of Hâjî Pîr,' *Force*, April 2004.

ix In the volume on 'Kashmîr' I had incorrectly given his name as Lâl Dîn.

x Pathik, op. cit., p. 351.

xi Pathik, op. cit., p. 354.

xii Qadir, Brig. Shaukat, '1965: Battle of Sialkot'.

xiii 'Ayub Khân's son drops a bombshell,' *Daily Excelsior*, 31 May 2005.

xiv 'Gohar stops short of naming mole: He was a DMO,' *The Times of India*, June 4, 2005.

xv Pathik, op.cit p.356.

xvi From the website: Library of Congress Country Studies: Pâkistân http://lcweb2.loc.gov/cgi-bin/query/r?frd/cstdy:@field(DOCID+pk0152)

xvii Tohid, Owais, 'Doctored report killed Pâkistânîs,' *The Times of India*, 4 June, 2005.

xviii Matinuddin, Lt Gen. Kamal, 'Gohar Ayub's revelations and the '65 war,' *Greater Kashmir,* 10 June, 2005.

xix From the website: Library of Congress Country Studies: Pâkistân http://lcweb2.loc.gov/cgi-bin/query/r?frd/cstdy:@field (DOCID+pk0152)

xx http://www.subcontinent.com/1971war/west.html

xxi Chibber, Maj. Gen. R,N., VSM (Retd.), *The Battle of Pooñch-1971*, unpublished manuscript (June 2005). This section is based on Maj. Gen. Chibber's paper, R. Saksena's article and oral histories.

xxii Chibber, Maj. Gen. R,N., op. cit.

xxiii Chibber, Maj. Gen. R,N., op. cit.

xxiv Chibber, Maj. Gen. R,N., op. cit.

xxv Chibber, Maj. Gen. R,N., op. cit.

xxvi Chibber, Maj. Gen. R,N., op. cit.

xxvii R. Saksena, 'Battle of Thanpir,' *Force*, February 2005.

xxviii *The Indian Armour: History of the Indian Armoured Corps - 1941-1971-* Vision Books-Delhi page.488, quoted by Maj (Retd) Agha Humayun Amin, in *The Battle of Chamb 1971*

xxix Maj (Retd) Agha Humayun Amin, in *The Battle of Chamb1971*

xxx Gaurav C. Sawant, 'Here jawans live on after they die' *The Indian Express*, Monday, June 17, 2002

xxxi http://www.defencejournal.com/2001/november/ismat.htm

xxxii From a letter to the editor of a Pâkistâni defence journal, perhaps published in March or April 2002 and posted on the internet.

xxxiii From a paper entitled 'Battle of Daruchian' published in the book *India's Wars Since Independence*

xxxiv 'Army suffers casualties at Darûchiâñ,' from The Liberation Times, a 'newspaper' posted on the Web. For this section I have also consulted the oral accounts of senior officers present in the Pooñch sector.

xxxv "Land forces of Britain, the Empire and the Commonwealth" http://www.regiments.org/wars/20thcent/71indopk.htm

xxxvi Kishtwâri, Wali Mohd. Aseer, op. cit., p.377.

xxxvii Kishtwâri, Wali Mohd. Aseer, op. cit., p.399.

xxxviii *Report on an IPS Fellow's Visit to Jammû: The Hard Realities of Jammû* by Ershad Mahmud and published in *The News* (Pâkistân), July 25, 2001

xxxxix This figure, calculated by neutral observers, including the scrupulously balanced and secular Aseer Kishtwâri (page 450), is based on the 1981 census. Mr. Kishtwâri's account is entirely sympathetic towards the displaced Kashmîrî Pañdits.

xl Op. cit., p. 567.

* * *

17

Regional Histories

Akhnoor town

(Jammû district) *The Akhnoor fort:* Work on this fort began in AD 1762, at the behest of Raja Tegh Singh. His son, Raja Alam Singh completed it, in 1802. Akhnoor was then an autonomous principality. There is a two- storeyed palace next to the fort. It has decorated arches, as well as paintings on its walls. Most of the fort is in ruins. However, some of the palace walls are still intact.

On the eastern side there are steps leading down to River Chenâb. Though constructed in the 18th century, most of them are in good shape. The turret (*burj*), also still intact, is called the Kishore Singh *burj*, after Maharaja Gulab Singh's father, who was a close associate of Tegh Singh.

The Jeo Pota (or Jia Pota) *temple*, in Akhnoor proper, on the banks of River Chenâb, has a huge sedimentary rock that has been used as a royal throne. It was on this rock that Maharaja Ranjit Singh of Punjab gave the *raj tilak* (anointment as king) to 21 year old Gulab Singh on the 16th June 1822. Gulab thus became the Raja of Jammu and later the Maharaja of Jammu, Kashmir and Ladakh.

The magnanimous Ranjit left nothing to chance. He summoned all the top chieftains of Jammu province to witness, and thus endorse, this 'coronation.' Mian Nihâl Singh was the pre-eminent Rajput leader of the time. He pierced his finger and with his blood applied the *tilak* on Gulab's forehead: thus signalling that he, and othe other hill chiefs, accepted Gulab as their king.

The Kâmeshwar temple is extremely significant for scholars and national- integrationists. Its courtyard has yielded 6th or 7th century inscriptions- pilgrim records- in a Dravidian script. These are shell inscriptions on rough pebbles.

Ambaran

(28km. from Jammu.) This is the most important archæological site in Jammu province. It is near Akhnoor town, on the right bank of River Chenâb.

A large number of Buddhist terracottas were excavated from Ambaran/ Pamberwan throughout the 20th century. Many of them were sent to the Lahore Museum and other museums across the world. They include Buddha- heads, as well as the 'heads' of sundry men and women. These heads are all of high quality and come in different sizes. The most celebrated of the lot is the Great Buddha. Charles Fabri, working at the Lahore Museum, felt that they belonged to around AD 700. The fourth century AD is now considered a more accurate date. Other artefacts found here date to the 4th, 5th and 8th centuries.

The people shown wear fancy headdresses. Interestingly, they all have matted hair. However, Charak and Billawaria assert that the Akhnoor school of terracotta is 'unique [and] free from Græco-Buddhist influence... They reveal the Gandhara influence, and though some specimens are devoid of spontaneity and freedom of the early Gandhara...[they are] the earliest examples of such an art in this region.'

In April 2001 archæologists made an extremely exciting, and important, set of discoveries here. They found a silver casket, gold and silver leaves, pearls, coral, carnelian, amethyst and three copper coins, all dating to between the 1st and 4th centuries AD. This author is not aware of a similar treasure trove, especially one that old, having been excavated from any other part of the state.

And the treasure wasn't even the best part. The place where it was found was. This was the 6m. x 6m. base of a Sarirka Stupa. A copper reliquary was found half a metre above the base. The aforementioned treasures were inside the reliquary, and inside the silver casket were a gold casket, some bones and ash. Ambaran was, clearly, an important Buddhist site in ancient India.

The exteriors of the stupa were made of moulded and plain bricks. Its core was filled with pebbles and earth. Dr. Mani writes, 'The stupa was constructed in the style of Stupas at Kalawan and Jaulian at [Takshashila]. Some votive stupas around it were also constructed during Kushan and late- Kushan period.'

Other artefacts found at this site are basins, beads, copper coins, bowls, lamps, lids, pots with handles and spouts, small sculptures

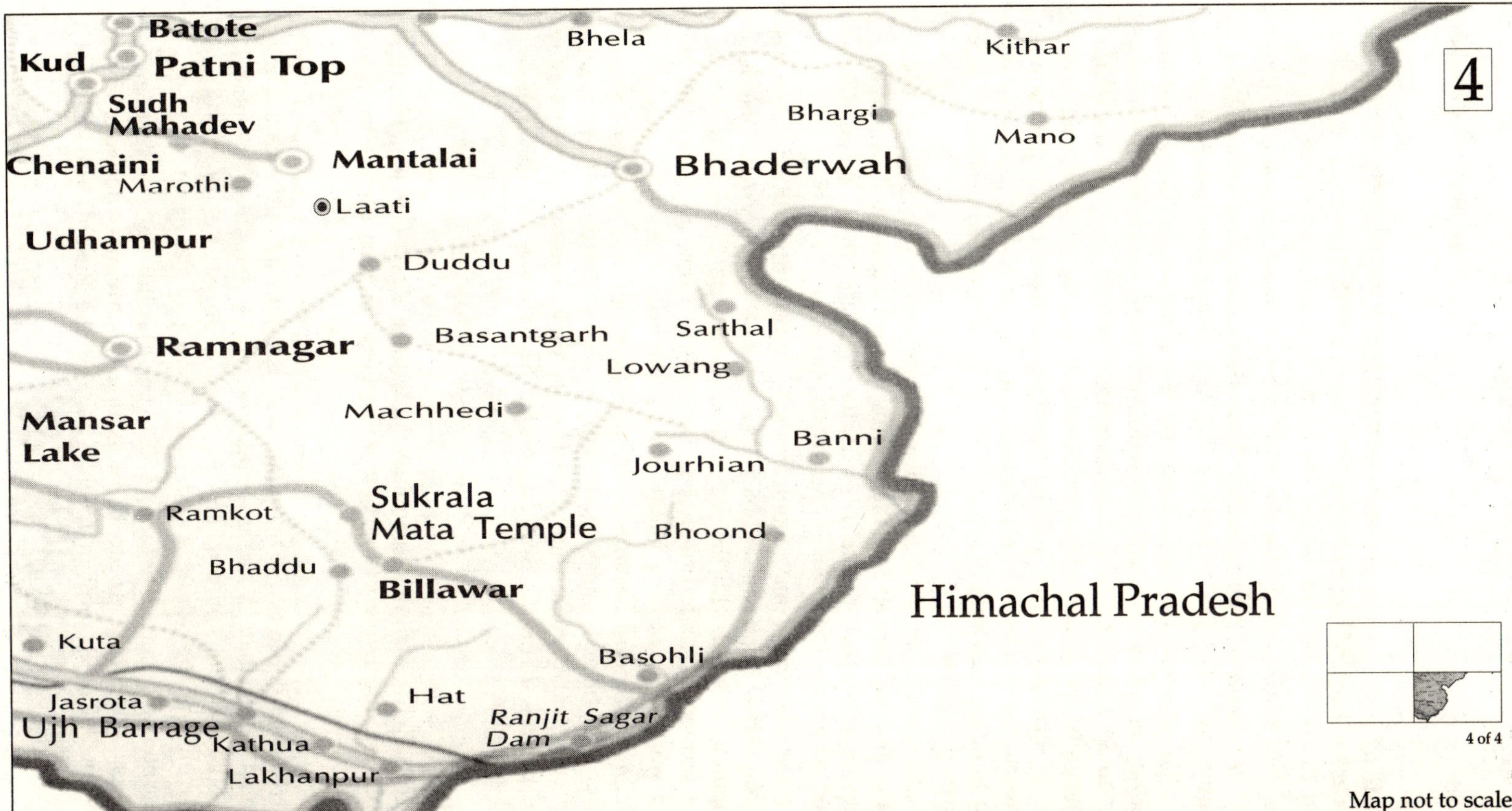

Doda, Udhampur, Kathua (Basohli, Banni, Billawar)

made of stone, sprinklers, terracotta human figures and vases. Things made of iron and copper have also been found. Huvishka, Kanishka and Soter Megas had issued the coins excavated at Ambaran.

The history of Ambaran- Pamberwan can be summed up thus:

Pre- history: People seem to have first settled here around the 2nd century BC. Till the 1st century BC, the village was quite small.

The Kushan period: Going by the richness of the art of the period, an advanced civilisation flourished here in the Kushan period (1st to 3rd centuries AD). Considerable building activity took place: especially the grand stupa mentioned above. Around the same time (1st-3rd centuries AD) a large building, prhaps a monastery, was constructed nearby. Floods damaged it. In the 4th- 5th centuries AD the building was rebuilt, only to be renovated and expanded several times thereafter.

The artists of Ambaran- Pamberwan were obviously in touch with- and influenced by- their better known Gândhâr counterparts. They mainly stuck to the Takshashila style. Red ware dating to the Kushan period has been found at Ambaran.

The Gupta period: Samudragupt brought the Sialkot- Jammu region (Madr Désh) under his control in the 4th century AD. Classical Gupta art merged with the previous style to produce something new. The terracottas that Ambaran is known for belong to this period. . Red ware dating to the Gupta period has been found at Ambaran.

The sixth and seventh centuries AD: Red ware dating to this period has been found at Ambaran. By now the rims of the bowls and cups had become thin. This reveals sophistication of technique. The pottery of the Kushan and Gupta periods was thicker- rimmed and broader.

Bafli(y)âz

(Pooñch district) Apparently the village has been named after Bunifales, the horse of Alexander the Great, which died here.

Basohli

(Kathuâ district) The word Basohli is a corruption of its ancient name Vishwasthali. Vishwa means 'the world' and sthal 'the place.' So, Vishwasthali could mean 'the place of the world' or 'the place that contains the whole world,' most probably the former.

About the period before 1630, when Basohli must have been a smaller state, what we do know is that the Mughals defeated Raja Krishan Pal of Basohli in 1590. After that the Basohli kings started going to the Mughal court. Raja Sangram Pal became a friend of the Mughal prince Dara Shikoh.

Raja Bhupat Pal is considered the founder of present- day Basohli. It was he who, around AD 1635.

During the reign of of Sangram's grandson, Raja Kirpal Singh (1678- 95), we have the first evidence of painters flourishing in Basohli.

Battalkote

(Poonch district) The village was originally called Bhatta Kote ('the town of the Kashmiri Pandits'). The army of Sultan Mehmood of Ghazni surrounded and laid siege to Loran (then Lohar Kote) in AD 1021. The Sultan then tried to launch an attack on Kashmir. The Kashmiri army that successfully fought the Sultan got its weapons made at Battalkote, because of its tradition with iron.

Behram Gallâ

(Poonch district) Till AD 1542 this village was known as Bharo Gali. That's the name by which the *Rajatarangini* refers to it. It got its present name after Behram Naik, the local jagirdar (overlord).

1542 looms large in the history of this village. That was the year when the Mughal Emperor Akbar used it as the base camp for his invasion of Kashmir. It retained this position for a long time thereafter: several battles were fought there. The ruins of Behram Naik's stone fort are testimony to the village's bloody past.

Bhaderwah

(Dodâ district) This hauntingly beautiful mountain kingdom was known in ancient times as Bhadrakashi ('a good place to rest at') or Bhadravaksha ('the happy region' or 'the good bosom').

Mostly history (and some legends)

The region: The Bhaderwah jagir (principality) measured 533 square miles. It always consisted of the valleys of River Neeru and the Kargad or Bhalessa nallah. Both rivers are tributaries of the Chandrabhaga or the Chenâb.

The jagir normally included Bhaderwah proper and, from time to time, Bhalessa, Thâthri tehsil, Ramban tehsil, Assar, Batote, Marmath, Ruggi and Galihan.

Earliest references: The *Rajatarangini* refers to its existence as an inhabited area in AD 112- 128. It is believed that this region used to have an ancient capital called Dughanagar (present day Satingal).

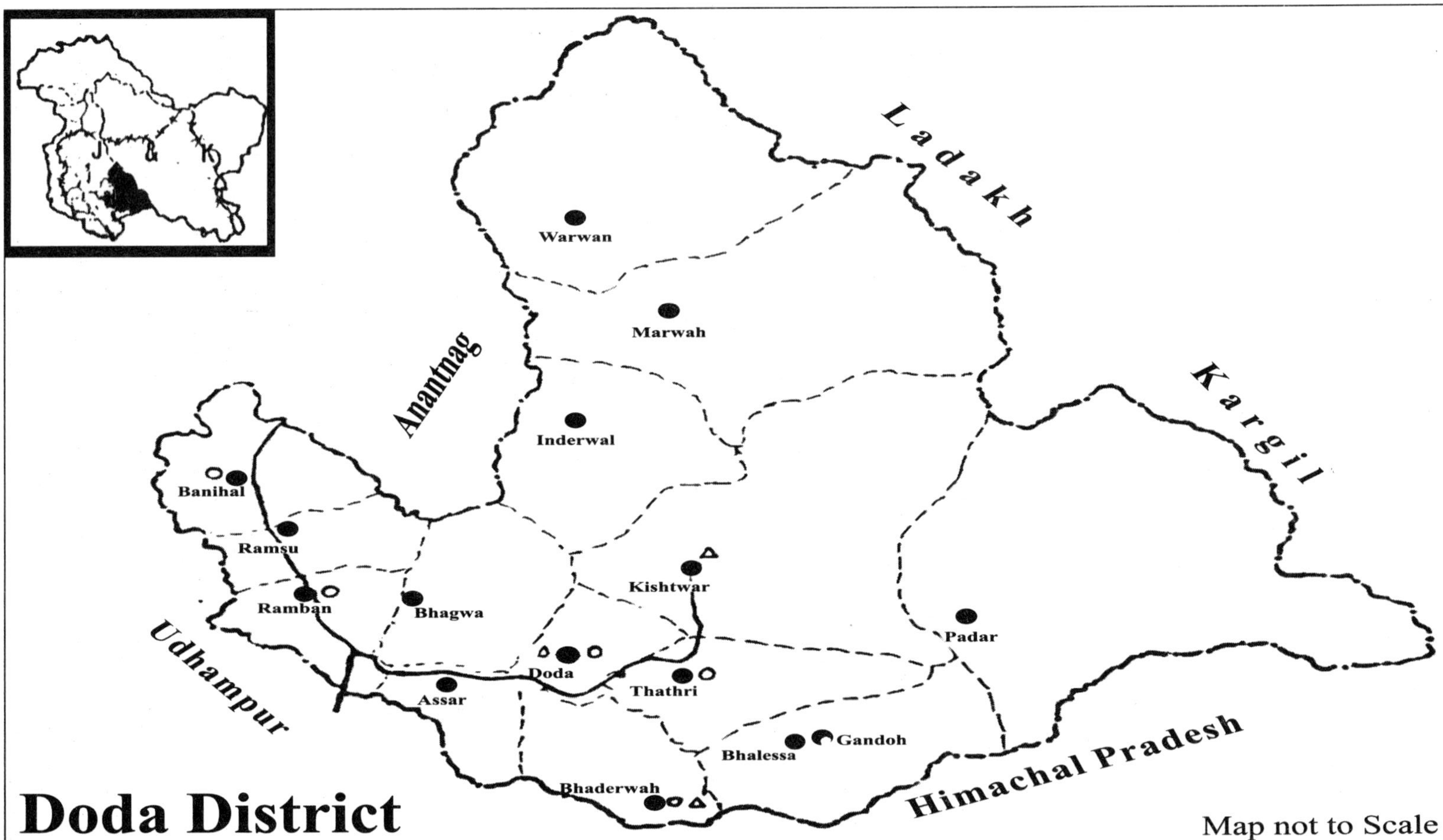
Ladakh
Kargil
Anantnag
Udhampur
Himachal Pradesh
Warwan
Marwah
Inderwal
Banihal
Ramsu
Ramban
Bhagwa
Kishtwar
Doda
Thathri
Assar
Padar
Bhalessa
Gandoh
Bhaderwah
Doda District
Map not to Scale

It is said that the Pândavs defeated Jobnath, the last king of that dynasty.

Bâsak Nag: Bâsak (Vâsuki in Sanskrit) Nâg, the snake god, is the patron deity of Bhaderwah. He is also believed to have been its first king. He belonged to Kashmir but fled to Bhaderwah's highest peak, the Kaplas Kund, when Garuda, the bird whom Lord Vishnu would ride on, chased him out of Kashmir.

Goddess Kali was the ruler of Bhaderwah at that stage. She took pity on Bâsak (who, it turns out, was her favourite brother) and let him rule in her stead. (Her shrine in Bhaderwah, right behind that of Bâsak Nag, is claimed to be the oldest in South Asia.) They had two other brothers as well, Mahl Nag and Savar Nag. The brothers agreed that whichever of the three would be the first to see the rays of the sun the next morning would get to be the king of Bhaderwah.

The Goddess Kali hid the sun from the other two, so that Bâsak could win the contest. There is a major pilgrimage to the lake (*kund*) atop the Kaplas (spelt Kamalas by some) peak (14,241')

The establishment of the state: Thereafter (now *this* is history), Bhaderwah and Bhalessa were ruled by the Ranas. This was in contrast with the rest of the Chenâb valley which was controlled by the Thakurs. A branch of the Billawar royal family, led by Radhik Pal, established the princely state of Bhaderwah not before the 10th century AD and possibly as recently as in the twelfth century AD. (W.M.A. Kishtwari puts it around the 15th century.

Later the Chamba kingdom (of HP) would subjugate Bhaderwah. Off and on, Billawar/ Basohli and Kishtwar, too, exercised control over it. Kashmir almost certainly did not in the ancient and mediæval periods.

Radhik's kin ruled Billawar, Bhaddu, Kulu (HP) and Batol. Batol is probably the ancient Vartula, near Ramban. (The Batol rulers accepted Islam is the late 17th century.)

King Nag Pal: The first king of Bhaderwah about whom we know anything at all is Nag Pal, a contemporary of Emperor Akbar (16th century). Apparently his mother, Rani Kandani, was the daughter of the king of Kishtwar. Her husband, Bishamber Pal, King of Dughanagar (and, thus, of Bhaderwah) died within six months of marriage, without having, er, successfully planted his seed. So, the newly widowed Kandani was left in the temple of Bâsak Nag for a night. She became pregnant. In response to her prayer her son was born with a snake's hood on his back, to ensure that there were no doubts about his legitimacy. The boy was, naturally, given the name Nag Pal. He was also known as Than Pal.

According to a local legend, King Nag Pal had once been invited to the Mughal court at Agra. The occasion was a convention (*durbar*) of the kings and chieftains of the Mughal Empire. The Bhaderwahis believe that their king alone refused to bow before Akbar. He merely saluted the Emperor, which offended Akbar. Akbar got a low door constructed so that Nag Pal would have to bend when he entered the court. So, Nag Pal started entering that door backwards. Akbar asked him to explain his behaviour. Nag Pal said that he would bow only before Bâsak Nag.

Others say that Nag Pal's servants had a fight with Akbar's staff early one morning. They insisted that they should be the first to draw water from the emperor's well.

Either way, Nag Pal got into an argument with Akbar about the powers of Bâsak Nag. He also insisted that it was the duty of all devotees to offer the snake- god the first water that they drew from their wells every morning.

Akbar was not impressed by all this talk about Bâsak Nag. He wanted proof. And proof he got.

That night the snake- god came to Nag Pal in a dream. He asked the king not to worry but to wear a loose turban when he went to Akbar's court the next day. In the court the five- headed Bâsak Nag snake popped out of Nag Pal's turban and 'threatened to ascend the throne on which Akbar was seated'. Akbar was terrified and told King Nag Pal that he'd grant him a wish if he'd call the snake- god off. 'This Nag Pal did and obtained the privilege of the royal drums (*naubat*), which were used at the palace; and down to the present day are beaten in the temple of Bâsak Nag at Bhaderwah'. (Both quotes from Hutchison and Vogel who wrote this in 1933. The drums continue to be beaten in the twentyfirst century as well.)

Akbar also gave Nag Pal ornaments made of gold and silver and robes of honour made of silk, so long as he took the mighty snake away. These robes are known as *patt* in the Bhaderwahi language.

When Nag Pal returned to Bhaderwah, he wanted to let all his subjects know about his triumph at the Mughal court. However, he did not call them all together. He reasoned that if all his subjects- especialy the military men- were missing from their homes on the same day one of the neighbouring kings could easily invade Bhaderwah. So he spread the celebrations across three days.

The Mela Patt ('the festival of the royal robes') is held every year to celebrate this supposed victory of Nag Pal over Akbar. The festival lasts three days, because of the precedent Nag Pal had set. The king died in AD 1620.

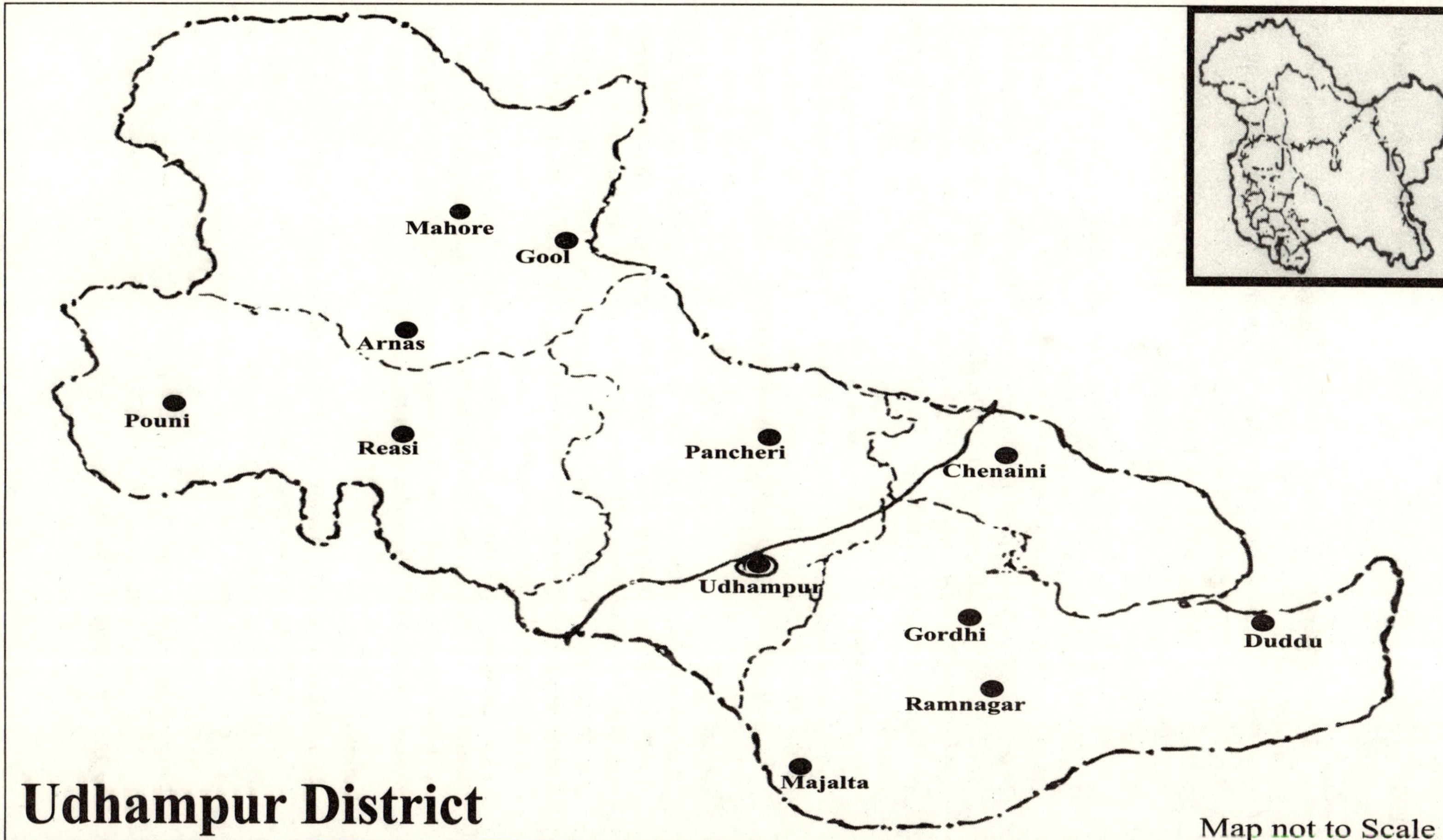
Mahore
Gool
Arnas
Pouni
Reasi
Pancheri
Chenaini
Udhampur
Gordhi
Duddu
Ramnagar
Majalta
Udhampur District
Map not to Scale

Bhaderwah comes under Chamba: Bhaderwah was awarded to Chamba during the reign of Char(h)at Singh (1821- 44), king of Chamba. (Charat was a minor when his mother, the regent, accepted this decision of Maharaja Ranjit Singh, and gave up the Rihlu area of Kangra in exchange.) Pahar Chand, the last king of Bhaderwah, saw that there was no point in resisting. So, he fled to Amritsar, where he later died.

The Dogra era: The Dogras of Jammu made an unsuccessful attempt, under Zorawar Singh Kahluria, to wrest Bhaderwah from Chamba. They succeeded in 1845. The Treaty of Amritsar of the 16th March, 1846, formalised this annexation. The Dogras ruled over Bhaderwah first through Administrative Officers and Kardars and later (1878- 81 and 1886- 1911) by giving it as a *jagir* (estate; fief) to Raja Sri Amar Singh who later ruled over it as his 'Private Dominion.'

In AD 1931 Bhaderwah was merged with the Udhampur district and its area reduced to 213 square miles. In 1948 it was made a part of the newly- created Dodâ district, first as a tehsil and later as a sub- division. That remains its position to this day.

Billâwar

(Kathuâ district) Scholars like Dr. Sukhdev Singh Charak state that the three oldest Duggar (i.e. Dogra) kingdoms were Jammu, Prunts and Billawar- Basohli. Billawar was then known as Vallapura, from which its present name has been derived. Ancient texts like the Rajatarangini suggest that Vallapura was the capital of a 2600 sq. km. hill state of the same name.

It remained so till AD 1630, when the capital shifted to Basohli. According to these scholars, Bhaderwah was a part of this kingdom. Just as Jammu and Prunts (Poonch) later broke up into smaller kingdoms, so did Billawar- Basohli.

Chenaini

(Udhampur district) Chenaini used to be the capital of a tiny kingdom till 1822, when Raja Gulab Singh annexed it first to the Lahore empire and then to the Jammu state. And yet its ruling dynasty is one of the oldest in India, having ruled uninterrupted for 45 generations, roughly from AD 850 to 1822. However, since at least Ranjit Dev's time it had been subordinate to Jammu and before that to the Mughals.

The ruling clan came from Chanderi (Bundelkhand, central India) in the 9th century. The name Chenaini is derived from Chanderi.

Chiñgus

(Rajouri district) (Rhymes with 'bus.' Also spelt Chingas.) Chingus means 'intestine' in Persian. In AD 1627, the Mughal Emperor Jehangir was travelling from Srinagar to Agra. He died in the royal howdah when his caravan passed through a village called Khanpur. His queen, Noor Jehan, wanted to influence the selection of the next emperor. She knew that if news of Jehangir's death reached Agra before she did, his sons (and their supporters) would try to kill each other for the throne. Therefore, Noor Jehan tried to keep Jehangir's death a secret.

So she got a trusted surgeon to remove Jehangir's intestines, which were buried in Khanpur (c.2,000' above the sea). Jehangir's body was propped up in the howdah. However, a fly came and perched itself on Jehangir's nose. Jehangir was obviously in no position to swat the fly. Those in the caravan who saw this knew that he was dead. Poor Noor Jehan's scheme did not work.

A major Mughal monument, a caravan sarai, was later built around the 'grave' where the intestines were buried. The village came to be known as Chingus after its most famous possession.

Dodâ district

The pre 2006 district was not only proud of being almost as big as all six districts of Kashmir put together, its residents remind you that Dodâ's history is much older. Dodâ was inhabited, they point out, when Kashmir was a mere lake, called Satisar.

Dodâ apparently got its name from a man called Deeda, a craftsman who made metal plates, cooking pots and other utensils. Deeda belonged to Multan (in what is now Pakistan). One of the kings of Kishtwar invited Deeda to establish in his kingdom a factory where metal utensils were made and also to settle in the district. At that stage the kingdom of Kishtwar consisted of most of the present day Dodâ district. Deeda set up base in a village now called Dodâ.

Though much of history the district (as well as the Deng Batal area of the Mahore tehsil of Udhampur) has been divided into two rival kingdoms, Bhaderwah and Kishtwar. Kishtwar has always been the bigger of the two. It also has a much older history- one that has been closely intertwined with the history of Kashmir, in all ages, ancient, mediæval and modern. Its fortunes have also been linked with those of neighbouring Zanskar (Ladakh).

Ghorhâ Galli

(Udhampur district) A treasure- trove of large stone sculptures, mostly reliefs, but some *a roundel* exists in these dense mountain forests near Gool (of Gool- Gulabgarh fame). Like everything else that was created in the state in ancient times, these stones were personally sculpted by the Pândavs during the age of the Mahabharat, when they passed this way.

Guru Baba ka Tilla

(Jammû district) This is an important archæological site near Gajansu in the Marh block. This site seems to have been active during four periods: pre- historic, early historic, Kushan and mediæval. Among the more exciting finds are three fully intact Kushan cups, a marble plate and a carved, decorated stone medallion (all 1st-3rd century AD) and a bone plaquette (2nd- 1st century BC).

Pre- historic grey ware culture has been found here. Also discovered from this period were fine plain black ware, red ware and coarse red ware. Dr. Mani says that 'the characteristic form' was 'convex and straight sided bowls and dishes.'

The early historic period continued with many of the pottery traditions of its predecessor. It also produced basins with 'nail headed' rims and vases shaped like pears.

The Kushan period saw even more sophisticated pottery. The rims of cups were sharper. Their sides tapered to a flat base. Spouted vases in red ware and sprinklers have also been found from this period.

What is called *the 'mediæval' period* of this site is really a late ancient period: 1st to 5th centuries AD. This period has yielded the ricchest pickings: animal figures, balls, coins made of copper and silver, a marble plate and terracotta heads.

Jâfar Chak

(Jammû district) (19km. west of Jammu, in Marh block.) Dr. B.R. Mani and his team from the ASI conducted excavations at Jafar Chak in 1998-99. Artefacts found here date to between the sixth and eighteenth centuries AD.

Dr. Mani notes, 'Decorated bricks [from the 6th and 7th centuries AD] were reused in succeeding periods.' He adds that 'structures [built between the 13th and 18th centuries AD] show deterioration of settlement [because] large size pebbles were also used with bricks, reused bricks and brick bats... A sunken brick paved floor of a room measuring 3.70 x 2.45m. was encountered.'

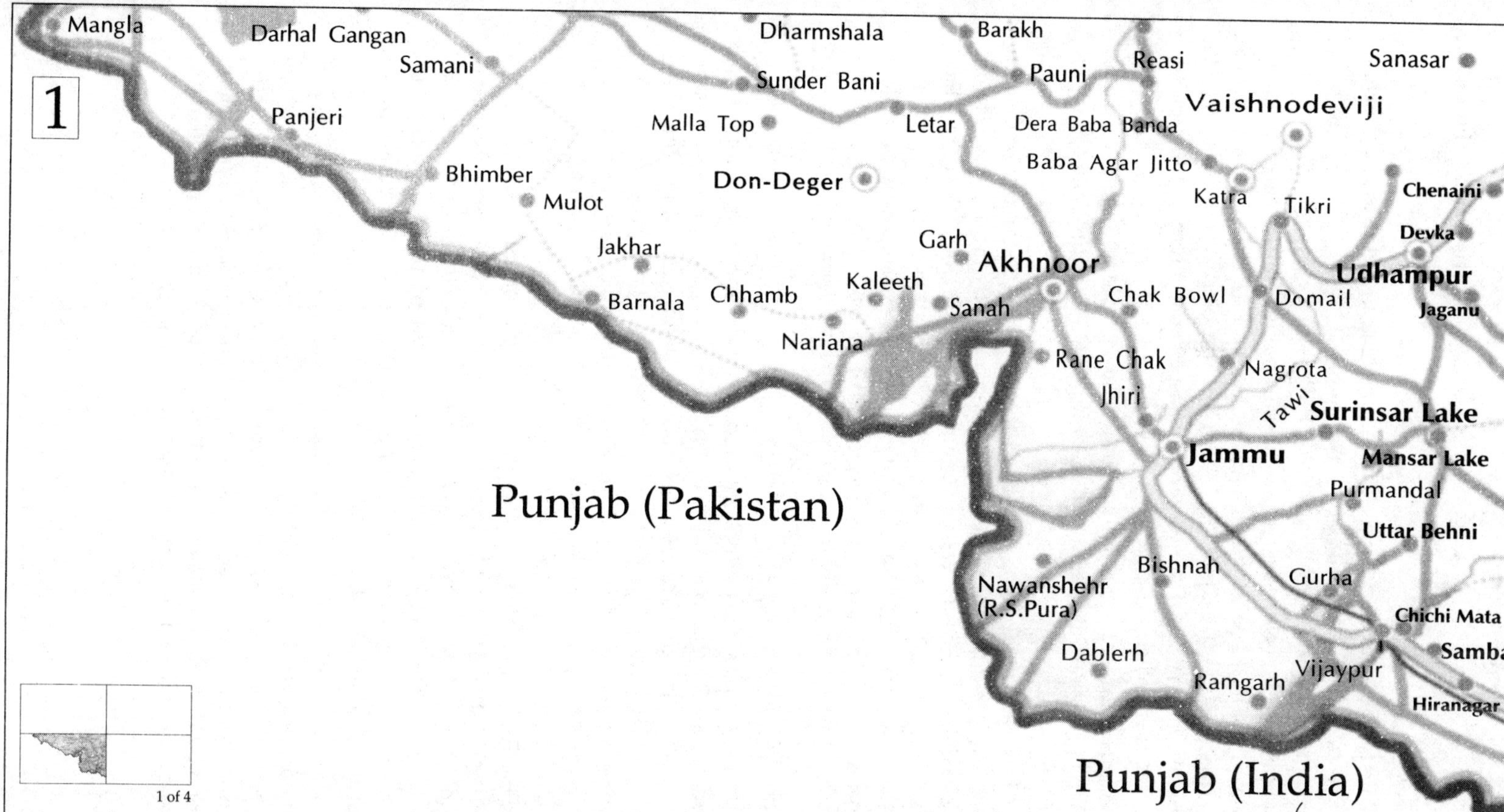

Jammu, Udhampur

Map not to scale

Most of the pottery found at Jafar Chak is red ware. It seems to have been used there in every period studied. Over the centuries, styles and shapes changed somewhat, though.

Other artefacts excavated at Jafar Chak include basins, bangles (made of shells), beads (made of stone as well as glass), bowls, jars, pots (plain as well as painted black) and terracotta figurines. As at Ambaran, the rims of bowls grew sharper and more sophisticated over the centuries.

A silver bracelet decorated with semi- precious stones was one of the most exciting discoveries. Things made of iron and copper were also found.

Above all, a copper coin minted for Zain ul Abedin aka Budshah, Sultan of Kashmir (1420- 70), was found from the layer that corresponds to the thirteenth century. The coin had, thus, reached Jafar Chak soon after it was minted. This discovery has far reaching implications, especially in view of claims by contemporary Kashmiri historians that Budshah had conquered all of undivided Punjab. (His elder brother's father in law was the king of Jammu.)

Jasrotâ

(Kathuâ district) This kingdom derives its name from that of its founder, Jas Dev, a Jamwal (i.e. 'of Jammu town') Raja who came here in AD 1019 or 1195. His descendants, a sub- sect of the Jamwals, came to be known as the Jasrotia Rajputs. This was a largeish kingdom which, by the 19th century, consisted of 13 *parganas* (small, mediæval districts) and stretched from present- day Hiranagar to the Ravi.

Details: Autar Dev was the king of the Jammu area. (c.1175). Nothing is known about the successors of Autar's son Jas Dev, except their names. Twenty five kings ruled over Jasrota after Jas Dev. Ranbir Singh (19th century) was the last of the lot. He had no children. So his brother, Bhuri Singh, administered the kingdom for a while after his death.

Then, in 1834, Raja Gulab Singh conquered Jasrota on behalf Maharaja Ranjit Singh of Punjab. The Maharaja granted this area in the form of a *jâgir* (estate) to Gulab Singh's nephew, Raja Hira Singh to administer on behalf of the Punjab empire. In March 1846, when Gulab Singh became the Maharaja of Jammu and Kashmir, Jasrota was converted into a wazarat (district).

Jasrota was vanquished in 1845. It never recovered from that blow. The defeated royal family was exiled to Khanpur, near Nagrota (beyond Jammu town).

Kâlâkote area, the

(Rajouri district) *Old references:* The great grammarian, Pânini (c.300 BC), wrote in his famous book, *Asht Adhyâyi* that a place called 'Kalakakuda' was known for its coal. He specified that this place was in Apr Madr. Therefore, it must have been the present Kalakote.

Kathuâ district

There were at least six, possibly as many as ten, Rajput kingdoms in what now is Kathua district. Some of them were no bigger than a dozen villages. Others stretched over 500 square kilometres. Each kingdom had at least one fort or palace. Some of these 'palaces' were smaller than a Rajasthani haveli (manor). Others were important enough to get mentioned in Western fiction.

I seriously doubt that all- or even most- of Kathua district was ever united into one kingdom. Nor was present day Kathua town ever the capital of the region. In fact, it was Jasrota that was the headquarters of the *wazarat* (lit.: 'the domain of a minister,' loosely corresponding to the districts of the British Raj) that preceded today's Kathua district. Therefore, the history of the district is necessarily the sum of the histories of these individual principalities. The old kingdoms now within Kathua district are: Basohli, Bhaddu, Billawar, Hiranagar, Jasrota, Kathua proper, Lakhanpur, Mankote/ Ramkote and Trikote.

Kathuâ town and adjacent areas

(Kathuâ district) Jodh Singh, a noble of the Andotra group of Rajputs, is said to have shifted base, around the beginning of the Christian era, from Hastinapur (present day Delhi) to what is now called Kathua. His sons Teju, Kindal and Bhaju founded the clans of Tajwalia, Khanwalia and Bhajwalia and the villages of Taraf Tajwal, Taraf Manjali and Taraf Bhajwal respectively. Taraf Tajwal was where the Main Bazar of Kathua town is today. The other two villages are now known as Parli- Wand. (My problem with this version of history is purely linguistic: Did words like 'taraf' exist in North India in the first millennium of Christianity? Did even the 'f' sound exist in the local language then? Or the suffix '-wal'?)

In any case, these three villages were collectively known as 'Kathai', a name that over the centuries changed to Kathua. Strabo,

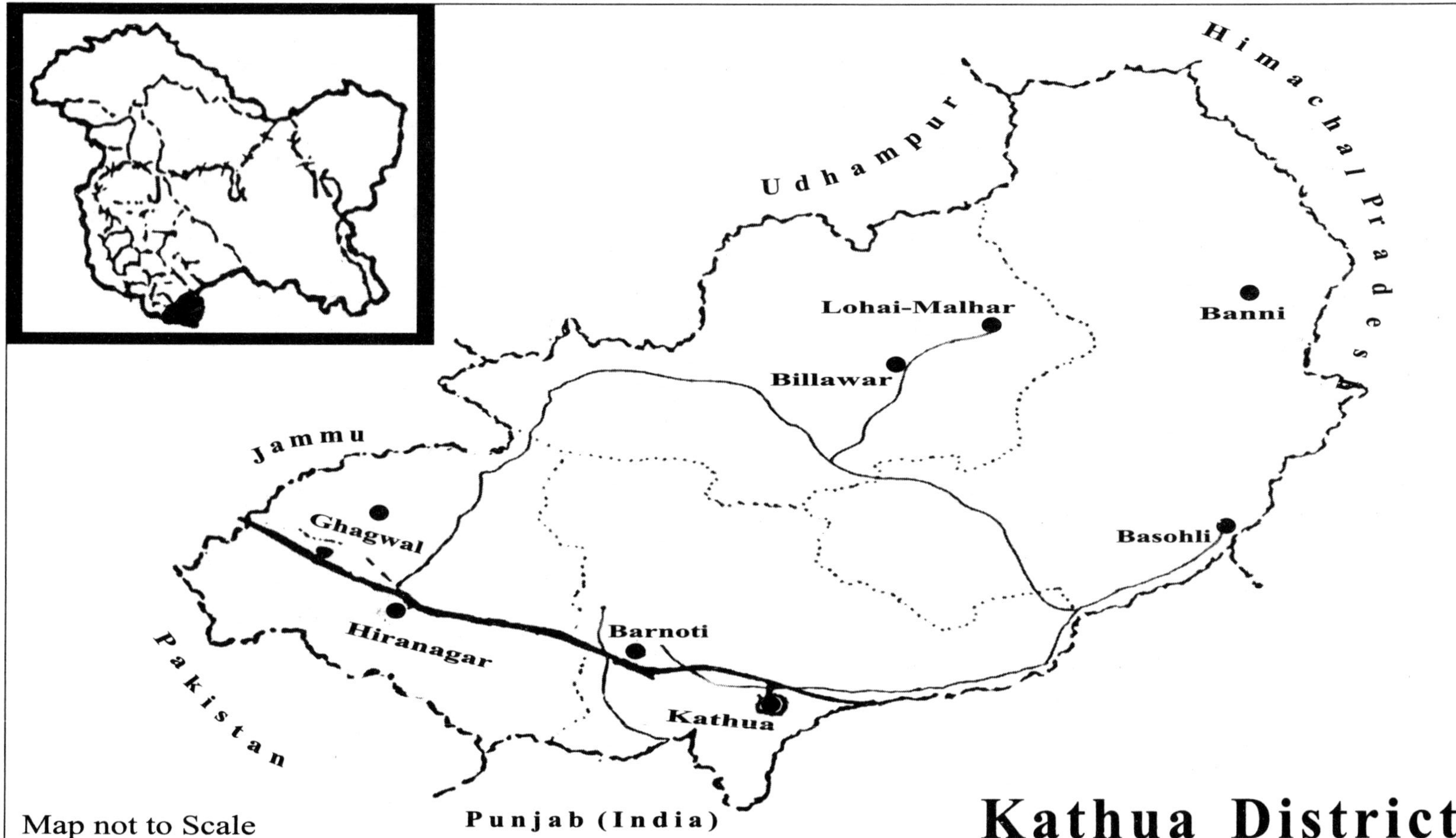

Kathua District

a Greek historian of the era of Alexander the Great refers to the powerful republic of 'Kathaioi' located in the foothills and on the banks of river Ravi. 'Kathaioi' is mentioned along with present day Poonch as one of the two major empires in the Jammu region of that age. The description fits Kathua exactly. Strabo wrote that the warriors of Kathaioi put up a brave fight against the invaders.

Kishtwar

The word Kishtwar is probably derived from its ancient Sanskrit name, Kashthavata: (Another theory credits the name to Kishat Rishi, an ancient saint.) Its boundaries have always been clear: Ladakh in the north, Kashmir on the west, Padar (J&K) and Chamba (HP) in the east and Bhaderwah in the south. Padar was merged with Kisthwar in 1836 by the Dogra rulers. There have been times when this kingdom also included all the Banihal areas between Dodâ and Ramban.

Jehangir, rivers and rope bridges: Jehangir, the 17th century Mughal emperor, wrote about the area in some detail in his memoirs. Since it was his army that annexed Kishtwar to the Mughal Empire, his concerns were mainly military. He saw the rivers Maru and Chenâb as Kishtwar's defences against invaders. The waters of these rivers flowed fast and were deep. The Chenâb, he wrote, was rather difficult to cross. Therefore, the people of Kishtwar would build rope bridges, called *zampâs*, wherever possible.

Jehangir described how the Kishtwaris would make bridges of rope. They would fix wooden planks between two parallel ropes. The planks were for people to place their feet on. Directly above these two ropes would be another pair of parallel ropes, three feet (a *gaz*) higher than the lower ropes. These were for people to clutch with their hands. The Kishtwaris would post armed guards near their bridges. Jehangir's army was twice stranded on the wrong side of the river because the retreating Kishtwaris had burnt their bridges behind them. That's when he must have realised how critical it was to guard bridges.

Its own currency: Certainly till the 17th century, and for a while later, too, Kishtwar had its own currency. Its silver Sanhasi coin was equal to two- thirds of a Mughal rupaya.

Its system of weights: The *man* (maund) of the rest of north India was equal to 40 *sers*, or around 30 kilograms. In Kishtwar a *man* equalled two *sers*.

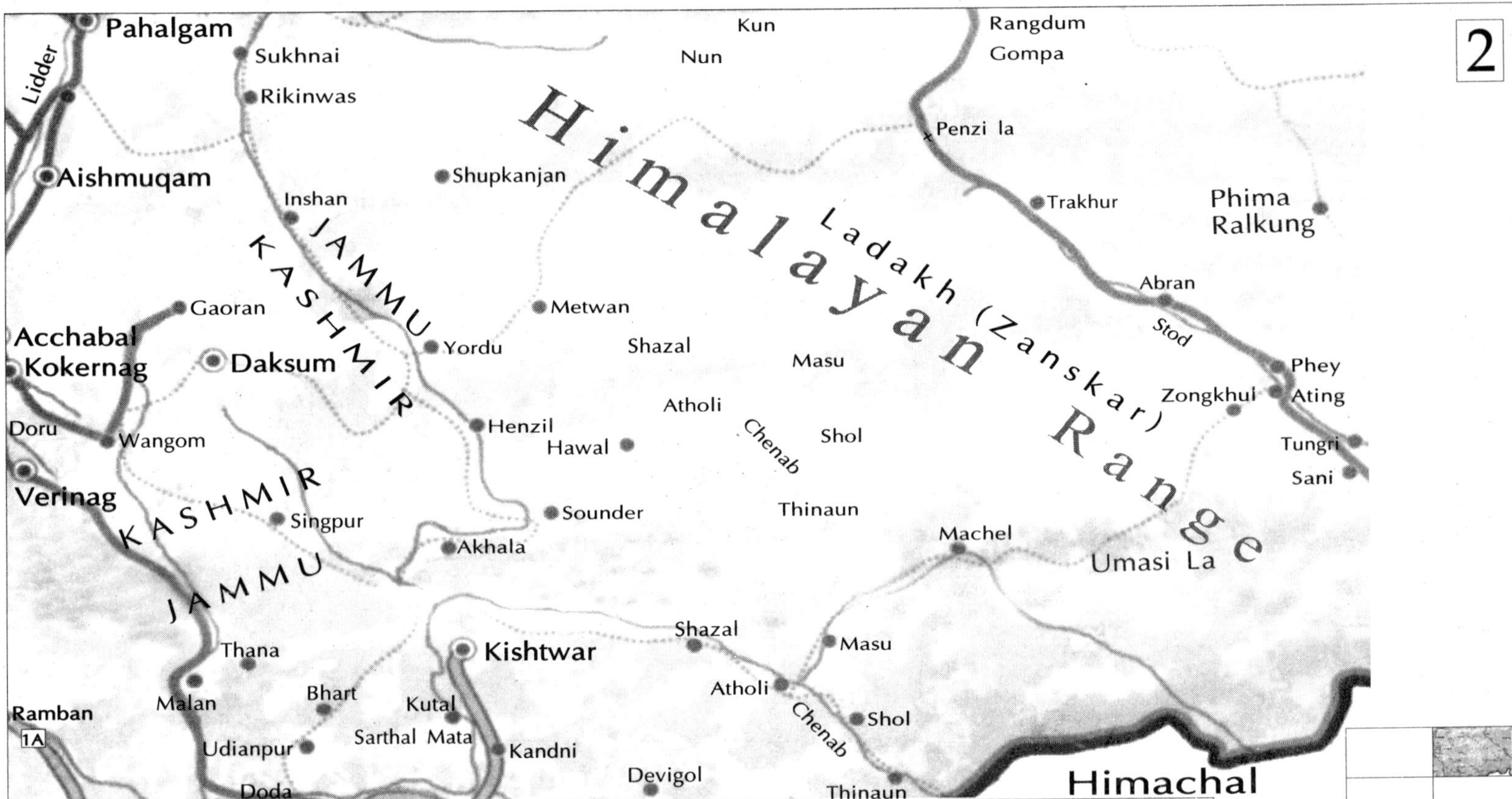

Doda, Kishtwar

Hazrat Farid ud Din and Hazrat Asrâr ud Din

The saints: Hazrat Farid ud Din's links are with Baghdad. Hazrat Farid reputedly had the power to stop earthquakes and give sight to the blind. (Kishtwar is part of a seismically active zone.)

He is said to have prayed for the early death of his own son Hazrat Asrâr ud Din, because the son had developed a spirituality that disturbed the father. A number of Islmic books have mentioned this. Some go on to say that Farid ud Din Saheb gave his son a bowl of water to drink. Asrâr ud Din Saheb died on drinking the water.

Mian Basheer, the eminent Gujjar leader, scholar and spiritualist, explained this to me differently. He said that Hazrat Farid was a conservative in religious matters. He believed that if a pious Muslim were to receive a divine visitation or a mystical vision in his dreams, he should keep the experience to himself. He should not talk about it. Hazrat Asrâr, on the other hand, believed in talking about the experience and sharing it with others. The father felt that such behaviour was outside the *shariat*, the Islamic law. Therefore, through his spiritual powers, H. Farid caused his son to die prematurely. (There are similar legends about Baba Reshi of Gulmarg and Sheikh Noor ud Din Noorani of Tsrar e Sharief.)

Historian Aseer Kishtwari disputes the veracity of these anecdotes. He says that Hazrat Asrâr ud Din died a natural death at the age of 18. He adds that the 'offer [of the bowl of water] and [its] acceptance amounted to the perfection of transfer of spiritual power and not unhappiness' [with the son]. Aseer then writes that 'one day Shah Asrâr ud Din Sahib (RA) was delivering a lecture on Islam which got interrupted by a voice "Oh! My friend come back' and Asrâr Sahib (RA) disclosed about his death. He took a white sheet over his head and left this mortal world.'

When he was just a teenager, Hazrat Asrâr ud Din brought a dead Hindu child back to life. This child used to play with the young saint. Asrâr ud Din Saheb saw his friend's corpse being taken for cremation to the north- western end of the chaugan. He prodded the corpse with his stick and said, 'Arise. You had promised to play with me.' The dead boy did just that. It is said that Hazrat Farid ud Din was disturbed that his son was going about performing miracles like this one.

Laddan

(Udhampur district) Dayal Chand, the Raja of Chenaini got two forts built in the 1820s: at Laddan and Shivgarh. That is when the Jamwal

Dogra rajas of Jammu had launched an aggressive spree to conquer all the neighbouring hill states, of behalf of Maharaja Ranjit Singh of Lahore. When the Lahore- Jammu army overran Chenaini, Dayal shifted the women and children of his family to Shivgarh. The Laddan fort never saw a battle.

Lakhanpur

(Kathuâ district) Lakhanpur was part of the Jasrota kingdom. However, in the 14th century it was given to Raja Sangram Singh (or Dev), the twin of the king of Jasrota. (The Jasrota family, in turn, was a branch of the Jamwal ruling clan of Jammu.)

The Jasrota kindom was split into two in the late 13th / early 14th century. Sangram Dev/ Singh, who was one of the twin sons Raja Kailash Dev of Jasrota, received the areas between the Ravi and Ujh rivers. Dr. Ashok Jerath says that this new state was founded in AD 1350 and 'with it was constructed the Lakhanpur fort.' (*Forts of Lakhanpur and Thein* by Dr. Ashok Jerath, Daily Excelsior, the 11th April, 1999.)

The state was also called Thein, because Thein was a summer capital of sorts. It is somewhat cooler because of the river nearby. Thein is a small township uphill on the road to Basohli. It is the last outpost of Kathua tehsil, on its boundary with Basohli tehsil. In all probability Thein always represented the northeastern limits of this state.

The Thein fort must have been quite impressive, if its ruins are any indication. The king of Nurpur (HP) captured it in the 18th century. Maharaja Ranjit Singh of Punjab conquered Nurpur in 1815. When he died, the British assumed that control of Thein was theirs by right. However, Ram Singh Pathania, a minister in the government of Nurpur refused to let the British take over either Thein or neighbouring Shahpur (HP). By raising a guerilla force and through brilliant military strategy he managed to hold out for quite a while. He even constructed a temple for the guardian deity of his clan. Maharaja Gulab Singh's army finally defeated him at Jasrota. It took him prisoner and delivered him to the British.

Loran

(Pooñch district) Loran, then known as Lohar Kote, was the capital of the Poonch area till AD 1542. Loran's legendary fort, now in ruins, was said to be impregnable. Raja Trilochan Pal of Loran defeated Sultan Mahmood of Ghazni at this fort.

Mahorgarh- Dhérgarh- Bapnérgarh

(District Jammû; near Samba)

History: The fort was certainly built by an emperor who was based in Delhi or Agra and was a Muslim. This happened around AD 1550. This much is definite. Nothing else is. The emperor concerned was either Akbar (1553- 1605) himself or Sher Shah Suri, a contemporary of Akbar's father.

The most plausible explanation is that Sher Shah's son Salim (or Islam) Shah Suri built this fort as a garrison for his forces. He stationed a *faujdar* (garrison commander) there. (Charak and Billawaria feel that Salim built the fort around 1550 'for the purpose of shelter in emergency.') The Mughals might have expanded the fort. They needed to station an army in the Jammu area because the hill chiefs would periodically rise against the Mughals. (See 'A History of Jammu' Chapter 5) Dr. Jerath quotes from some contemporary Mughal document to the effect that Mughal forces were needed near Jammu to suppress any possible revolt in the days to come.

The Mughal document says, 'Two *kos* from Sâmbâ, a fort was built and Muhammad Khân Turkmân was sent forward to take charge of Lakhanpur.' (The aerial distance between Mahorgarh and Sâmbâ is roughly 6 miles/ 10 kilometres.) Jerath adds, 'Alas this fort was not used afterwards. It took almost [one] year to complete the fort but [it] was used for [barely] a few months by [the] Mughal army. Either it was seized by the hill chieftains or the Mughals themselves deserted it.'

Mândâ

(Jammû district) This is an extremely important archæological site near Akhnoor, on the west (right) bank of the Chenâb. It is the northernmost Harappan site anywhere, and the only such site in Jammu province. The Harappans had reached Mâñdâ in the 4th century BC. Their culture continued to evolve at Mâñdâ till the 1st century BC.

In 1977 the ASI (Archæological Survey of India) made major excavations at Mâñdâ. They found Harappan and black- slipped ware as well as late- Harappan red ware and plain grey ware (the latter two being c.1300 BC). Among the more interesting finds was a double-spiral headed copper pin, done in a middle- Eastern style (c.2350 BC). Bangles and triangular tiles, both made of terracotta, potshards with Harappan writing and bone arrowheads have also been found. Terracotta heads from the 1st- 2nd century AD reveal men with very 'Aryan' facial features and perhaps Greco- Roman helmets.

Naushérâ

(Rajouri district) (Also Nowshera and Naushehrâ.) We know that Emperor Akbar had got a stone fort- cum- serai built here. His son Jehangir wrote in his memoirs that a police station was functioning in the fort. An official document says that its construction started around AD 1620. This can't be correct. By then Akbar had long since been dead. I would put its construction at around 1586, when Akbar needed it the most. It might have been expanded in 1620. The Mughals used it as a royal rest house on their way to Kashmir and back.

The Mughal Road

The Mughal road originated at the Mughal capital, Agra (in UP). It wound its way through Lahore (now in Pakistan) to Poonch, Rajouri and, thence, to Srinagar in the Valley. It's a pity that relations between India and Pakistan are what they are, because it would be so rewarding to recreate the Mughals' journey and see the wonderful buildings, forts, tombs and *sarais* (rest- houses) that they had got constructed along the route.

The Poonch segment of the road used to be called the Namak road (presumably, the 'salt road') till Jehangir (early 17th century) travelled on it and renamed it the Mughal Road.

Noori Chham(b)

(Pooñch district) *History and legends:* That the Mughal Emperor Jehangir camped near the fall a dozen, perhaps thirteen, times is beyond doubt.

We know from Mughal records that the Royal Caravan would camp here for a few days on its way to and from Srinagar. Jâgirdar Behram Naik, the feudal chief of the area, and Mehdi Naik would make all the local arrangements. The people of the area would serve as porters.

It stands to reason that his Empress Noor Jehan might have bathed under the fall each time they were there. Local legends go on to assert that the mirror currently fixed in a niche in the mountainside was where the Empress' mirror used to be fixed, for toiletry after the shower. Some assert that the present mirror is the very mirror that the Empress would use.

Mirror or no mirror, it was Jehangir who named (renamed?- for surely the fall must have had a name before) the fall after his wife.

When Jehangir reached Noori Chham in 1627 he was very ill. His doctors advised him to spend a few days near the falls. While there he spotted a deer. He asked one of his employees to kill the deer for him. The employee fell off a cliff, and died, while doing so. The emperor saw this accident happen. This ruined Jehangir's health further. He died a few days later, when his caravan was travelling between Noori Chham and Rajouri.

Pâdar

(Dodâ district) Padar 'block' has a population of around 20,000 (according to a 1999 estimate). In ancient times it was called Zanskar-Pardav. The region has been mentioned in *The Rajatarangini.* Its people belong to the Pangiyali, Zanskari- Lahuli and Paharhi ethnic groups. The culture of Padar is a mixture of these three. Padar is one of the most backward parts of the state. Literacy is lower than the average for the state.

The Hindus of the area worship Nag Devta, the snake god, and Shakti, the mother goddess. The Machail yâtrâ is the block's most celebrated pilgrimage.

Before the 17th century, the area was ruled by a number of Rana chieftains, who were ritually 'superior' to the Thakurs. Each Rana controlled one or two, at the most three, villages, was independent and often at war with his neighbour. Around AD 1650 Raja Chatar Singh, king of Chamba, conquered Pangi and then all of Padar. That was the first time in known history that Padar was united.

Chatar then constructed the Chatargarh fort near Atholi. His descendants ruled over Padar till the early 19th century. By 1820 Padar was only nominally under Chamba. Around then, Ratanu, a local Thakur (significantly, he was not a Rana), led the Padar army into Zanskar. He subjugated Zanskar on behalf of Chamba.

In 1834 Raja Gulab Singh of Jammu- Lahore sent a force under Zorawar Singh to Ladakh. In 1835, Zorawar, now in Zanskar, decided that a good route from Jammu to Ladakh would be through Padar. Therefore, he got Wazir Lakhpat to build a road from Jammu to Padar. Lakhpat subdued Padar, posted a Dogra thanedar (middle-rung police officer) there and moved on.

Ratanu roused the local people, took hostage the few Dogra policemen posted there and handed them over to the King of Chamba, who panicked. He did not want to offend either the mighty Dogra Raja, or the Sikh Maharaja on whose behalf Gulab Singh was theoretically acting. So the King of Chamba disowned Ratanu's action and sent the hosstages back to Jammu. However, Zorawar was furious. After the snow had melted he invaded Padar with an army of 3,000. Ratanu's men destroyed the bridge to Chatargarh. Zorawar was, therefore, unable to cross the Chenâb for two months. His force then set up a rope bridge across the river, using which they crossed over.

The Dogras captured the fort and totally wiped out the town around it. They executed a number of local people and maimed others. They also built a second fort for their soldiers. It was thus that Padar became part of Jammu.

Ramkote

(Kathuâ district) This is a small town on a hillock on the Dhar-Udhampur road, at the point where Kathua district meets Udhampur. It is close to Mansar Lake. Till the 19th century it was known as Mankote, by which name you will find it mentioned in books about Paharhi (hill) miniature painting. For a brief while miniature painting in the Dogra hill style flourished here. This 24 km. by 15 km. state was founded in the 13th century by Raja Manak Dev. Raja Suchet Singh (1822-43) gave Ramkote its present name.

Râmnagar

(Udhampur district) Ramnagar used to be a kingdom called Bandralta till Maharaja Ranjit Singh conquered it in the early 19th century, after defeating its much loved ruler Raja Dev. The Raja exiled himself to Subathu (near Shimla). It was granted as fief to the then Raja Gulab Singh's brother Raja Suchet Singh in 1822.

Suchet renamed the kingdom Ramnagar and built a fancy palace and fort there. The palace remains the chief tourist attraction of this tiny town. Suchet consciously offered refuge to people from places as far apart as Peshawar, Multan and Lahore (all now in Pakistan), Tonk (Rajasthan) and Kashmir.

Suchet attracted migrants to his state for much the same reason as underpopulated Australia, Canada and New Zealand do: to increase the population and stimulate economic growth. And he wound up attracting the same kind of refugees as some New World countries did in the beginning. To quote *The Gazetteer*, '(Suchet) made Ramnagar a city of refuge for runaways who had been guilty of no greater crimes than murder or slight political offence.'.

Kashmiris, especially shawl- makers, had started migrating from Kashmir around Suchet's time, mainly because of famine and the pashmina politics of the British. Vigne and Drew, wrote in *The Gazetteer*, 'There are a good many Kashmíris settled in Rámnagar; some of them are occupied with shawl- work, executing orders from Núrpúr and Amritsár [sic]; and some in making coarse woollen cloth.'

Réâsî

(Udhampur district) There are legends about spots in Reasi where the 19th century Dogrâ General Zorawar Singh hid the treasures that he had, er, purchased from Ladakh-and of snakes guarding them.

Vigne and Herrey, late- 19th century historians of the British Raj, were quite impressed by the Reasi 'castle.' *The Gazetteer* records their impressions thus: 'The situation of Ríasí has added prosperity to the town and importance to the castle…[which] is one of the strongest, perhaps the strongest and best constructed, in the country.' [By 'country' perhaps all of Jammu, Kashmir and Ladakh was meant.]

Sunderbani

(Rajouri district) The town came into existence as reecntly as in 1947, after refugees from southern Poonch and other parts of POK settled here. The *haveli* (manor) of Rai Ghulam Hussain was built on the Phulwari hillock in the early 20th century. The tract was called the Bhajwal *jâgîr (fief* or *estate*). The Rai was the local feudal chief (*jâgîrdâr*) and a much-respected descendant of the Jaral royal family of Rajouri. After he migrated to Pakistan, the refugees occupied his land and built the present Sunderbani on it.

In 1980 Sunderbani was made the headquarters of a tehsil of the same name. The tehsil includes Bhajwal (the estate of the Rai), Thandâ Pânî (the estate of Jagat Ram), Bakher (Thakur Basant Singh's estate) and Devak (Nâr Singh's estate). Maini estimates that the tehsil's 2001 population was around 42,000. Its area is 83,401 acres.

Surankot

(Pooñch district) The Rajatarangini refers to this pretty valley by its ancient name, Sawernik (prob.: 'the golden one'). 'Kot', as everywhere else in South Asia, means 'fort'. This town's fort was in existence in the eleventh century AD.

Thein

(Kathuâ district) (See 'Lakhanpur' above.)

Trikote

(Kathuâ district) For a brief while tiny Trikote, too, was a princely state. Located close to Jasrota, it was absorbed into its bigger and more powerful neighbour.

* * *

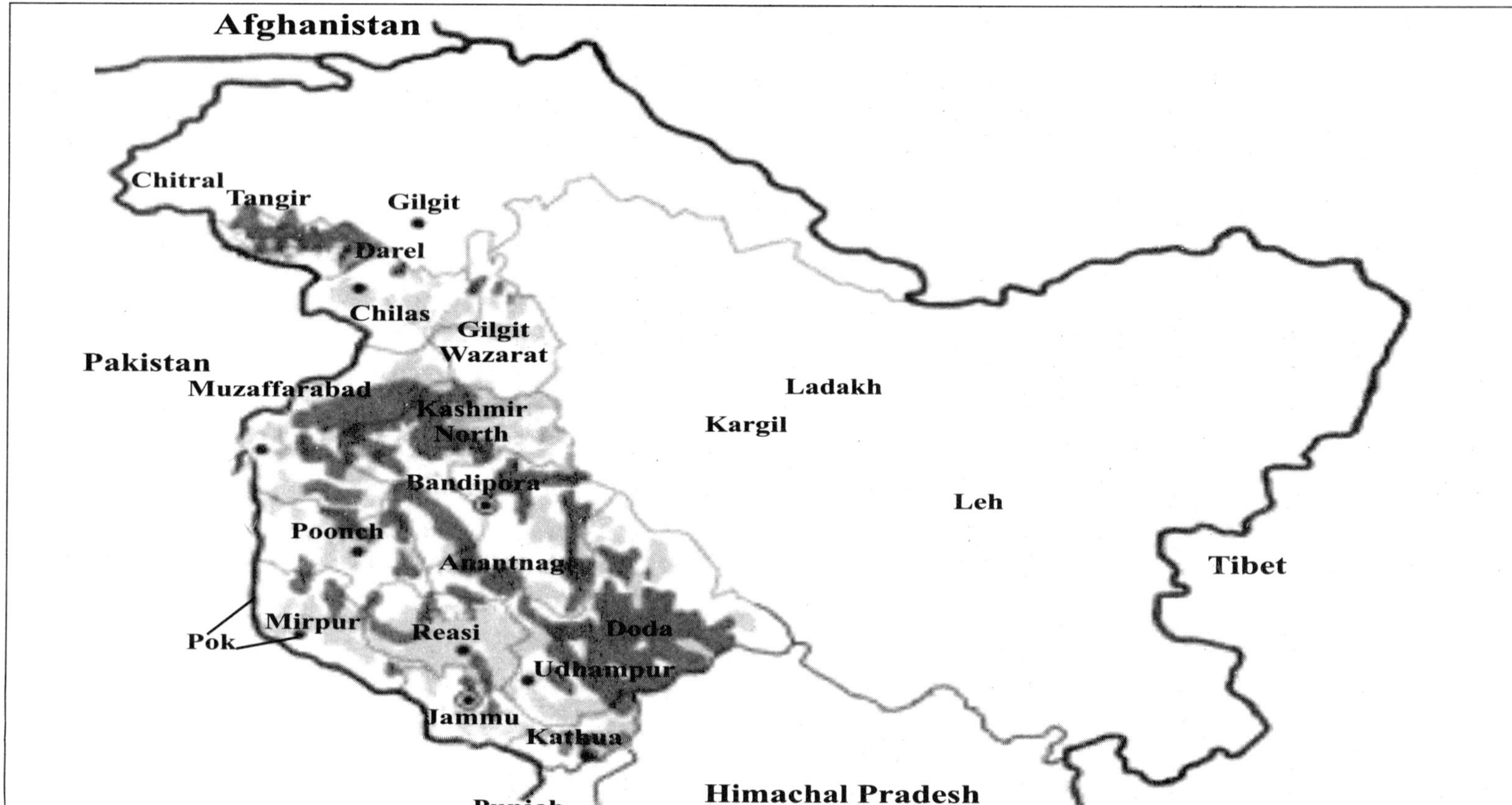

Forest map of Undivided Jammu & Kashmir

18

The Population of Jammû Province

The undivided Jammû province: In 1947, Jammû province was divided into five districts, each under a Wazîr é Wazârat. The districts, along with their tehsils (in brackets) and, in the case of Réâsî, niabats, were:

Jammû (Jammû, Sâmbâ and Akhnoor); Mirpur (Mirpur, Nausherâ, Bhimber and Kotlî); Udhampur (Udhampur, Râmban, Râmnagar, Bhaderwâh and Kishtwâr); Réâsî (Réâsî and Rajourî. Niabat: Gulabgarh) and Kathua (Kathuâ, Jasmérgarh and Basohli).

Jammû had an area of 12,401 sq. miles (approx. 32,200 sq.km.). In 1941, according to Daya Sagar, its population was 20,01,557 (i.e. 2 million). He is marginally off the mark. Journalist-historian B.P. Sharma has a slightly different figure for the population of Jammû province. Based on census figures, he puts it at 19,81,433.[1] Either way, the Muslims, with a population of 12,15,676 in 1941, were in an overwhelming, 61.53%[i] majority in Jammû province.

1. My figure, also based on the census, differs by 12. That's because my sub-totals are slightly different.

1941: The population of undivided Jammû province *(actual numbers)*[ii]

District	Total of district	Hindus/ Scheduled Caste	Hiñdus/ Others	Muslims	Christians	Sikhs	Buddhists	Jains	Others	Pârsîs	Tribes
Jammû	431362	51120	197053	170789	2297	1519	2	895	3	23	29
Kathuâ	177672	18949	112974	45214	204	431	0	0	0	0	0
Udhampur[2]	294217	21646	143175	128327	98	445	520[3]	6	1	0	0
Réâsî[4]	257903	15720	65005	175539	98	1541	0	0	0	0	0
Mîrpur	386655	3008	60568	310880	88	12111	0	0	0	0	0
Chenainî jâgîr[5]	11796	2670	6911	2205	0	10	0	0	0	0	0
Pooñch jâgîr	421828	410	23727	382722	3	14	0	0	0	0	0
Total	19,81,445	1,13,523	6,09,413	12,15,676	2,788	38,566	522	901	4	23	29

There were no Jews in Jammû province.

2. Includes present Dodâ but not Réâsî or Chenainî.
3. Presumably, mainly in Pâdar (now in Dodâ).
4. Includes almost all of present Rajourî district.
5. Now a part of Udhampur.

1941: The population of the present Jammû province ***(percentages)***

District[iii]	Hindus	Muslims	Christians	Sikhs	Buddhists	Jains	Others
Dodâ	42.22	57.35	N	0.15	0.26	N	0.02
Udhampur	66.53	33.17	0.03	0.22	N	N	0.08
Jammû	59.44	37.36	0.34	2.45	N	0.16	0.75
Kathuâ	74.19	25.45	0.1	0.24	-	-	0.12
Pooñch	13.25	85.59	0.01	1.15	-	-	0.01

1941: The population of undivided Jammû province ***(percentages)***

Year 1941[iv]	**Hiñdus**	**Muslims**	**Sikhs**	**Buddhists**	**Others**
Jammû	57.53	39.6	2.12	-	0.75
Kathuâ: Jasmérgarh[6] and Kathuâ tehsils	68.49	30.99	0.39		0.13
Mîrpur: Mîrpur and Bhimber tehsîls	20.03	76.06	3.88		0.03
Basohli tehsîl **(Kathuâ)**	82.85	17.07	0.02		0.06
Kotlî tehsîl **(Mîrpur)**	7.55	91.17	1.28		
Udhampur	56.02	43.62	0.15	0.18	0.03
Réâsî	31.30	68.06	0.60		0.04
Chenainî Jâgîr	81.22	18.70	0.08		
Pooñch Jâgîr	5.72	90.73	3.53		0.02
Total	**36.48**	**61.34**	**1.95**	**0.03**	**0.20**

6. Hîrânagar.

1961:[v] The population of the present Jammû province *(actual numbers)*

District	Buddhist	Christians	Hiñdus	Jains	Muslims	Sikhs	Religion not stated	Total
Dodâ	612	13	92797	0	174499	480	9	268410
Udhampur	0	0	165506	0	86059	2259	2	253826
Jammû	29	2010	428835	1418	51847	32788	0	516927
Kathuâ	0	0	177666	4	27005	2553	5	207233
Pooñch	0	0	58712	0	259082	8193	2	325989
Jammû Province	641	2023	9,23,516	1422	5,98,492	46,273	18	15,72,385

1961: The population of the present Jammû province *(percentages)*

Districts[vi]	Hindus	Muslims	Christians	Sikhs	Buddhists	Jains	Others
Dodâ	34.57	65.01	0.01	0.18	0.23	N	N
Udhampur	65.15	33.87	0.09	0.89	N	N	-
Jammû	82.96	10.03	0.39	6.34	0.01	0.27	N
Kathuâ	85.65	13.02	0.1	1.23	-	N	-
Pooñch	18.01	79.46	0.02	2.51	-	-	N

N = negligible.

Note: The tables on page 237 of the census report have very obviously interchanged the Sikh, Buddhist and Jain populations of Jammû with those of Udhampur. (All rows that begin on page 236 with the name of a certain district end on page 237 with the name of the same district. Only in the case of Jammû and Udhampur has the order been interchanged on page 237.) I have taken the liberty of transferring these figures back to where I think they should belong.

The census authorities' note: 'The break-up of Christians and Jains is not available separately in the Village Tables of [the] 1941 Census. The figures of these religions have, therefore been included in "Others"'[vii]

1981: The population of the present Jammû province *(actual numbers)*

District	Total	Hindus	Muslims	Sikhs	Christians	Buddhists
Dodâ	425,262	179,538		243,666	847	1,113
Jammû	943,395	824,209	40,309	72,034	5,413	
Kathuâ	369,123	336,503	25,699	6,082	N/a	
Pooñch	224,197	16,339	199,674	8,134		
Râjourî	302,500	118,705	176,302	7,325		
Udhampur	453,636	327,538	118,987	5,741	N/a	
Total	27,18,113	18,02,832	8,04,637	1,00,163	6,260	1,113
%		66.30	29.58	3.68		

2001: The population of the present Jammû province *(actual numbers)*

District	Total	Hindus	Muslims	Sikhs	Christians	Buddhists	Jains
Dodâ	691929	286849	400765	1942	439	1866	26
Jammû	1588772	1366711	90272	117490	11115	1155	1899
Kathuâ	550084	493966	44793	9152	1458	138	25
Pooñch	372613	19391	342512	10297	283	108	0
Râjourî	483284	180162	291067	11601	206	94	7
Udhampur	743509	542593	190112	7723	2632	211	57
Total	44,30,191	28,89,672	13,59,521	1,58,205	16,133	3,572	2,014
%		65.22	30.68	3.57	0.36	0.08	0.045

Literacy

Distt	Popn	Lit2001	R2001	M	F	Lit1981	R1981	Growth	Gender
J&K	98,86,585	53.57		64.6	41.61	32.68		3.41	900
Dodâ	6,81,152	46.08	10	62.49	28.30	18.5	13		
Udhampur	7,10,493	52.15	7	64.02	39.08	23.52	7		
Pooñch	3,68,544	50.60	8	64.81	35.28	34.79	2		
Rajourî	4,70,968	56.85	6	68.56	44.11	24.73	5		
Jammû	15,14,468	76.54	1	84.13	68.38	42.86	1		
Kathuâ	5,43,266	65.22	2	75.64	53.92	31.90	4		
Jammû province	42,90,871	63.07						3.09	890

Popn.= Total population (of the district, province or state mentioned); Lit2001= The percentage of the total population that was literate in the year 2001; M= the percentage of men who were literate in 2001; F= the percentage of women who were literate in 2001; Lit1981= The percentage of the total population which was literate in the year 1981; Growth= the average annual percent rate of growth of the population between 1981 and 2001; Gender= the number of women for every 1,000 men. R1981: 'Rank in 1981' or how the district ranked in 1981 in terms of literacy among the 14 districts of the state. R2001: 'Rank in 2001' or the district's rank in 2001 in terms of literacy among the 14 districts of the state.

Literacy and the peace dividend: Kathuâ is generally considered a nondescript district that has nothing to commend it other than its tradition of being the most peaceful district in Jammû and, perhaps, the state. (Budgâm has a similar peaceful reputation in Kashmîr and Kargil in Ladâkh.) Kathuâ carried this tradition forward into the 1990s when some other districts got involved with senseless, suicidal militancy. Kathuâ, along with Muslim-majority Kargil and Buddhist-majority Leh, stayed totally aloof from militancy.

The dividend was immediate. 'Colourless' Kathuâ suddenly became the 2nd most literate district in the state. (Leh and Kargil reaped similar benefits. And Jammû bettered its traditional no.1 status by becoming the educational capital of the state—as well as of the neighbouring districts of the Punjãb and Himâchal Pradésh.)

Considering that Jammû province as a whole reaped the peace dividend, why did Pooñch plummet from no.2 to no.8? Perhaps Pakistan-inspired troubles in the Surankot area made it drop to Pakistani levels of literacy. Neighbouring Rajourî dropped by only one rank, but drop it did, again because it had some problems, though insignificant compared to what happened in parts of Surankot (Pooñch). Dodâ, which, too, has had some troubles, *seems* to have climbed from rank no.13 to no.10. However, if you look at the percentage of literacy there, it is the worst in Jammû—and by a very large margin. It improved its rank only at the expense of Kashmîr, where the troubles were much worse.

Pooñch, Dodâ and Rajourî might have lost their relative ranks but, as in the rest of the province, the percentage of literacy in all six districts of Jammû improved, and noticeably.

References

i And not 66% as I had stated in the 'Kashmir' volume.

ii Census of India, 1941, Vol. XXII Jammû & Kashmîr, Parts I and II, Essay and Tables, by Capt. R.G. Wreford, Census Commissioner, Jammû and Kashmîr State, Jammû (1943) pages 341-343.

iii Census of India, 1961, Vol. VI Jammû & Kashmîr, Part 1-A (iii), General Report; MH Kamili, Superintendent of Census Operations, pages 236-237.

iv Census of India, 1941, Vol. XXII Jammû & Kashmîr, Parts I and II, Essay and Tables, by Capt. R.G. Wreford, Census Commissioner, Jammû and Kashmîr State, Jammû (1943) pages 346-347.

v Adapted from the Census of India, 1961, Vol. VI Jammû & Kashmîr, Part II-C Cultural and Migration Tables; MH Kamili, Superintendent of Census Operations, pages 272-273. Irritatingly, the total population of districts has not been given. Instead we have been told how many men and how many women there in each district. We are left to add the two figures together to get the total and sub-totals.

vi Census of India, 1961, Jammû & Kashmîr, Vol. VI Jammû & Kashmîr, Part 1-A (iii), General Report; MH Kamili, Superintendent of Census Operations, pages 236-237.

vii Census of India, 1961, Jammû & Kashmîr, Vol. VI Jammû & Kashmîr, Part 1-A (iii), General Report; MH Kamili, Superintendent of Census Operations, page 236.

Index